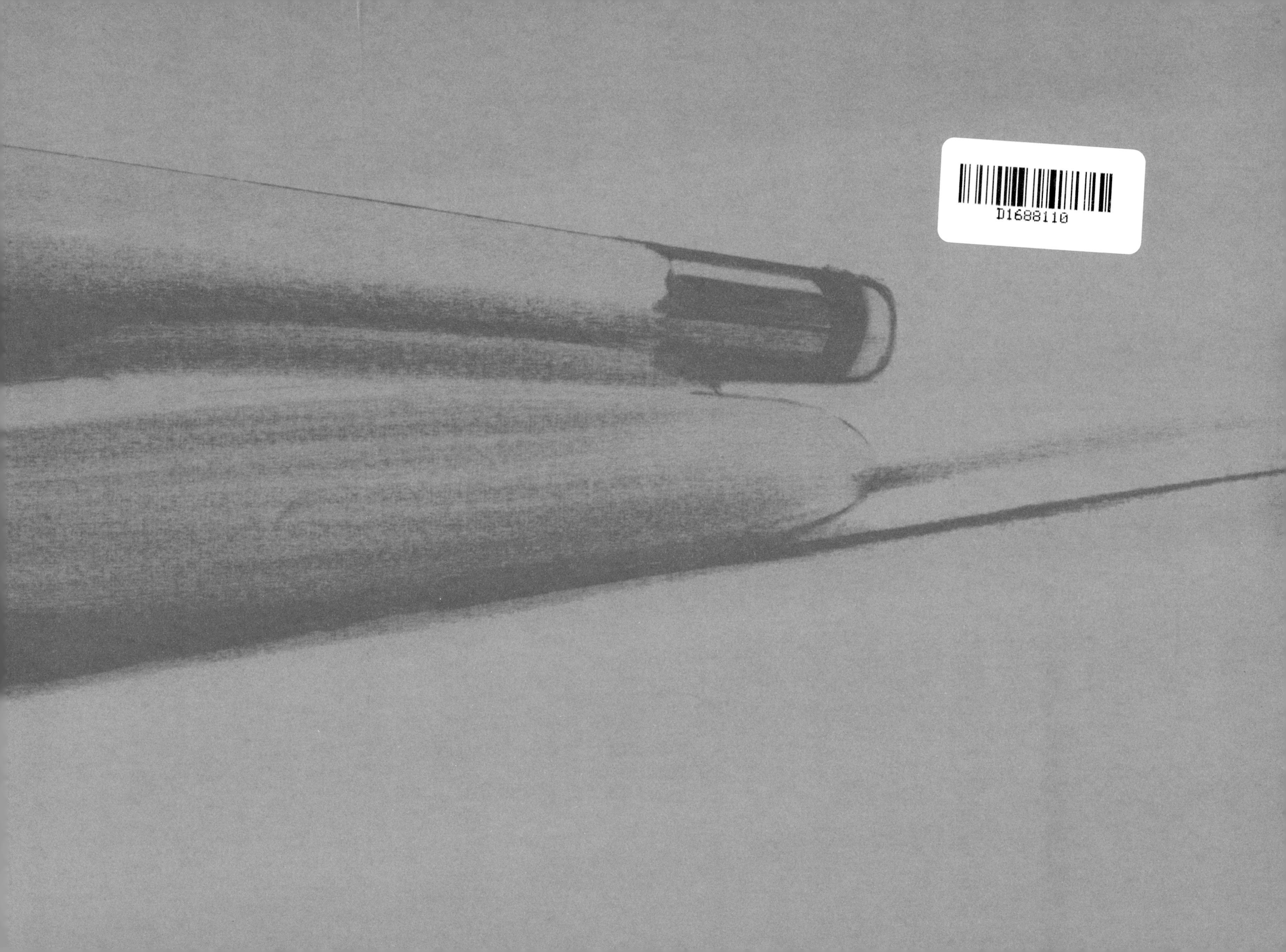

KEN ADAM DESIGNS THE MOVIES

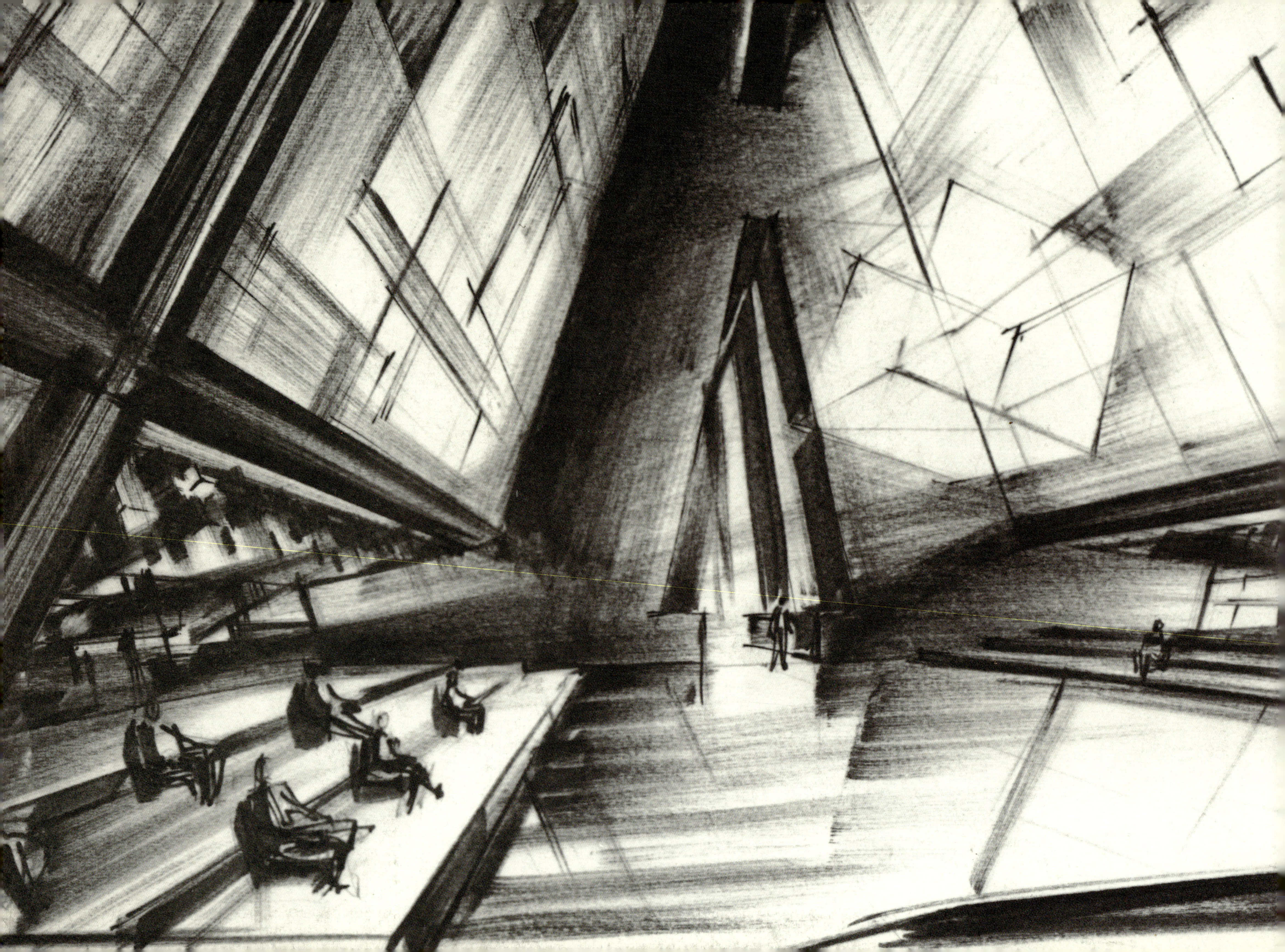

KEN ADAM DESIGNS THE MOVIES
JAMES BOND AND BEYOND

KEN ADAM AND CHRISTOPHER FRAYLING

with 265 illustrations, 155 in colour

Thames & Hudson

INTRODUCTION   6

1
ART DIRECTOR TO PRODUCTION DESIGNER

THE QUEEN OF SPADES	12
FOUR SHIPS	13
CHILD IN THE HOUSE	18
AROUND THE WORLD IN EIGHTY DAYS	19
NIGHT OF THE DEMON	21
THE BRIDGE ON THE RIVER KWAI	22
TEN SECONDS TO HELL	23
THE TRIALS OF OSCAR WILDE	24
SODOM AND GOMORRAH	28

p.1 Concept drawings of Stromberg's base, Atlantis, *The Spy Who Loved Me*, 1977.

pp. 2–3 Final concept drawing of Drax's Pyramid Control Room, *Moonraker*, 1979.

left Ken Adam working in his studio.

CONTENTS

2
WORKING WITH STANLEY KUBRICK
DR. STRANGELOVE — 32
BARRY LYNDON — 44

3
DESIGNING JAMES BOND
DR. NO — 51
GOLDFINGER — 56
THUNDERBALL — 68
YOU ONLY LIVE TWICE — 75
DIAMONDS ARE FOREVER — 80
THE SPY WHO LOVED ME — 88
MOONRAKER — 96
GOLDENEYE: ROGUE AGENT — 110
ANOTHER SPY: THE IPCRESS FILE — 114

4
THE THEATRE OF HISTORY
CHITTY CHITTY BANG BANG — 119
GOODBYE, MR. CHIPS — 126
SLEUTH — 128
THE SEVEN-PER-CENT SOLUTION — 132
SALON KITTY — 135
PENNIES FROM HEAVEN — 136
KING DAVID — 144
AGNES OF GOD — 146
THE LAST EMPEROR — 148
CRIMES OF THE HEART — 152
THE FRESHMAN — 155
THE MADNESS OF KING GEORGE — 159

5
TWO OPERAS
THE GIRL OF THE GOLDEN WEST — 166
WOZZECK — 172

6
DRAWINGS COME TO LIFE
PETER PAN — 177
ADDAMS FAMILY VALUES — 180

7
DESIGNING THE FUTURE
LORD L — 186
STAR TREK – THE MOTION PICTURE — 189
THE CINEMA OF THE FUTURE — 194
THE FANTASTICKS — 200

8
BACK TO BERLIN
BERLIN MILLENNIUM EXHIBITION — 204
TAKING SIDES — 209
'THE CABINETS OF DR. CALIGARI' — 214

9
CONCLUSION: THE ART OF KEN ADAM — 222

Ken Adam Filmography — 227
Bibliography — 228
Picture Credits — 229

INTRODUCTION

'Treating reality in a theatrical way'

Countless books have been written about famous film stars, directors, producers, writers and even cinematographers, but surprisingly few have been written about production designers. And yet it is the production designer who is the person most responsible for transforming words on the page into images on the screen, and for doing so in a visually coherent and distinctive way. In close consultation with the director and cinematographer, it is the production designer who, in Ken Adam's words, 'establishes a style and visual progression for the film, and then physically realizes it'. Whether the film is shot on the street or on a soundstage, the production designer has decisively shaped the visual experience.

Some of the most memorable images in the history of film – the village of Holstenwall in *The Cabinet of Dr. Caligari*, the city centre of Fritz Lang's *Metropolis*, the yellow brick road to Oz, the plantation house at Tara, Charles Foster Kane's Xanadu, the airport in *Casablanca*, the Bates Motel and mom's California clapboard mansion on the hill in *Psycho*, the alternative futures of science-fiction epics – have been the work of successive generations of art directors or, since 1938 when the phrase originated, production designers. And not just these studio fantasies. It was in the post-war period, under the influence of the Italian neo-realists, that many Hollywood film-makers turned the city streets into their studio – beginning with *The House on 92nd Street*, and using in the notable case of *West Side Story* a mixture of the two. The art director's role in this might be less immediately visible, but it was equally decisive.

In 1938, independent producer David O. Selznick wrote a famous memo during pre-production on *Gone with the Wind*. He wrote, 'I hope to have *Gone with the Wind* prepared almost down to the last camera angle before we start shooting.' And of art director William Cameron Menzies's role he added, 'His work in this picture, as I see it, will be a lot greater in scope than is normally associated with the term "art direction".' So the credit 'Production Designed by William Cameron Menzies' was born. As an independent, Selznick was able to make unilateral decisions like this. A very large proportion of *Gone with the Wind* was filmed in the studio. Directors came, directors went, but Menzies's storyboards held the film – as a visual experience – together.

From the 1950s onwards, the art director's role expanded – though, to start with anyway, seldom to the extent of *Gone with the Wind* – until 'production designer' became a familiar credit. However, perhaps because film studies and film criticism tended to grow from literary roots, the visual aspects of film were rarely given the prominence they deserved – hence the relative neglect of the production designer in bibliographies of film. What exactly does a 'production designer' do? A set designer creates the sets, a construction manager co-ordinates the building of the sets, a cinematographer is in charge of the photography and lighting – but where does a 'production designer' fit in? And how is his/her role distinct from that of an art director?

When asked about this with regard to the various craft skills within the art department, Ken Adam tends to reply: 'Ideally speaking, the production designer supervises everything that is visual: sets, locations, props, co-ordination of costumes within the settings.... I personally like to be involved from a very early stage – in script discussions, if possible, with the director and the cinematographer. In order to allow me more creative freedom, I always like to have an art director collaborating with me, who, like a personal assistant, is responsible for the practical organization and the budget. It is the production designer who assembles the art department – the art director, set decorator, the draughtsmen and the construction co-ordinator. As production designer, one always depends a great deal on the efficiency of the art department and its effectiveness as a team.'

Ken Adam was one of the first in Britain to be given the credit 'production designer'. This was in 1959. He had entered the industry as a junior draughtsman in 1947, having studied architecture followed by very active service as a fighter pilot in the RAF. Then he became an assistant art director, and a fully fledged art director in 1956. Already in that year he had written an article called 'Designing Sets for Action', in which he argued that for him the point of art direction was to create an *idea* of place rather than a real place; that realism was in any case a style that changed with the times, and that he much preferred to work for directors who gave him 'the opportunity to be creative and less reproductive'. In the article, he downplayed the precise delineations of the draughtsman in favour of the dramatic intensity of the film-maker, and noted his own gravitation towards a more theatrical approach which was nearer drama and narrative than architecture. Merely imitating reality was a dull thing to do. Much more interesting would be to create a different kind of reality. Already, his philosophy of film design was well thought out. It was somewhere between the documentary look on the one hand, and the theatrical 'cinema of quality' on the other, and at its heart was the ambition *to create an effect* in the mind of the audience.

Ken Adam has been doing that ever since. In a career that started during the studio era and has flourished for well over half a century (he designed the computer game *Goldeneye: Rogue Agent* in 2004–05), Adam has been responsible for a succession of some of the grandest illusions of all. The most memorable of these include the monochrome Lloyd's of London with the 'names' all dressed in black and white, and the waiters in scarlet, in the otherwise full-colour *Around the World in Eighty Days* (1956); the Marquess of Queensberry's two-colour reception room in a Scottish castle, with the actors all in black, in *The Trials of Oscar Wilde* (1960); the antique and modern villain's headquarters, with the Goya portrait of the Duke of Wellington propped up on an armchair, in *Dr. No* (1962); the huge triangular Pentagon War Room with its giant poker table and light ring in *Dr. Strangelove* (1963); the Aston Martin DB5, complete with such essential accessories as an ejector seat, an oil-slick squirter and wheel scythe, in *Goldfinger* (1964); the London warehouse that looks like an Eastern European prison in *The Ipcress File* (1965); the missile launcher hidden beneath a lake and inside a Japanese volcano – at the time, the largest set ever constructed in Europe – in *You Only Live Twice* (1967); the ship's body of an early Rolls-Royce combined with the front of a Bugatti, which turns into a hovercraft and a flying machine, in *Chitty Chitty Bang Bang* (1968); the English baronial hall full of tricks, mechanical dolls and automata, which many thought was a real National Trust country-house interior, in *Sleuth* (1972); the astonishing, candle-lit, eighteenth-century rooms – all from *real* country houses this time – in *Barry Lyndon* (1975); the mammoth supertanker that digests into a single compartment three nuclear submarines in *The Spy Who Loved Me* (1977); the mobile space station, made up of bolted-together metal cylinders, in *Moonraker* (1979); the 1930s city of the night, inspired by American painters and photographers of the period, in *Pennies From Heaven* (1981); in a lasting three-dimensional homage to the celebrated *New Yorker* cartoons the weird, gingerbread gothic interiors belonging to Morticia and Gomez in *Addams Family Values* (1993); and the mixture of historical locations and stylized design in *The Madness of King George* (1994).

Hidden within this astonishing list are two Oscars and two British Academy Awards for *Barry Lyndon* and *The Madness of King George*, three Oscar nominations, and five further award nominations. As a favourite industry one-liner put it: 'Adam created James Bond seven times over; Bond did not make Adam.' Another, in reply to the question, 'Who is the real star of James Bond? Connery, Lazenby or Moore?' has it: 'The real star is Ken Adam.' He even designed an inflatable multimedia cinema in the early 1980s, to recapture for modern audiences the thrill of movie-going in the golden age of the picture palace (sadly, it never got beyond the drawing board). When he received a knighthood in 2003, he was the first-ever production designer to be honoured in this way.

Ken Adam has kept a very extensive personal archive of concept sketches, drawings, set stills and photographs, from every stage of his career. This book presents visually – for the first time – the whole cycle of his production designs from initial concept right through to what actually appears on the screen. Early concept sketches and roughs, set and prop drawings, storyboards, set photographs and production stills are accompanied throughout by insights from Adam as well as background context from both authors. The roughs and early drawings are particularly interesting. Nearly always in black and white, these bold expressive sketches are as much about light as about physical space, shaped with a broad wedge-shaped Flowmaster pen. They eliminate unnecessary details, have a strong vanishing point, and it is they – rather than technical drawings – that are Adam's starting-point. 'This is,' he says, 'something to do with the way my mind works.'

This book aims to be at the same time a design book, a sourcebook, an album, a portfolio, an archive. It takes the reader behind the scenes and into the visual thought processes of the classic James Bond films, of *Dr. Strangelove* and *Barry Lyndon*, of *Sleuth* and *Pennies From Heaven*, of *The Madness of King George*, as well as many Hollywood films set in the past, the present and the future. It also examines Ken Adam's projects outside the film industry – including two operas, a computer game and that inflatable cinema. It explores the production designer's role through what he actually *does*.

Using case-studies from the 1950s through to the present day, *Ken Adam Designs the Movies* goes beyond the designs themselves to reveal changes in the structure of the film industry – and the evolving role of the art director and production designer within it – from big soundstages to the digital fantasies of the early twenty-first century. Most film books tend to approach the subject from a literary or biographical point of view: they are about the words rather than the images. This book is about how the images, the illusions, are created. Ken Adam calls the process 'treating reality in a theatrical way'.

British film director Michael Powell once said of the production designer, 'It is not generally recognized by the public that the most genuinely creative member of a film unit, if the author of the original story and screenplay is excluded, is the art director/production designer.... It is not sufficiently acknowledged that the production designer is the creator of those miraculous images up there on the big screen.' *Ken Adam Designs the Movies* puts the record straight through the work of one of the most significant miracle-makers in the history of film, who is also the most distinguished production designer of his time. He has rightly been dubbed 'the Frank Lloyd Wright of *décor noir*'; a man who has, as one critic put it, 'had a profound influence not just on his profession but on the whole look of modern film'.

Christopher Frayling
June 2008

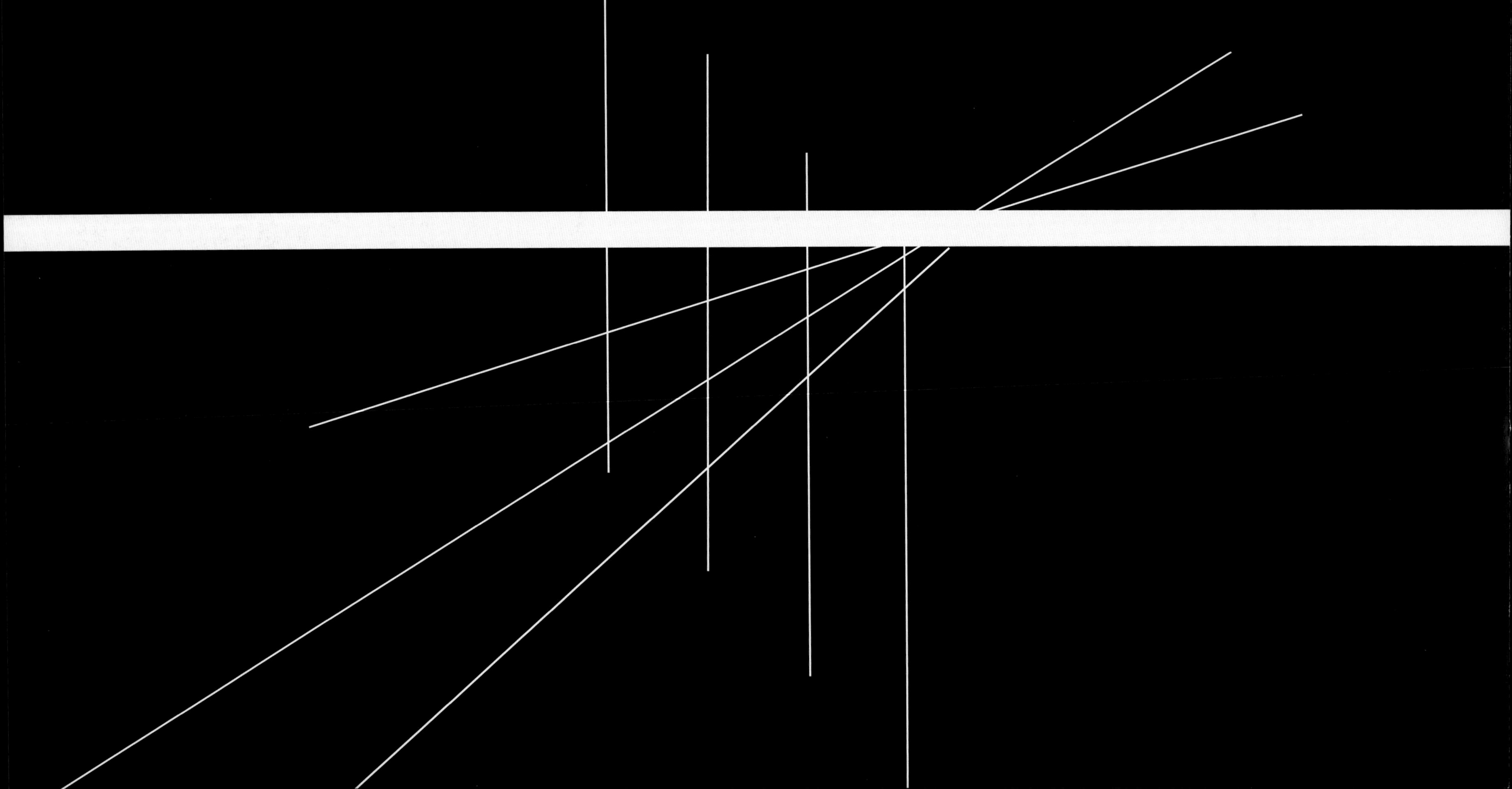

1 ART DIRECTOR TO PRODUCTION DESIGNER

THE QUEEN OF SPADES [1949]

Thorold Dickinson's *The Queen of Spades*, adapted from Pushkin's novella, was set in St Petersburg in 1815. It was designed by Oliver Messel, very well known at the time for his work in the theatre, and was shot at Welwyn Studio in 1948. The project was a major one for a recent recruit into the industry, and was Ken Adam's first costume film. 'Even though I was in a very junior capacity,' he says, 'Oliver liked me and I liked him. He liked my freehand drawing … and he taught me a lot about period design.'

THE CAPTAIN'S APARTMENT Prop drawing for the apartment of the main protagonist, Captain Herman Suvorin.

FOUR SHIPS

'I got *Hornblower* by a fluke because the man in charge of Warner Bros. in England decided to send me to the South of France to see if I could find a ship suitable for conversion into Hornblower's 24-gun frigate. First I did some research at the National Maritime Museum, then I had meetings with experts. In the end, we found this old three-masted schooner. After that, I began to have a good time designing ships….'

ON DECK Cast and crew, including Gregory Peck and Virginia Mayo, on the deck of Hornblower's flagship while filming *Captain Horatio Hornblower R.N.* at Denham Studios in 1949.

ART DIRECTOR TO PRODUCTION DESIGNER

CAPTAIN HORATIO HORNBLOWER R.N. [1950]

For Raoul Walsh's *Captain Horatio Hornblower R.N.*, set during the Napoleonic Wars, Ken Adam was assistant art director responsible for Hornblower's flagship—full-sized and on the set at Denham Studios—as well as other ships. The flagship was a converted three-masted schooner called *La France*, found on the French-Spanish border. Another Napoleonic ship—a schooner of the period—was an adapted ketch from Marseilles called the *Marie Annick*. Somehow, Ken Adam was becoming a specialist in maritime design.

left and below **THE SCHOONER** Filming on the schooner *La France*, transformed by Ken Adam into a 24-gun frigate for *Hornblower*.

ART DIRECTOR TO PRODUCTION DESIGNER

right and below right **THE BALLOON SEQUENCE** Burt Lancaster and Nick Cravat taking off from the fort in Ischia, during *The Crimson Pirate*'s elaborate balloon sequence.

below **THE PIRATE GALLEON** The *Hornblower* flagship transformed into Burt Lancaster's pirate galleon, crossing from Nice to Ischia in June 1951.

'We needed a balloon with a basket gondola. I remember having to climb up one of the 120-foot towers supporting the balloon traveller, and halfway up that tower I froze. I couldn't move. Vertigo.'

THE CRIMSON PIRATE [1952]

As associate art director on Robert Siodmak's *The Crimson Pirate*, Ken Adam assisted Paul Sheriff – another theatre designer, best known to film-goers as the designer of Laurence Olivier's *Henry V* – by recycling *La France* and the *Marie Annick* as eighteenth-century pirate vessels. Having revamped *La France* in Marseilles, Adam sailed on her to the island of Ischia, where filming was based, during a gale – 'an incredible experience'. When it was decided that the film's original script – by blacklisted writers – did not work as a conventional pirate story, it was rewritten as a spoof. Ken Adam, from day to day during shooting, had to create increasingly outlandish gadgets, including a rowing boat that became a submarine and a camouflaged hot-air balloon that bombarded a fortress – as Adam says, 'like a sort of period James Bond'.

THE MASTER OF BALLANTRAE [1953]

Ken Adam worked as associate art director on William Keighley's *The Master of Ballantrae*, which was loosely based on the classic 1889 adventure story by Robert Louis Stevenson. While the art director Ralph Brinton designed the sets in England, Adam worked on location near Palermo. Again, he was responsible for the ships, and also for customizing the local harbour wall.

THE HARBOUR The entrance to Arenella harbour in Sicily redesigned by Ken Adam – with the ships from *Hornblower* revamped yet again.

ART DIRECTOR TO PRODUCTION DESIGNER

'For the "thousand ships" of Helen of Troy, I designed one real ship. I loved doing it because my only references were Greek vases of the period and experts in museums who were never 100 per cent sure about how things worked.'

HELEN OF TROY [1955]

Ken Adam—again credited as associate art director, this time under art director Edward Carrere—helped to launch the fleet of a thousand ships in Robert Wise's epic *Helen of Troy*. In actual fact, nine hundred and ninety-nine of the ships were painted in. Adam designed a single Greek galley. He bought a coal barge, then took an entire family whose ancestors had been shipbuilders for centuries from Torre del Greco to Fiumicino near Rome, where they helped him convert the barge by hand, using period adzes to carve the timbers into the classic sweeping lines of Greek ships. Adam also co-ordinated the rest of the art department based in Rome, responsible for the city of Troy, its forty-foot walls, the Greek siege towers and the wooden horse. Two units filmed simultaneously at Anzio (the Greek galley) and Cinecittà Studios (the city of Troy), where the set caught fire one lunchtime. Eventually Raoul Walsh was called in, uncredited, to help keep the mammoth show on the road.

THE GALLEY Constructing the full-sized Greek galley—on a coal-barge base—at Fiumicino, in 1953.

CHILD IN THE HOUSE [1956]

Cy Endfield's *Child in the House*, starring Mandy Miller as the eponymous child, Phyllis Calvert as her censorious aunt and Stanley Baker as her father on the run, was shot at Walton-on-Thames Studio in 1956. The plot offered Ken Adam the opportunity to 'stylize slightly' with two sets — the child's dancing academy and Baker's squalid London hideout. The dancing academy was where the little girl got away from her repressive aunt: these sequences were filmed in Expressionist style, quite unlike the rest of the film. Adam wrote at the time that 'when designing the dancing academy, I always had in the back of my mind the ballet-school paintings of the French Impressionist painter Degas.... With this in mind, I attempted to create a dreamlike atmosphere by inclining the walls inwards, like those elongated French windows on one side and a wall mirror with the practice bar on the other.'

THE ACADEMY OF DANCING Drawing of the interior of Professor Topolski's Academy of Dancing.

right **THE REFORM CLUB** The card room of the Reform Club at MGM Studios, Elstree – with Trevor Howard, Ronald Squire, Robert Morley and Finlay Currie – filmed in 1955.

below **THE EMPLOYMENT AGENCY** Two production drawings, for Ken Adam's guidance, of the exterior of the London Employment Agency in Victoria Square and the interior.

AROUND THE WORLD IN EIGHTY DAYS [1956]

Around the World in Eighty Days was the brainchild of flamboyant showman Mike Todd, who thought the best way to attract audiences away from television was to bring together exotic locations, the widest possible screen and as many named stars as would agree to appear in cameo roles. William Cameron Menzies was associate producer and, under his guidance, Adam – whose name was mis-spelled on the credits – was responsible for the English and European legs of the journey: the Reform Club, Lloyd's of London, the Employment Agency and the elaborate crowd scene at the Place Vendôme in Paris. Menzies, 'the father of modern production design', encouraged Adam to be adventurous in the stylization of sets and the use of colour. 'Even though the designs were not originated by me,' says Adam, 'I had to translate them into reality.'

HAUNTED

NIGHT OF THE DEMON [1957]

Jacques Tourneur's *Night of the Demon* was based on M. R. James's celebrated short story 'Casting the Runes', with the central character changed from an English academic to a sceptical American scientist, played by Dana Andrews. The film was shot at Elstree in 1956–57, and Ken Adam recalls 'really going to town on those sets', creating an atmosphere of accumulating menace, with the diabolist-villain's country house, a séance parlour, a rural farmhouse near Stonehenge and, at the climax, a giant medieval-style Fire Demon. This monster was 'designed under protest', at the producer's request.

opposite **THE FIRE DEMON** Study of the demon, for the climax of the film.

right **THE SÉANCE SEQUENCE** Drawing of the cluttered séance interior.

'The big problem came when the producer, Hal E. Chester, decided that he wanted to show the monster. Jacques Tourneur and I both felt that huge footprints – with steam rising from them – were enough. We lost that battle. So I had to come up with a believable monster, a fire demon. I can't remember doing any research, but I must have seen something!'

below and right **FILM BROCHURE**
Drawings for the brochure issued at the première of *The Bridge on the River Kwai*, October 1957.

THE BRIDGE ON THE RIVER KWAI [1957]

David Lean's *Bridge on the River Kwai* was about the decision of Colonel Nicholson (Alec Guinness) to build the best possible bridge across the river to carry the Burma-Siam railway — also boosting troop morale and showing the superiority of British engineering. The bridge in the film was designed by art director Don Ashton and engineered by Husbands of Sheffield (as the credits proudly stated). Its three-frame profile deliberately echoed the Forth Railway Bridge, although the actual bridge just had a series of trestle bents. Ken Adam designed the brochure that launched the film.

22 ART DIRECTOR TO PRODUCTION DESIGNER

TEN SECONDS TO HELL [1958]

Robert Aldrich's *Ten Seconds to Hell*, another film made in Europe by 'an old pro' from Hollywood, was about ex-Wehrmacht soldiers who were bomb-disposal experts in the rubble of Berlin just after the Second World War. American actors played the leads. The film was shot almost entirely at the old UFA Studios in Tempelhof during 1958, and 'because the Berlin Wall didn't yet exist, half the studio workers commuted from the East'. This was also where Fritz Lang's *Metropolis* had been filmed in the mid-1920s. It was the first time Ken Adam had returned to Berlin since the war, and he had in the back of his mind that many of the UFA staff must have worked under the Nazis.

BERLIN BUNKER One of the earliest of Ken Adam's bunkers, in the ruins of postwar Berlin.

THE TRIALS OF OSCAR WILDE [1960]

Ken Hughes's *The Trials of Oscar Wilde*, with Peter Finch in the title role, was filmed at speed at Elstree in 1960, in competition with another Oscar Wilde project being made at exactly the same time. *The Trials* won. 'Because of budget limitations,' Ken Adam says, 'I was forced to do a lot of stylization.' This included the concept of having each set make a distinctive colour statement. The sketches, rather than being done in Adam's by now characteristic loose style, were made with pen and ink and watercolour, because 'I felt it was more suitable for an historical film set in Late Victorian England'.

above right and right **AFTER THE FUNERAL** Design for the interior of Kinmount House, ink and watercolour on paper, and corresponding film still, with Lionel Jeffries as the Marquess of Queensberry.

ART DIRECTOR TO PRODUCTION DESIGNER

ART DIRECTOR TO PRODUCTION DESIGNER

above **ST. JAMES'S THEATRE FOYER**
Four set drawings, from different
perspectives, of the foyer of the
St. James's Theatre.

ART DIRECTOR TO PRODUCTION DESIGNER

THE TRIALS OF OSCAR WILDE

FOYER - ST. JAMES THEATRE

left and above **ST. JAMES'S THEATRE FOYER** Final design concept, ink and watercolour on paper, and corresponding film still, with Peter Finch as Oscar Wilde and John Fraser as Lord Alfred Douglas.

ART DIRECTOR TO PRODUCTION DESIGNER

'Bob Aldrich, the director, rang me and said, "Ken, we'll have some fun. Come over to Rome and find some locations. We shouldn't be more than six weeks." Well, we worked for a year and a half on *Sodom and Gomorrah*!'

SODOM AND GOMORRAH [1962]

Sodom and Gomorrah, Ken Adam's third collaboration with director Robert Aldrich, was based on a couple of verses in the Old Testament, and from these Adam had to conjure up authentic-looking 'twin cities of the plains'. He found a town in Morocco called Aït Benhaddou, with no road to it but containing his idea of biblical architecture. Adam designed a huge main gate, flanked by two guard towers; streets and temples; and, of course, the destruction sequence. The chosen idiom was 'a bit Egyptian', with local mud-brick architecture too. The interiors, such as the torture chamber, were built and filmed at Cinecittà in 1960–61. The film was not well received – one critic said the most expressive actor was the pillar of salt – but the sets and costumes attracted better notices. One critic wrote, 'Few designers would have had the nerve to attempt such wild colour harmonies as shocking pink and raspberry against orange and bluish-purple.'

this page **THE UNDERGROUND CHAMBER** The underground Sodomite prison and torture chamber, built at Cinecittà.

opposite **THE DESTRUCTION SEQUENCE** Storyboard of the destruction of Sodom, including mushroom cloud, 1960.

DESTRUCTION SEQUENCE OF SODOM

①	②	③
1 EARTH QUAKE	2 LIGHTENING	3 EXPLOSION
④	⑤	⑥
4 BLACK WHIRLWIND	5 DUST CLOUD FORMING	6 DUST CLOUD RISES
⑦	⑧	⑨
7 DUST CLOUD OBLITERATES	8 DUST CLOUD CLEARS	9 HILL ONLY REMAINS

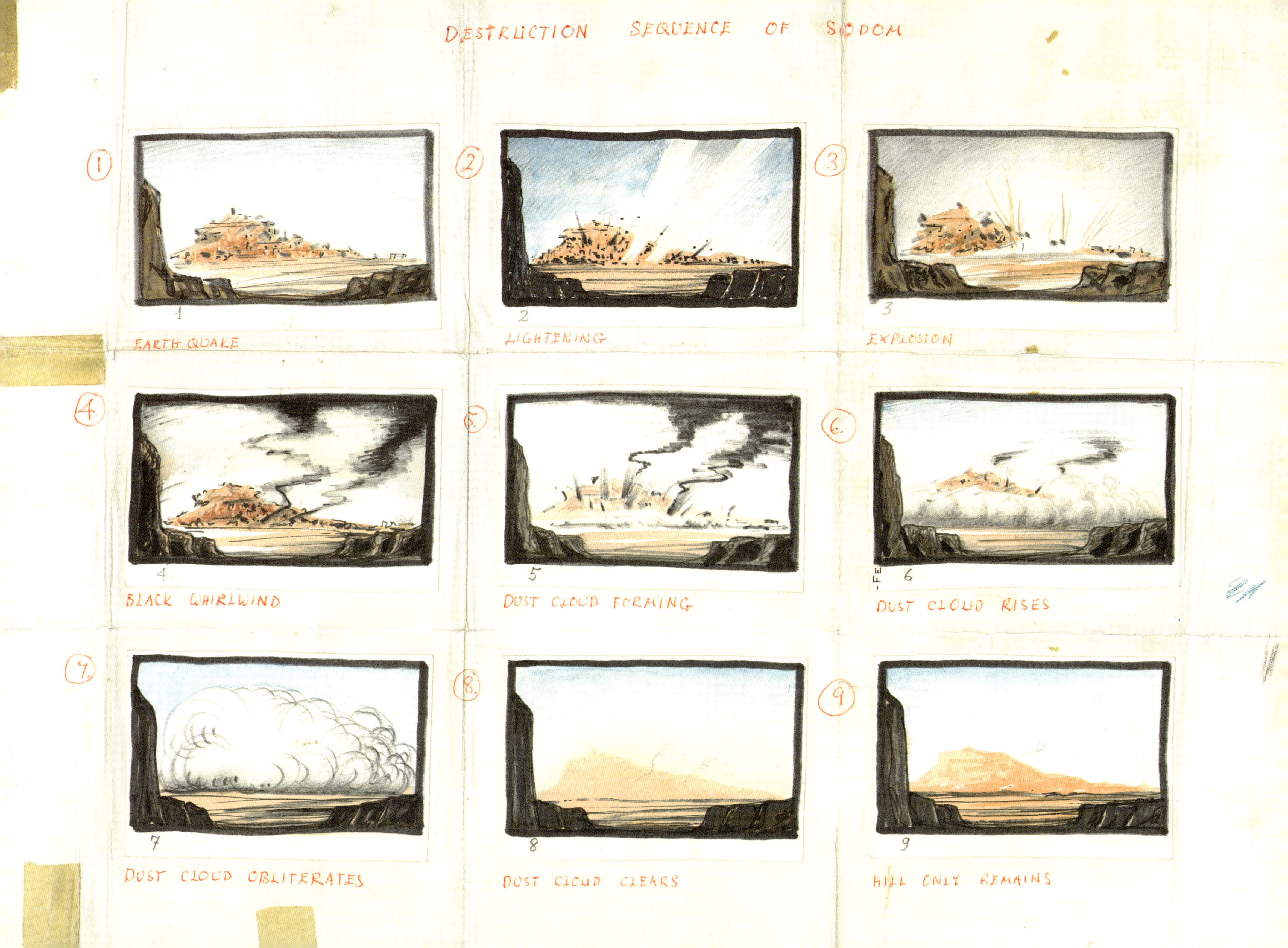

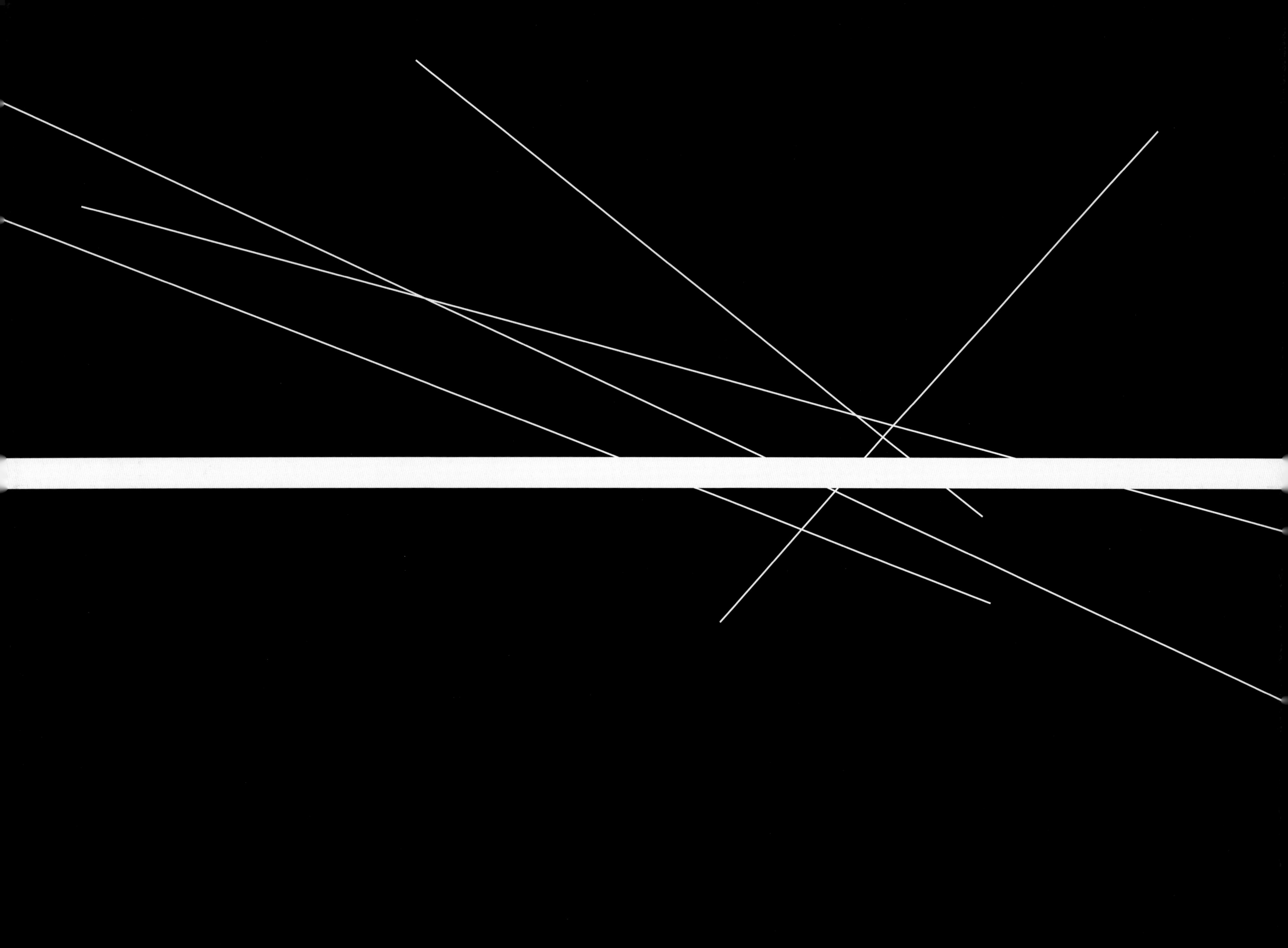

2 WORKING WITH STANLEY KUBRICK

DR. STRANGELOVE OR: HOW I LEARNED TO STOP WORRYING AND LOVE THE BOMB [1963]

Stanley Kubrick's 1963 film was a black satire on the taboo subject of world nuclear destruction. It also proved a vital step in Ken Adam's development as a production designer. He had to design three main sets: Burpleson Air Base, the interior of the B52 bomber carrying nuclear weapons to Russia and, most famously, the War Room beneath the Pentagon. The siege of the air base was shot like a hand-held newsreel, the B52 like a military documentary and the War Room like a piece of Expressionist cinema – complete with an ex-Nazi nuclear advisor with one black glove, played, like US President Muffley and the very British Group Captain Lionel Mandrake, by Peter Sellers. Kubrick and Adam worked very closely together on the visual concepts for the film, without any official military co-operation – for obvious reasons. The result was, for both of them, a masterpiece.

left **THE B52 BOMBER** Drawing of the B52 bomber, 1962.

opposite above **THE WAR ROOM** Stanley Kubrick and Peter Sellers on Ken Adam's War Room set at Shepperton, showing the large illuminated maps.

opposite below **THE WALL OF MAPS** Design for the wall of maps, with dimensions, 1962.

'The most important set for Stanley was the War Room. I had some stills of the North American Air Defence control centre, but they weren't interesting enough. So I came up with gigantic maps, which had to show the tracks of nuclear bombers approaching Russia. In the end, we used thousands of lightbulbs for these, behind sheets of plywood with cut-out squares, covered with Perspex and the maps.'

'I'd come up with a two-level set, which Stanley very much liked, so I thought I was in business. Three weeks later, as so often happened with him, he changed his mind. I flipped. I was walking through the gardens at Shepperton taking Valium. Then I came up with a basic, one-level, leaning, triangular shape. Stanley was standing right behind me as I was scribbling away'

above **THE WAR ROOM** Six drawings, from 1962, showing the evolution of the War Room design, from the initial two-tier set through to the final concept of a cavernous, triangular bunker with a circular table and circular light ring above to illuminate the actors – like a nuclear fallout shelter where a poker game is being played for the future of the world.

following pages **DR. STRANGELOVE** Ken Adam in the War Room, which Steven Spielberg once called the finest set in the history of film; the Strategic Air Command map; the enormous circular table; the final concept drawing (1962, extended 1999); a still of the final custard pie fight, cut from the film as released.

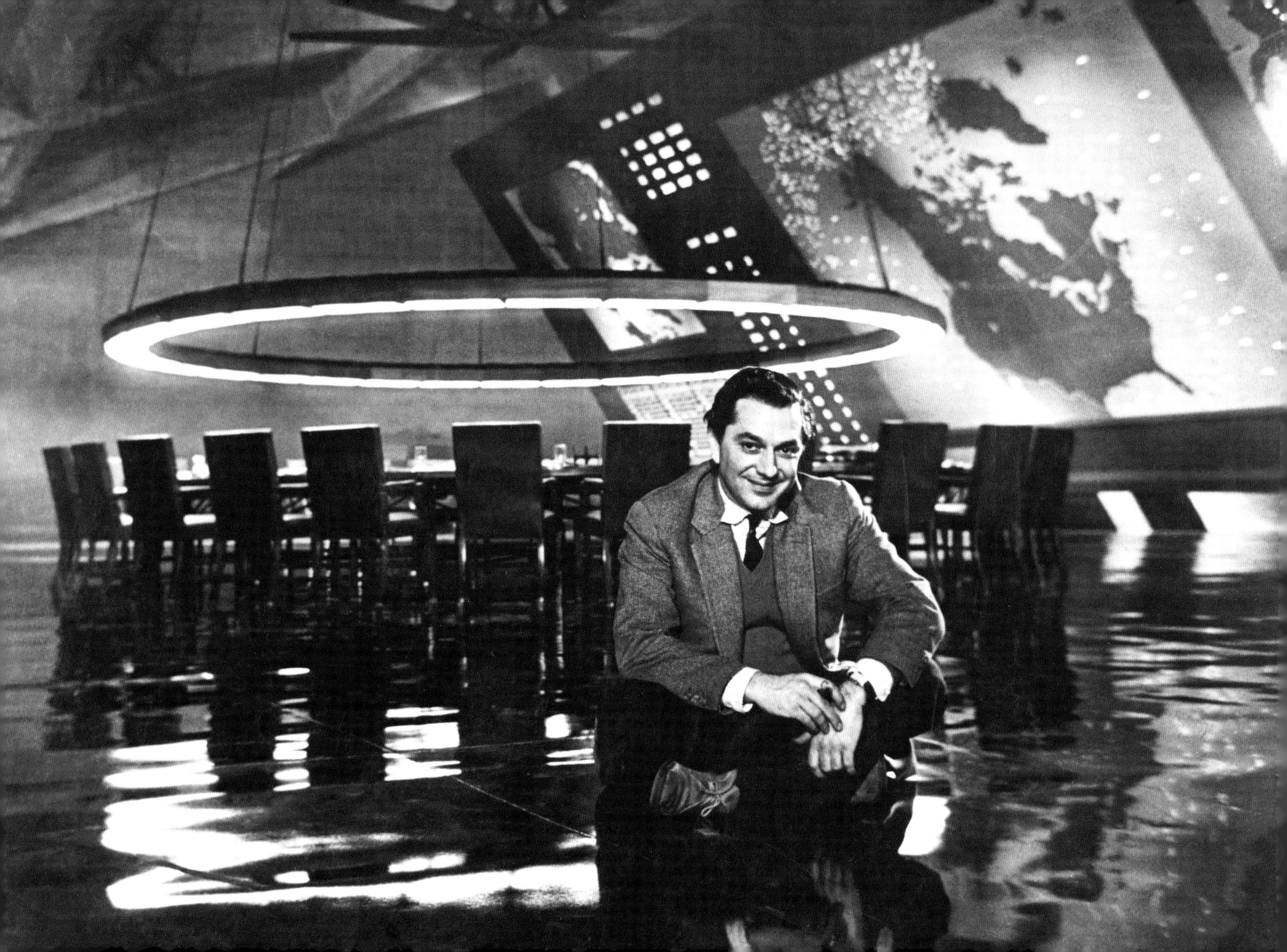

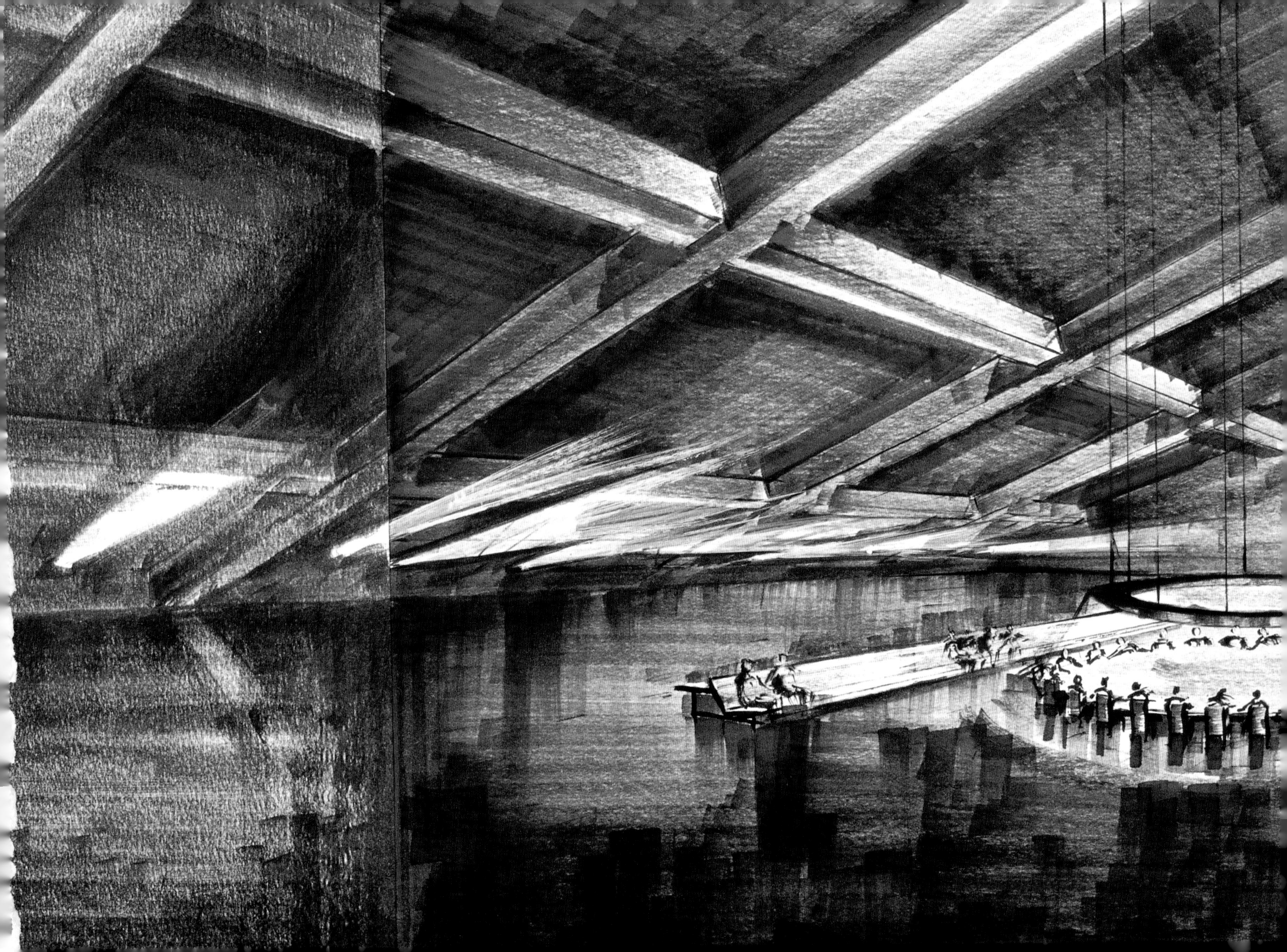

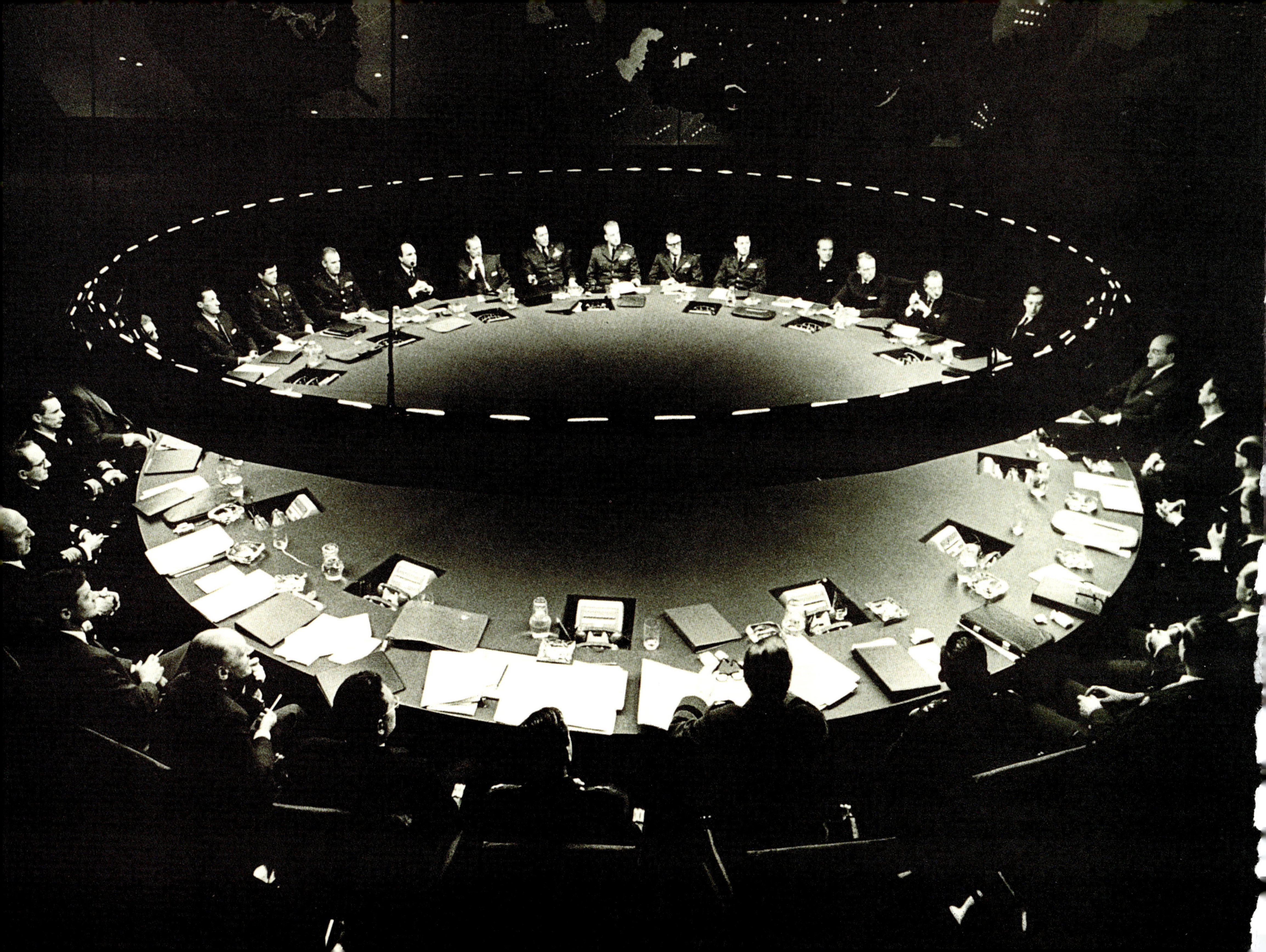

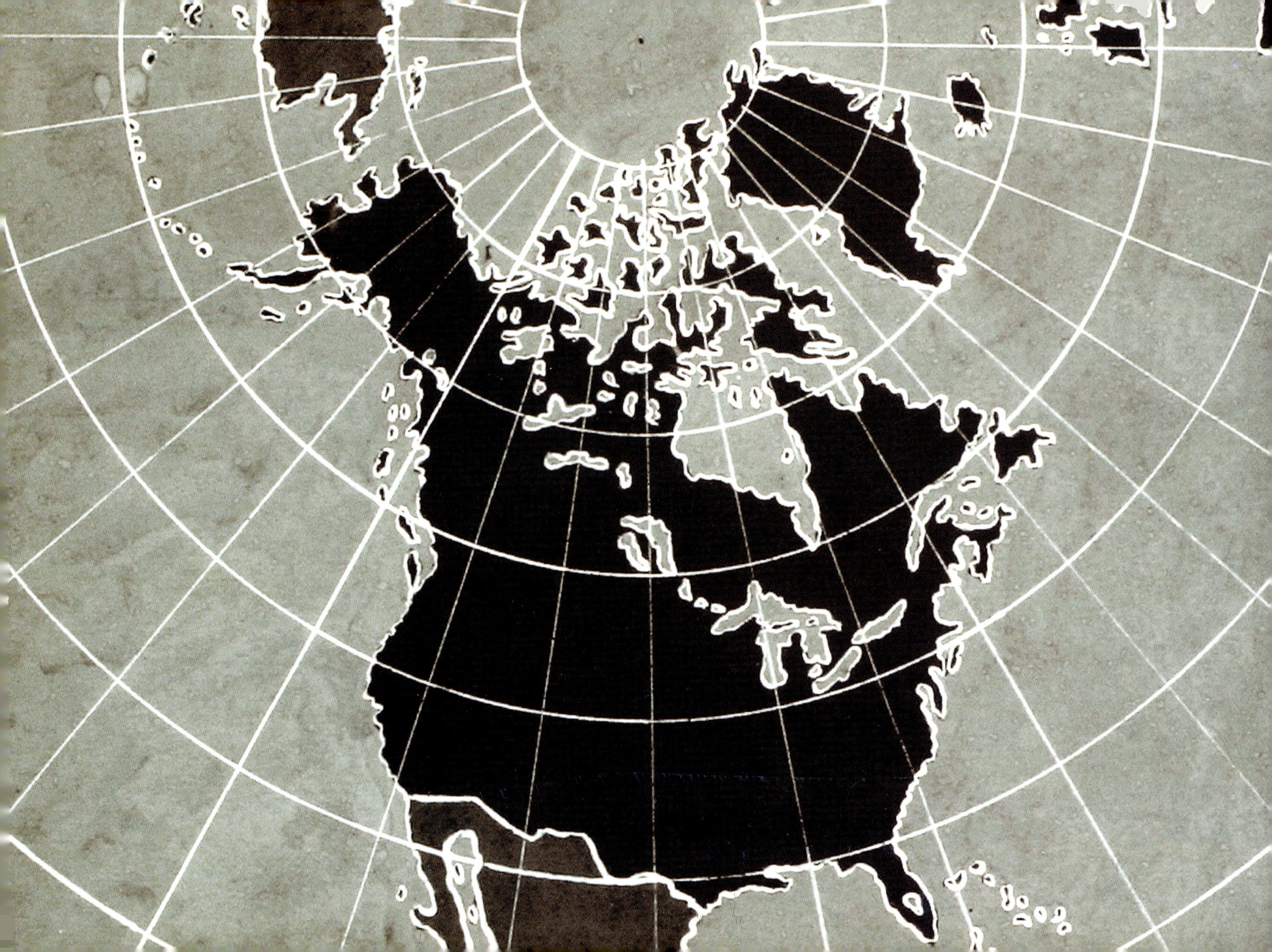

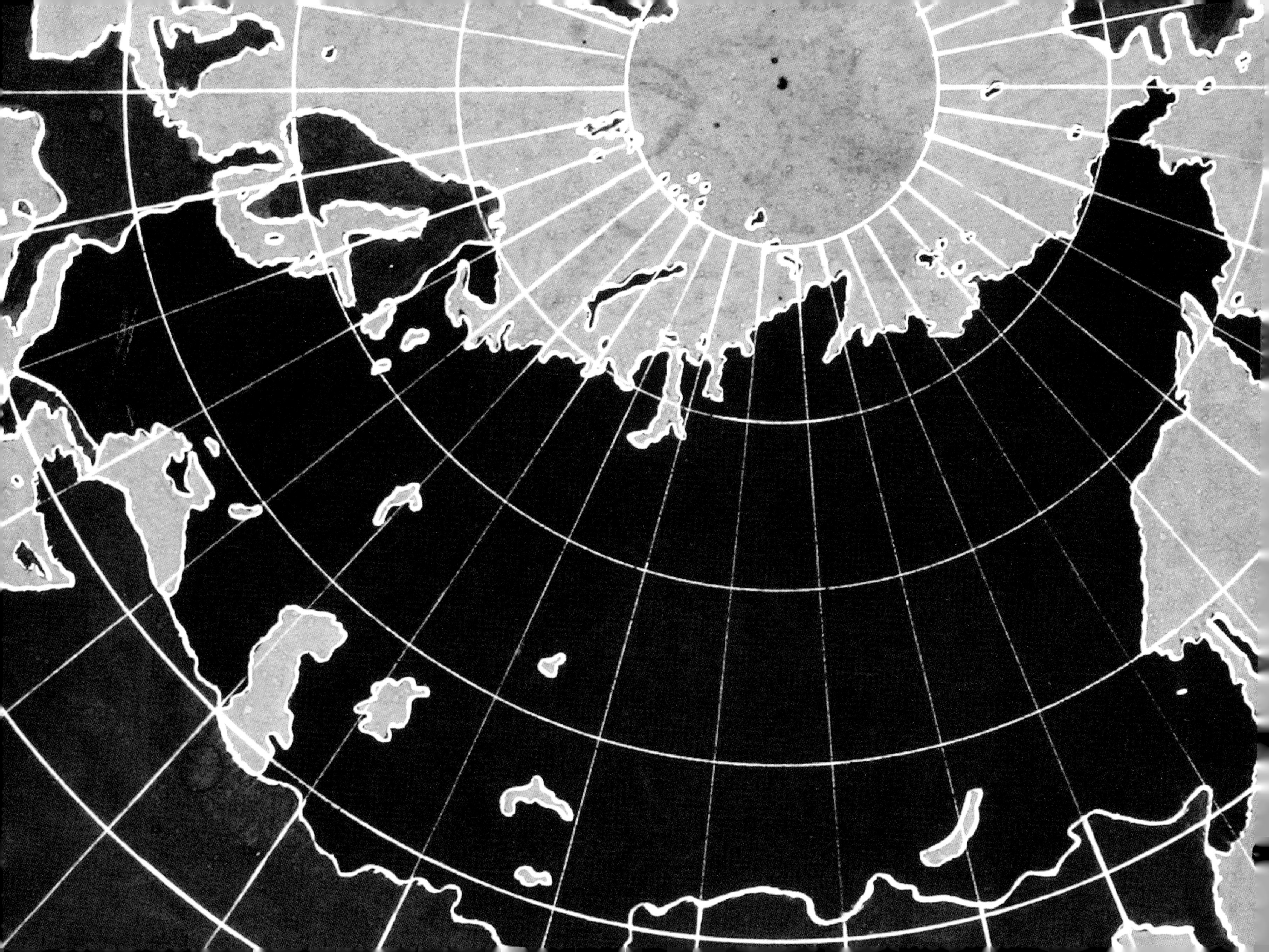

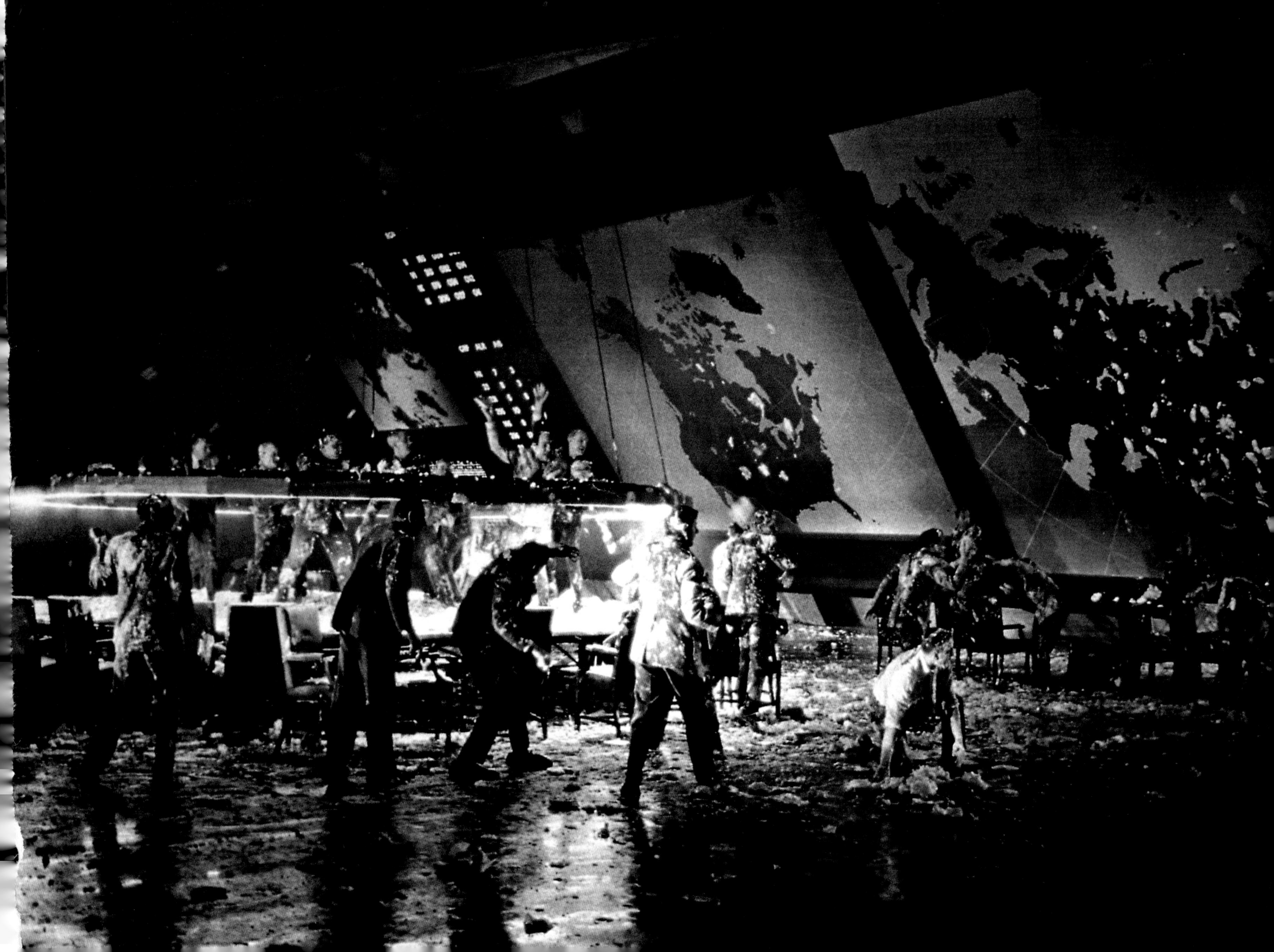

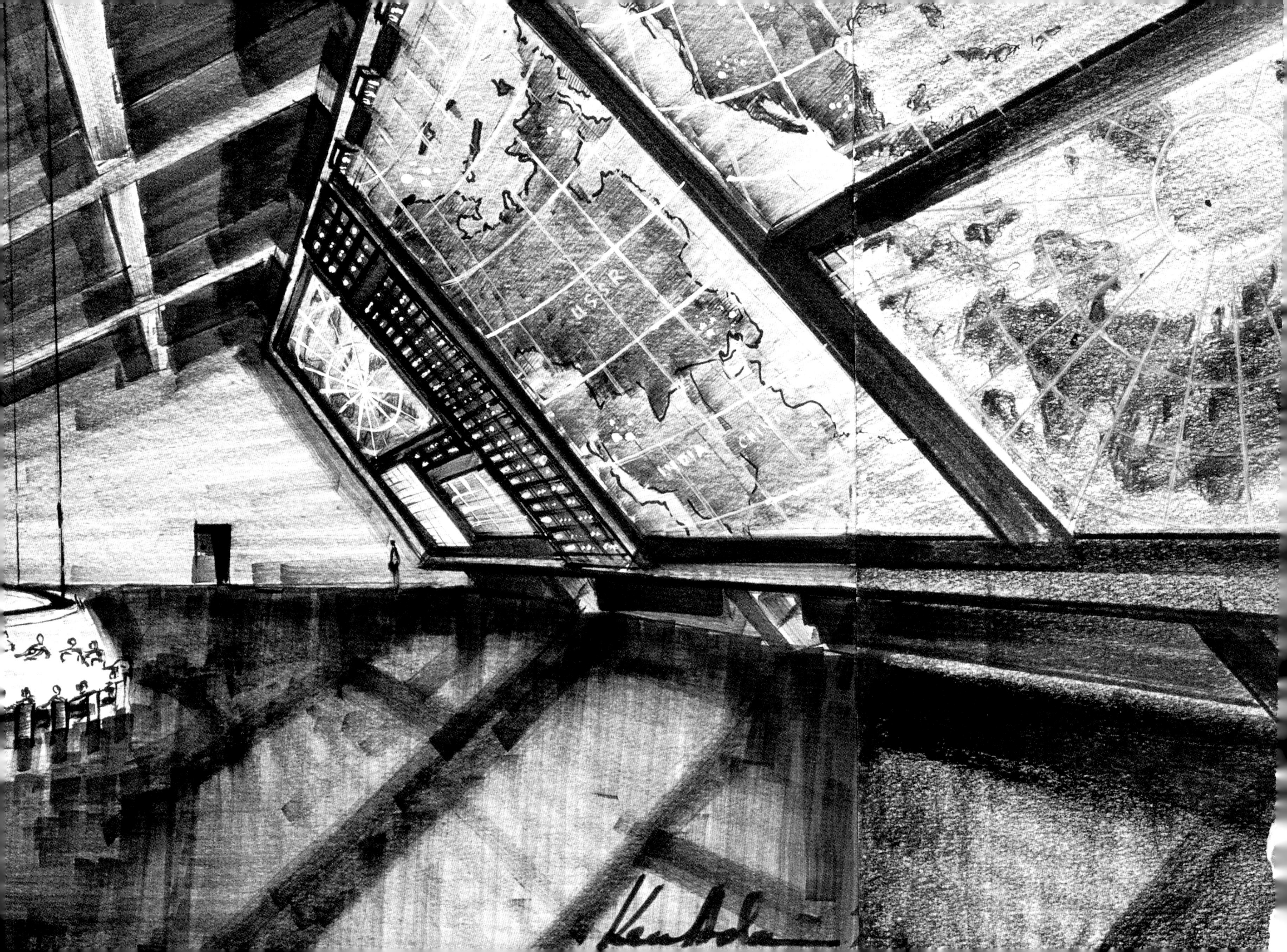
USSR

'We had decided that the scenes in the B52 bomber should be as realistic and detailed as possible, complete with bomb bay holding nuclear warheads with Second World War-style drawings and messages scribbled on them. But when Slim Pickens, the cowboy actor and stunt rider, replaced Peter Sellers as Major T. J. "King" Kong, Stanley decided he should "ride" one of the bombs like a bucking bronco.'

THE BRONCO RIDE Final drawing of the bombs and warheads, with Slim Pickens preparing to ride the weapon through the open bomb door.

DR. STRANGELOVE

right **THE BOMB BAY** These drawings show various initial concepts of the two nuclear bombs with their warheads, for the bomb-bay sequences aboard the B52 bomber, 1962.

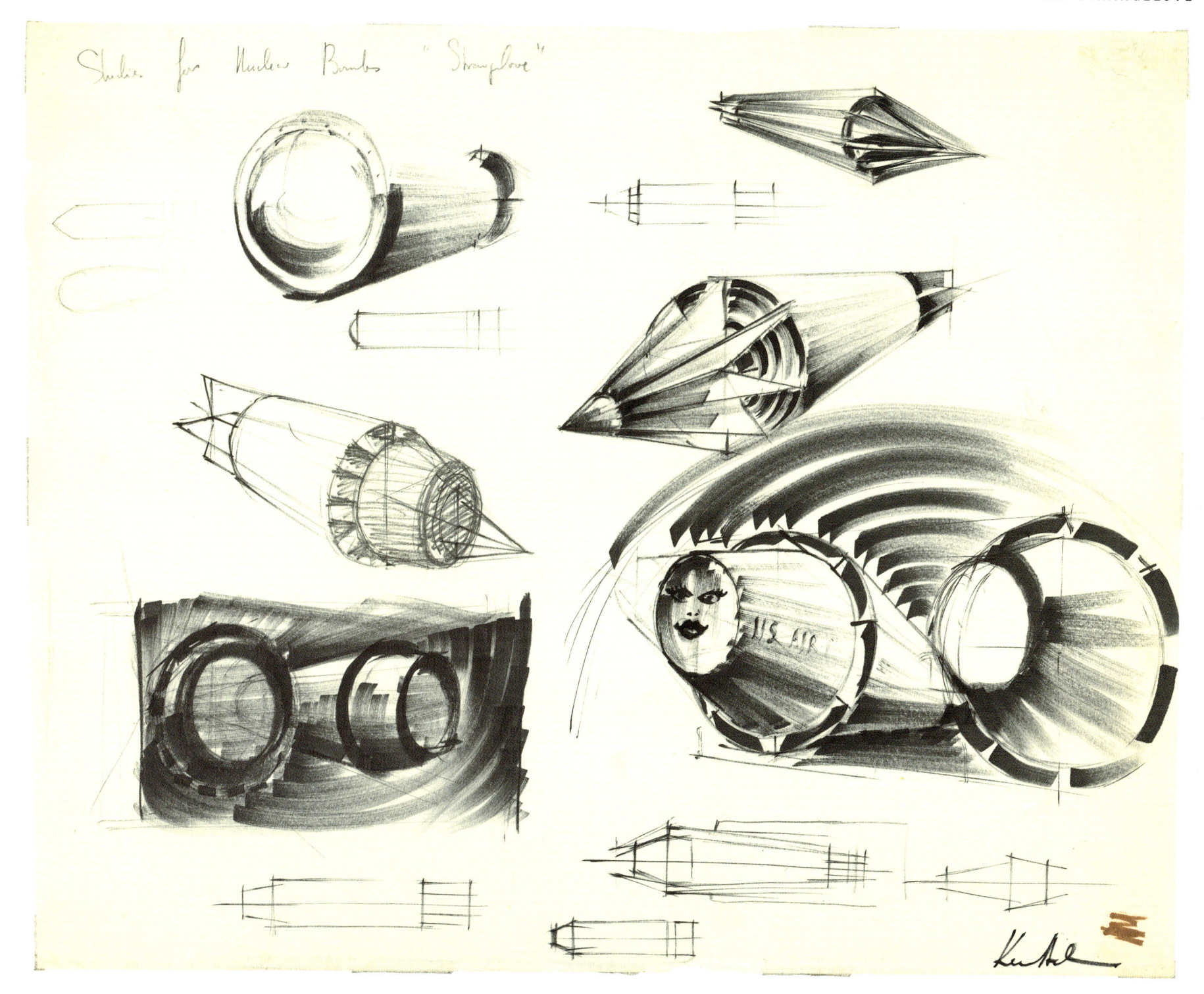

WORKING WITH STANLEY KUBRICK

BARRY LYNDON [1975]

'We did enormous amounts of research,' says Ken Adam of Stanley Kubrick's ambitious mid-1970s attempt to make 'an accurate documentary of mid-eighteenth-century England'. The film was based on *The Luck of Barry Lyndon*, William Makepeace Thackeray's novel about a penniless Irish adventurer who wants to be a gentleman. Historic houses, paintings of the period, music, garments, maps and landscapes were initially researched in 'a miniature war room in the garage of Stanley's house'. The word 'costume' was banned – this was supposed to be an historical documentary, after all – and the interiors were to be shot by candlelight. Adam 'never did one single sketch … the only sketches were done by a brilliant assistant', but he was in charge of the overall visual concept of the film, which was shot over a two-year period in Ireland, England and Potsdam. Kubrick's obsession with detail made the experience very stressful. It was ironic that it was for *Barry Lyndon* that Adam won his first Academy Award – as 'Best Art Director' – because 'somehow I felt that my purely creative and imaginative contribution on other films might have been more deserving of the award. This film was shot entirely on location. I felt it was more reproductive than imaginative.'

POTSDAM Still of the Potsdam sequence, filmed by the second unit in 1974. Stanley Kubrick had originally wanted Ken Adam to direct this sequence.

'Stanley wanted to base the pictorial elements on paintings, but he had a brilliant eye and it was much better when he *didn't* copy.'

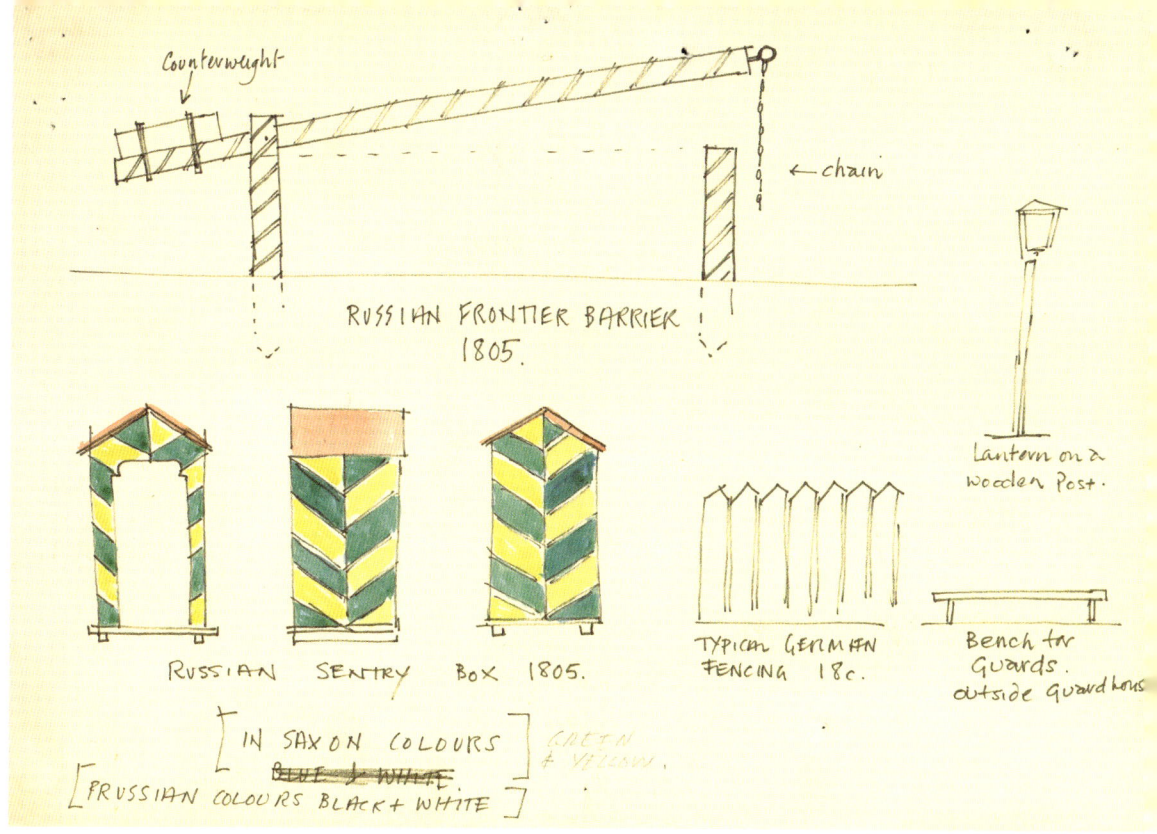

above and below **BORDER POST** Two drawings by Ken Adam's assistant, Ivor Beddoes, of the details of a mid-eighteenth-century border post.

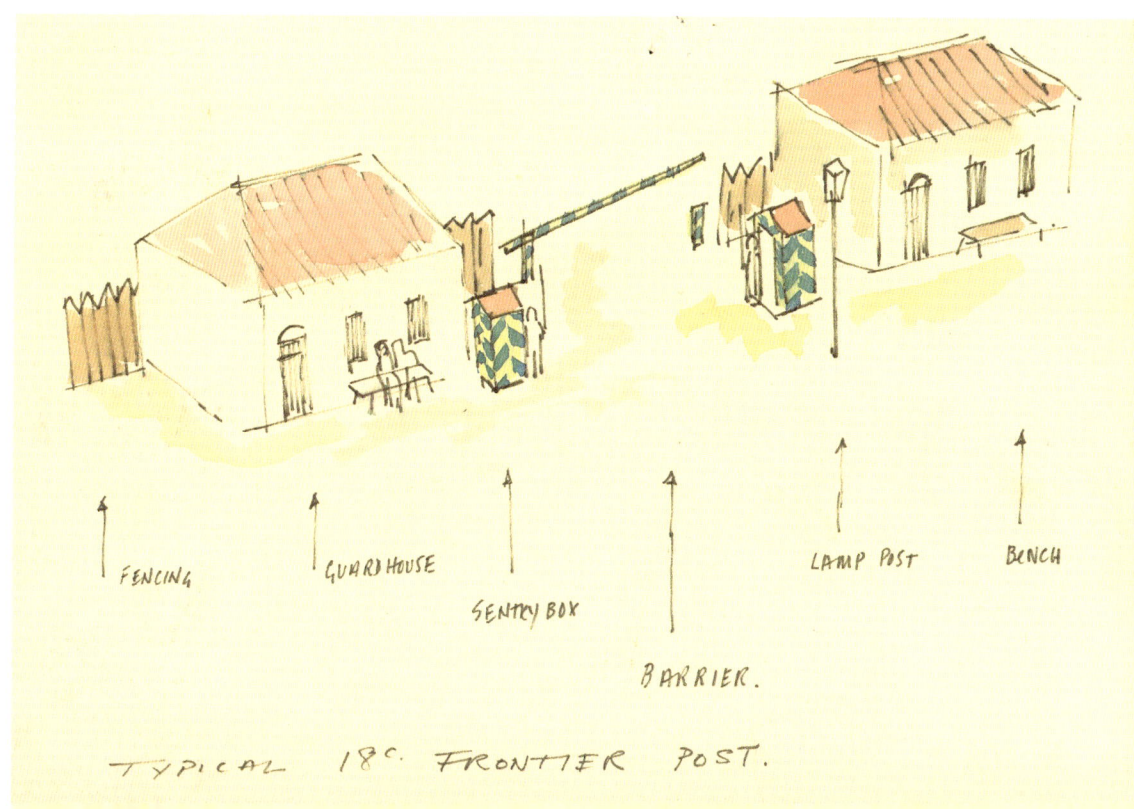

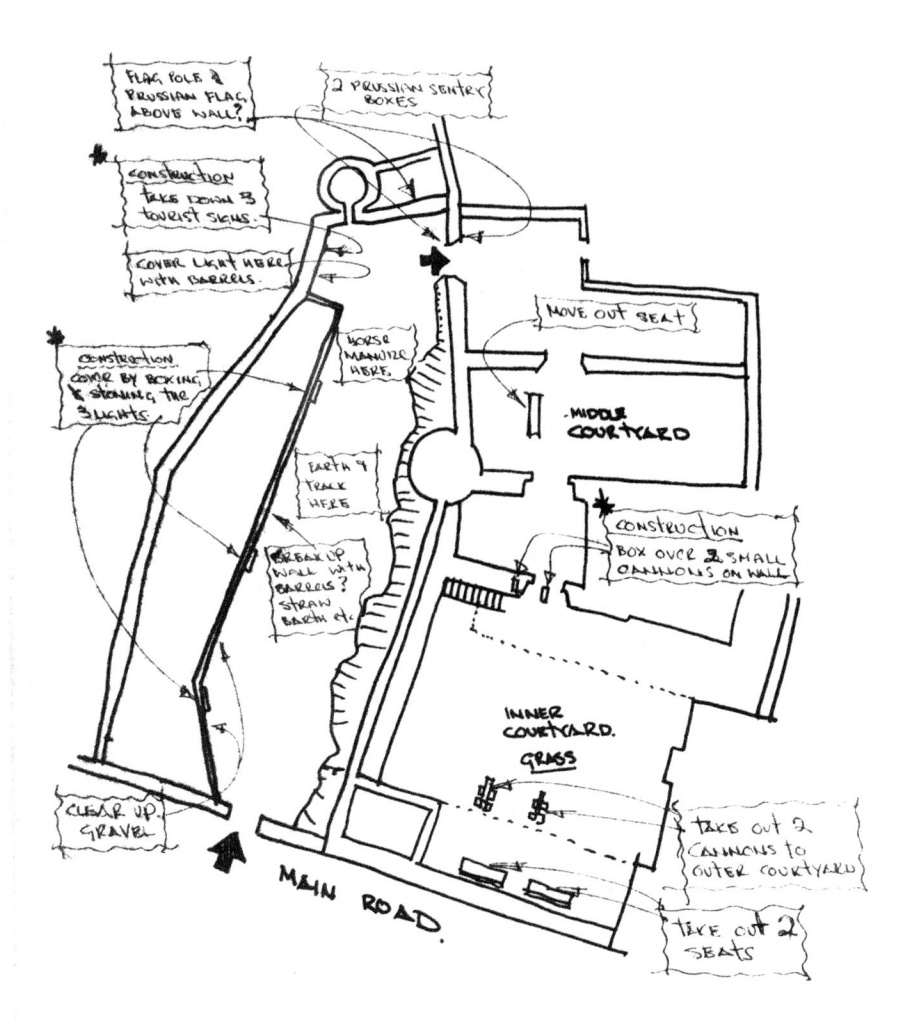

above and right **CAMERA POSITIONS**
Drawings showing possible camera positions on locations at Cahir Castle and Cappoquin in Ireland.

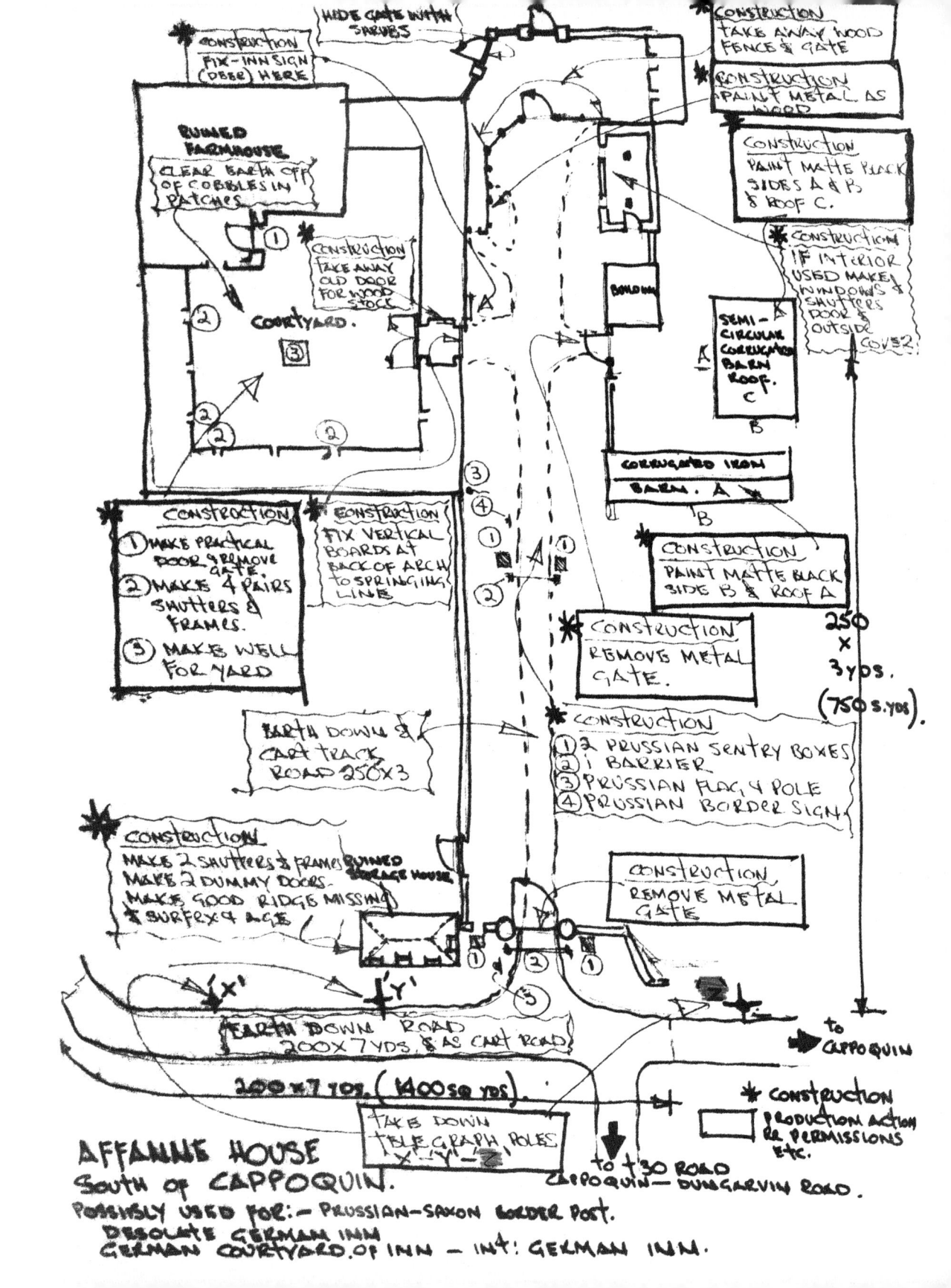

BARRY LYNDON

RESEARCH DRAWINGS
Four research drawings by Ivor Beddoes: Prussian border guards; the interior of Lady Lyndon's Hackton Castle; civilians watching a military parade; recruiting outside a village pub.

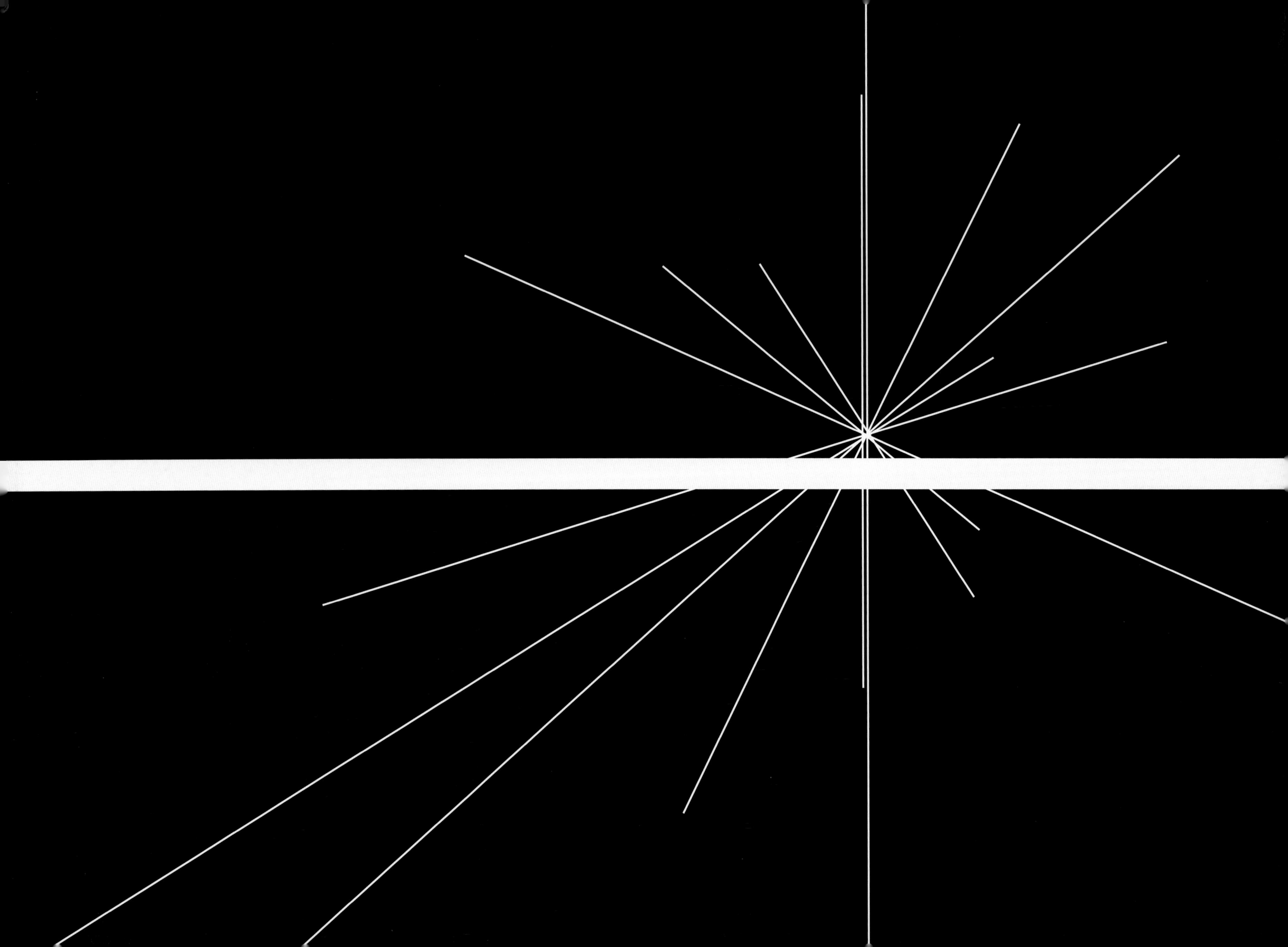

3
DESIGNING JAMES BOND

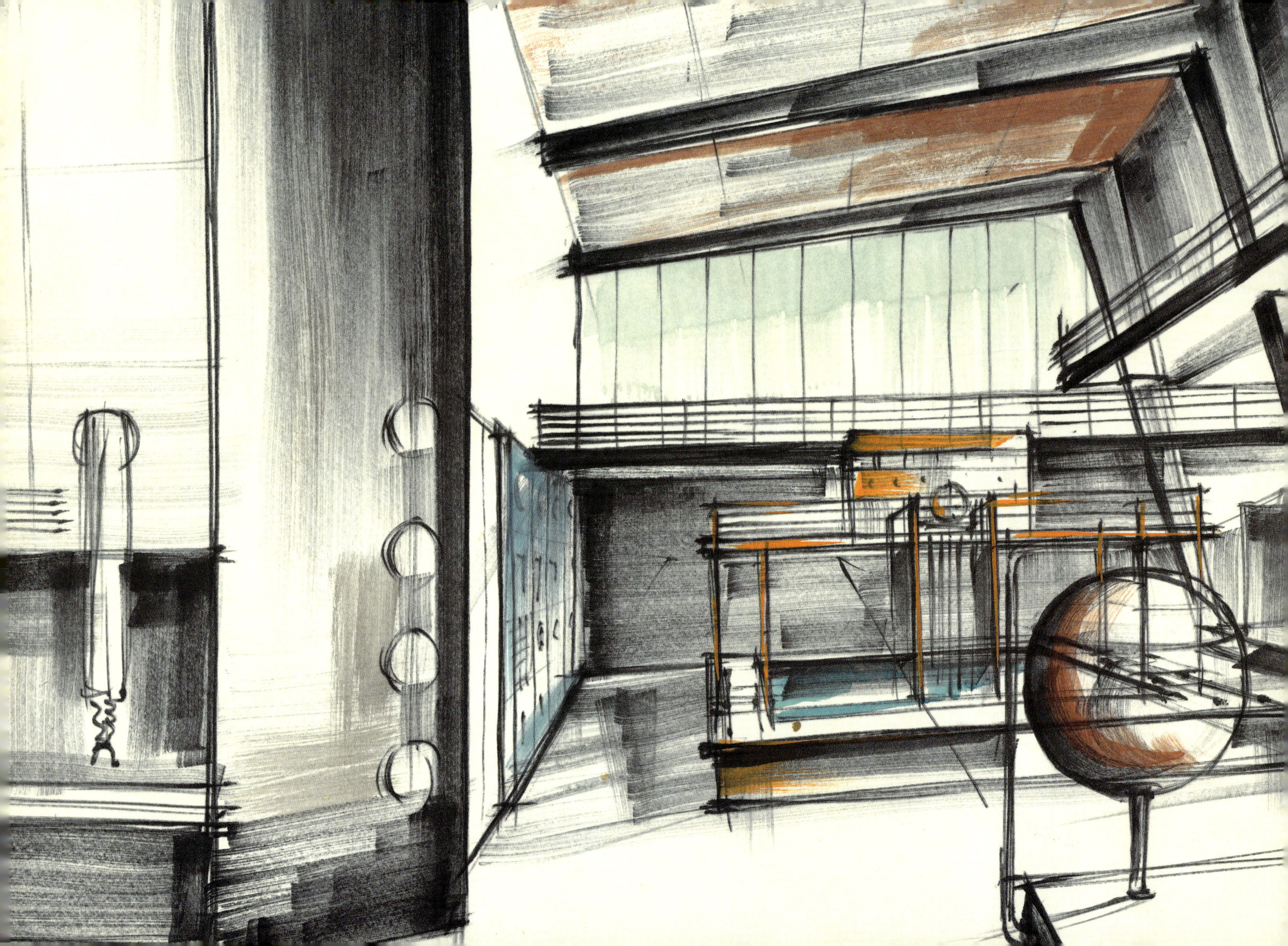

DR. NO [1962]

For the first of the James Bond films, Ken Adam had an initial budget of £14,000, out of a total of £350,000. For this, while the main unit was filming in Jamaica, he created various sets at Pinewood, including the casino (based on Les Ambassadeurs), Bond's Chelsea apartment and M's wood-panelled office. Design features such as the spider-web-like grille in the Doctor's ante-room ceiling and the metallic Piranesi-like corridors meant that 'a small whodunnit' became a franchise very different in tone to the Ian Fleming books. From *Dr. No* onwards, the stories of Bond films would usually resemble the Greek myth of Theseus and the Minotaur: the hero enters the maze of the villain's lair, gets captured and tortured, manages to escape with special equipment, blows up the villain's lair, saves the Western world with his quick thinking and professionalism, and, in a final joke, gets together with a warrior woman from the underworld. The Minotaur, meanwhile, has a public face that is high-tech and a private face that is that of a crazy Renaissance banker-prince.

left **THE REACTOR ROOM** Concept for Dr. No's nuclear reactor room, 1961.

below **PINEWOOD** Still of author Ian Fleming visiting Sean Connery on the reactor-room set constructed at Pinewood.

DR. NO

DESIGNING JAMES BOND

'After we encounter Dr. No – his voice anyway – on the island of Crab Key, I adopted a slightly tongue-in-cheek, slightly ahead-of-contemporary approach: the mixture of antique and modern in his underground apartment, with the Goya Wellington portrait propped up on the couch and a magnified aquarium in the stone wall.'

opposite and this page **DR. NO'S RECEPTION ROOM**
Design of Dr. No's underground reception room, and contact-sheet of stills of the finished set.

DR. NO

DENT'S OFFICE

opposite **PROFESSOR DENT'S OFFICE**
Design of Professor Dent's office, with display cabinet, plus overhead view of set layout, 1961.

above **DR. NO'S GUEST BEDROOM**
Dr. No's underground guest bedroom, where Bond and Honeychile Rider change into surprisingly well-tailored clothes, 1961.

GOLDFINGER [1964]

Goldfinger was the third of the James Bond films, following the huge and unexpected success of *Dr. No* and *From Russia with Love* (which Ken Adam did not design—he was working on *Dr. Strangelove*, *Woman of Straw* and other films). This time, the budget was considerably higher and the fantastical elements of the story could be brought to the fore—a golden opportunity to imagine another 'secret place' like the War Room and make it larger than life, though the script was still mostly faithful to Ian Fleming's original novel. The pre-credits 'Mexican' sequence, with light-hearted pay-off, was added at the script stage, but derived—more or less distantly—from Fleming were Goldfinger's stud farm in Kentucky, his 'Rumpus Room' for harness and tack (school of Frank Lloyd Wright) which converts into a gas chamber, his Laser Room and Bond's Aston Martin DB5, with all its gadgets.

left **SETTLING OF ACCOUNTS** Sean Connery as Bond and Harold Sakata as Oddjob, on the Fort Knox set at Pinewood, 1964.

right **FORT KNOX** Final design concept of the Fort Knox interior, 1963. The climax of the film takes place in the bullion rooms, which Ken Adam envisaged as a gigantic cathedral built of steel and granite, with downlighting from a vaulted ceiling. Unlike a real gold vault, the room was to be stacked high with gold, behind bars as in a prison.

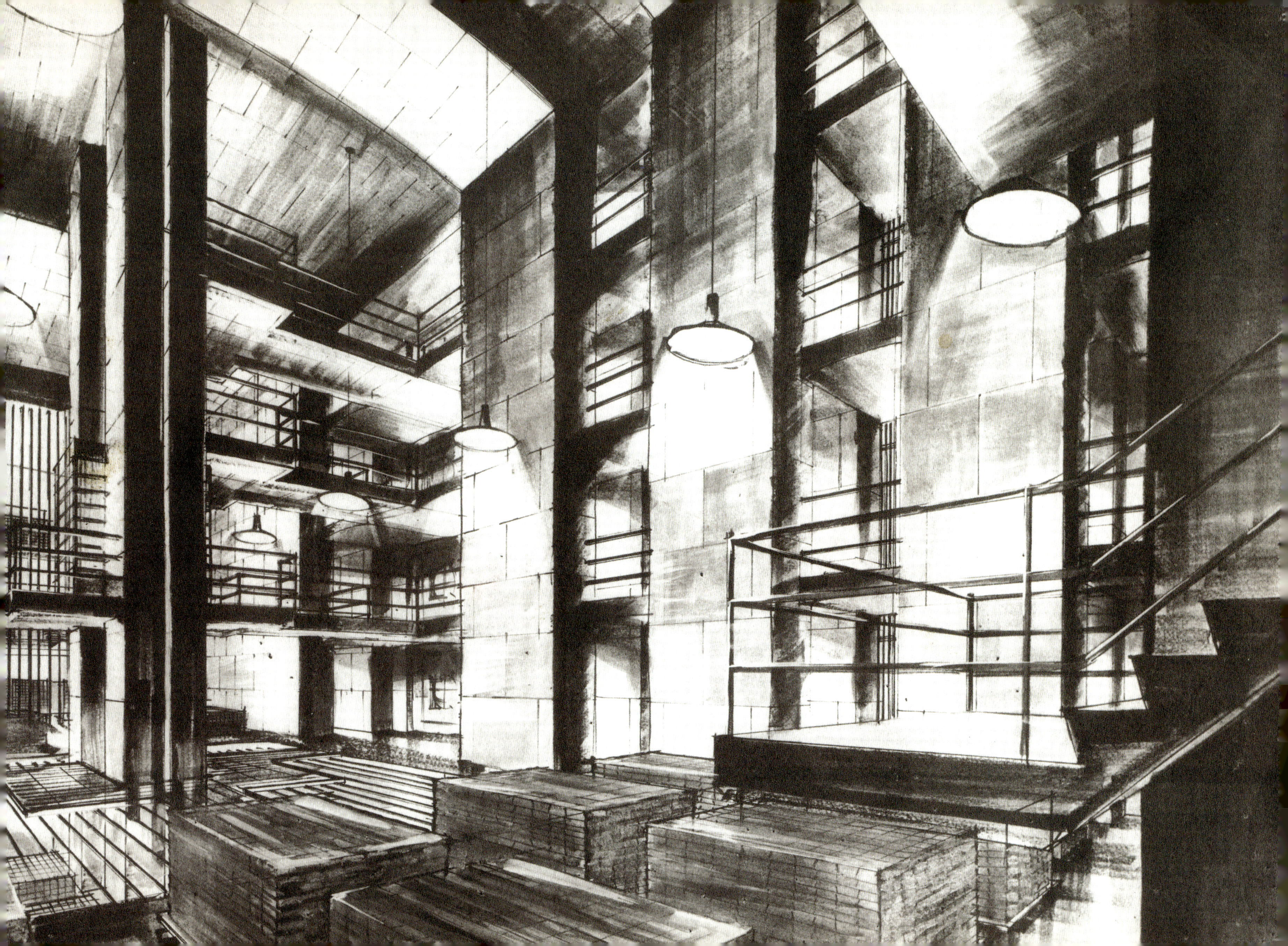

'I'd seen the interiors of the gold vaults at the Bank of England, and found them most uninteresting – a series of low tunnels really. So I decided to use stylization. And I had quite a battle about whether it was over the top. I wanted to build a cathedral of gold, almost forty foot high – completely impractical; gold is too heavy for that. But it worked.'

this page and opposite **FORT KNOX** Initial visual concepts for the Fort Knox interior, with characteristic perspective, 1963, and (opposite) final design concept, from the establishing angle used in the film.

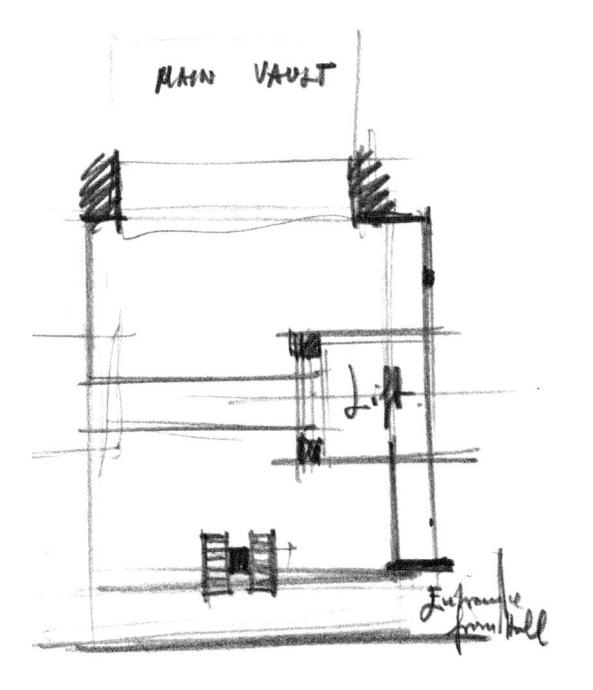

DESIGNING JAMES BOND

GOLDFINGER

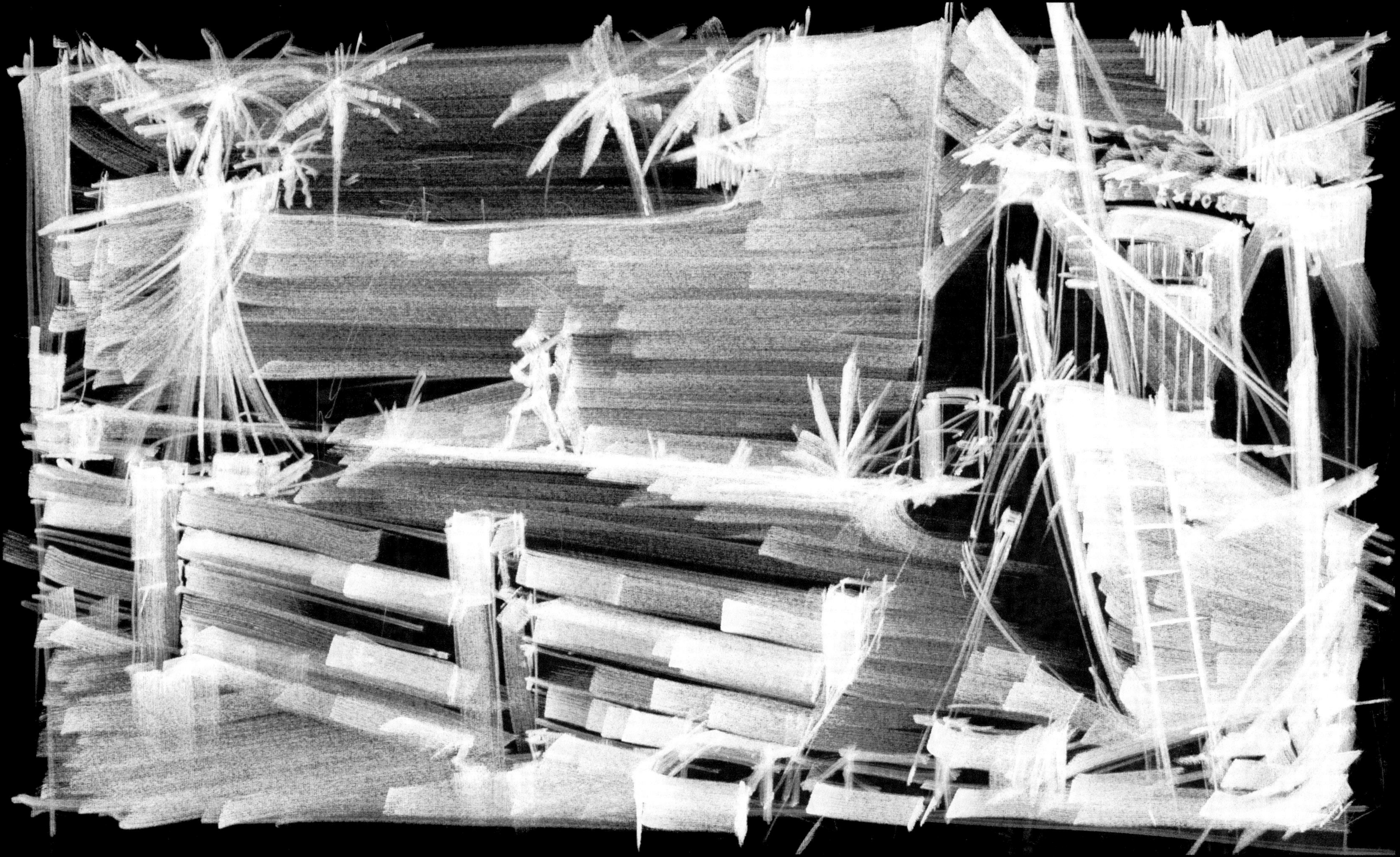

GOLDFINGER

opposite and above **PRE-CREDITS SEQUENCE**
Concepts for the pre-credits sequence, showing the quayside where Bond arrives (opposite) and an interior with characteristic round roof grille (above).

DESIGNING JAMES BOND   61

GOLDFINGER

THE ASTON MARTIN DB5 Sketches, 1963. In the book, the Aston Martin DB3 comes with 'certain extras', such as reinforced bumpers and a gun in a hidden compartment. For the film, Ken Adam was largely responsible for thinking up the gadgets – the machine-guns, the wheel-scythe that was a *Ben-Hur* in-joke, the ejector seat, and the over-riders that came out like boxing gloves – to create an Andy Warhol-like icon of destructive technology.

'We decided the Aston Martin DB5, the most expensive and sexy British sportscar of the period, would be the right prop for Bond. So I went with Johnny Stears, who was the brilliant special-effects engineer, to the plant at Newport Pagnell. After the picture came out and Aston Martin's sales went up by about 60 per cent, we had no problems getting cars from anybody!'

DESIGNING JAMES BOND

GOLDFINGER

THE STUD FARM Concept drawing of Goldfinger's Kentucky stud farm, the exterior of which was actually built at Pinewood, 1963.

GOLDFINGER

this page and opposite **THE RUMPUS ROOM** Four drawings, showing the evolution of the design, from initial idea through to final concept, in which it transforms into a gas chamber, 1963, and (opposite) a set still of the room, as constructed at Pinewood, complete with harnesses, tack, billiard table and rotating bar, 1964.

DESIGNING JAMES BOND

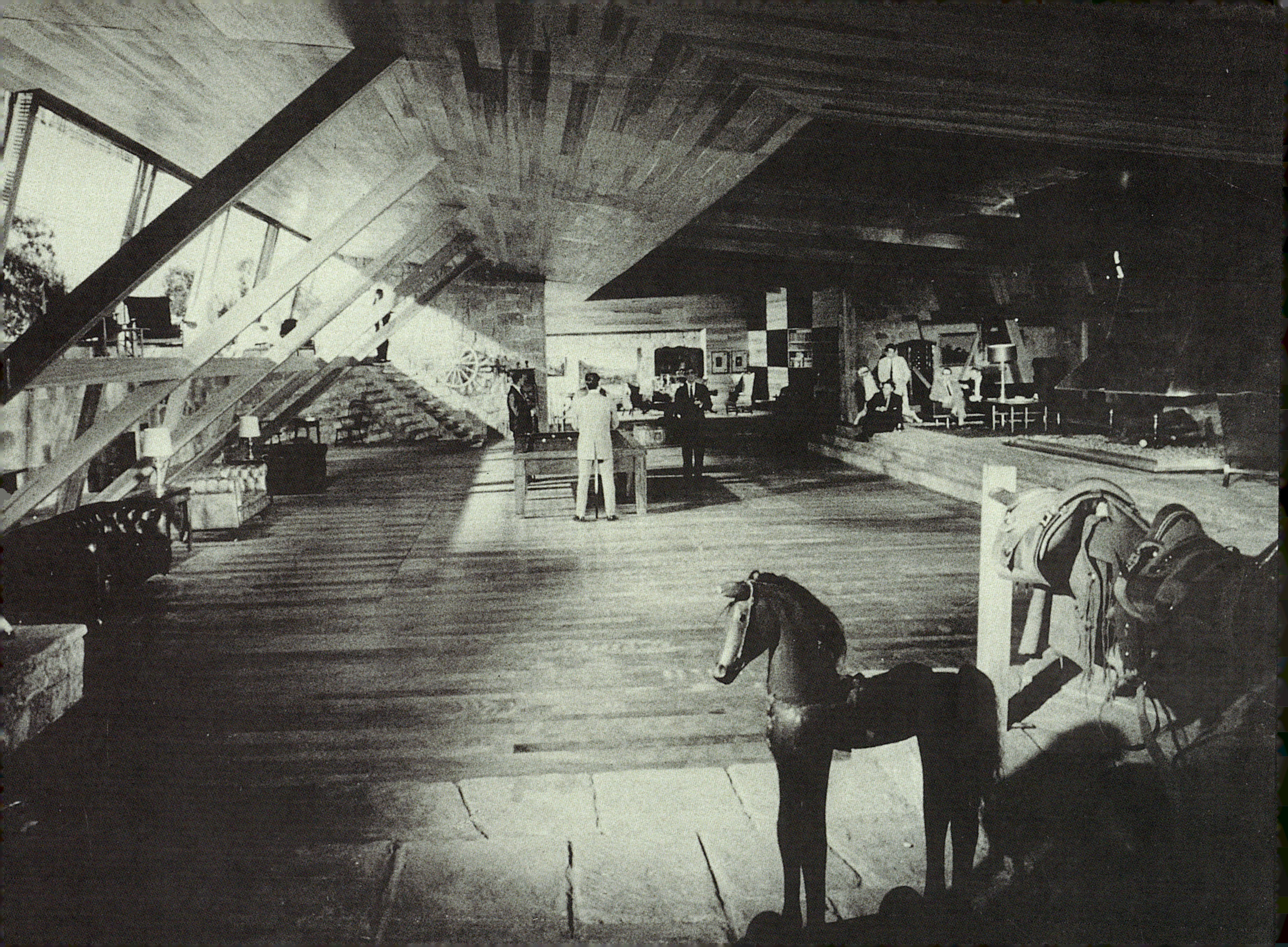

left and below **THE LASER ROOM** Set still and final concept drawing for the Laser Room in Goldfinger's Swiss factory, 1963–64.

opposite **THE PRIVATE JET** Interior of Goldfinger's private jet, for the villain's final appearance and disappearance, 1963.

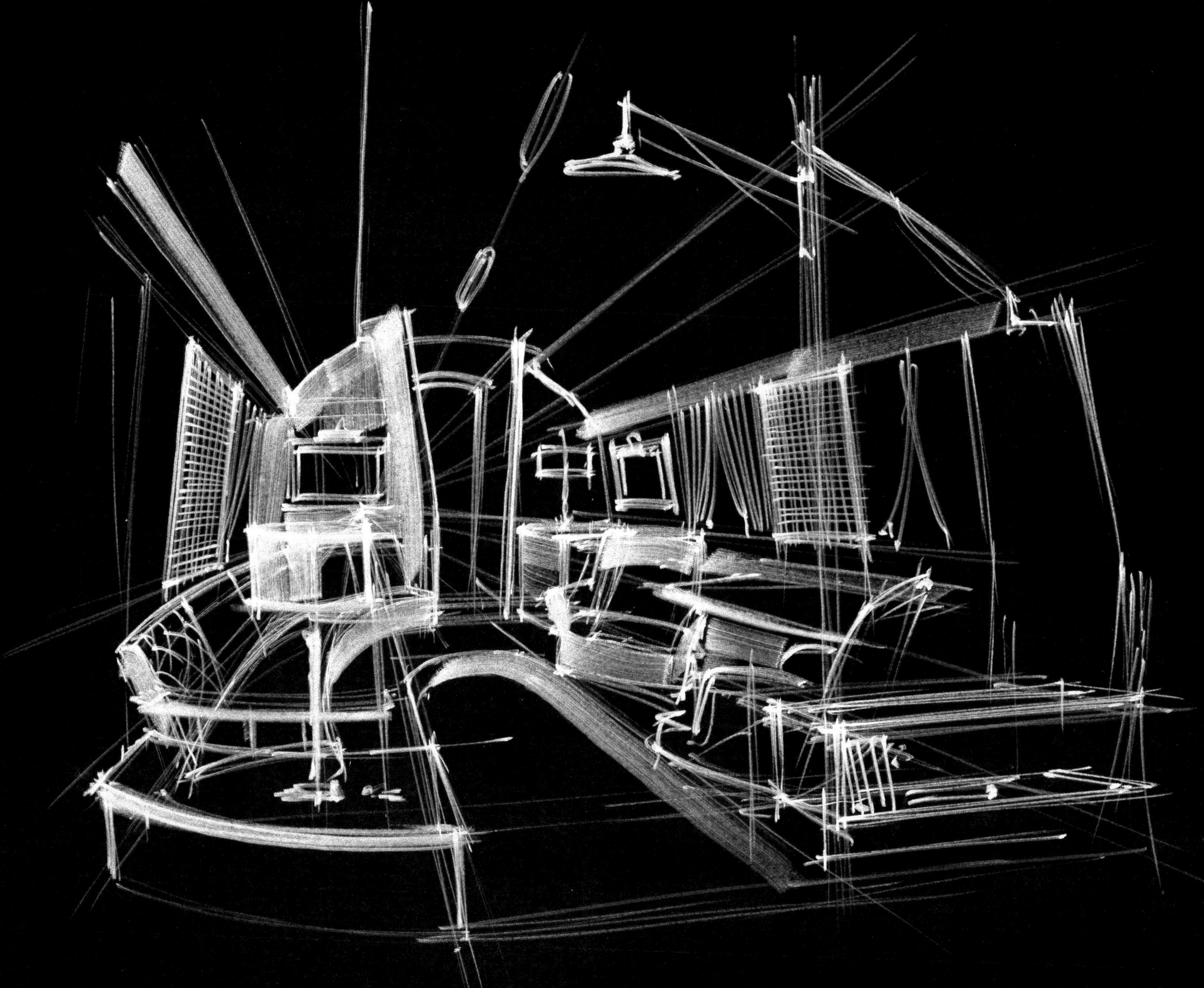

THUNDERBALL [1965]

With *Thunderball*, 'the design, the visuals, were becoming more and more important', and there was a much more substantial budget to match. But this film presented a particular design challenge: much of the action takes place on or beneath the sea, in the Bahamas, where the villain Largo—who has hijacked two nuclear bombs—has his base. There was, as usual, M's Combined Command Centre— this time with Vatican chairs and large tapestries that rise to reveal strategic charts—and there was the SPECTRE headquarters, with its wired-up office furniture like padded electric chairs, of which Ken Adam now says, 'I was getting fed up with boardrooms and long tables.' But once the action shifts to the Bahamas, the sea takes over—and Adam had never created contemporary maritime designs before. He came up with concepts for the villain's superfast and streamlined luxury yacht, the *Disco Volante*, which has a hydrofoil hidden inside it; a sunken Vulcan bomber; assorted bomb carriers and mini-submarines; frogmen, harpoon guns and sharks. 'We were,' Adam recalls, 'getting less and less input from the Fleming books, and the producers relied more and more on spectacle. That's why they gave me a reasonably free hand. The key was to create designs that looked as though they actually worked, and to find a team of specialists who could make them real.'

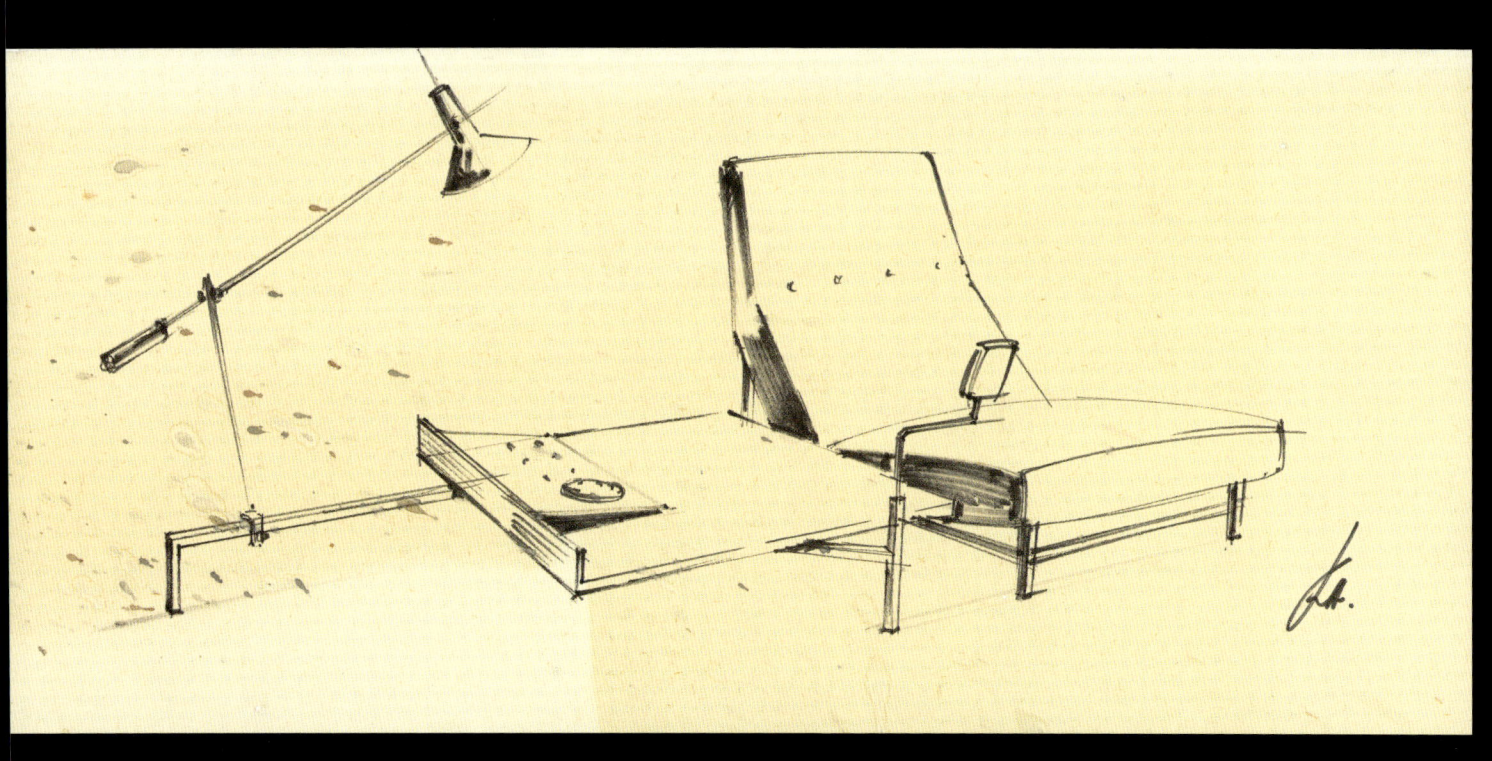

above and right **SPECTRE HEADQUARTERS**
Design concepts for the boardroom interior of SPECTRE's Paris headquarters—the office furniture and the room itself, 1964.

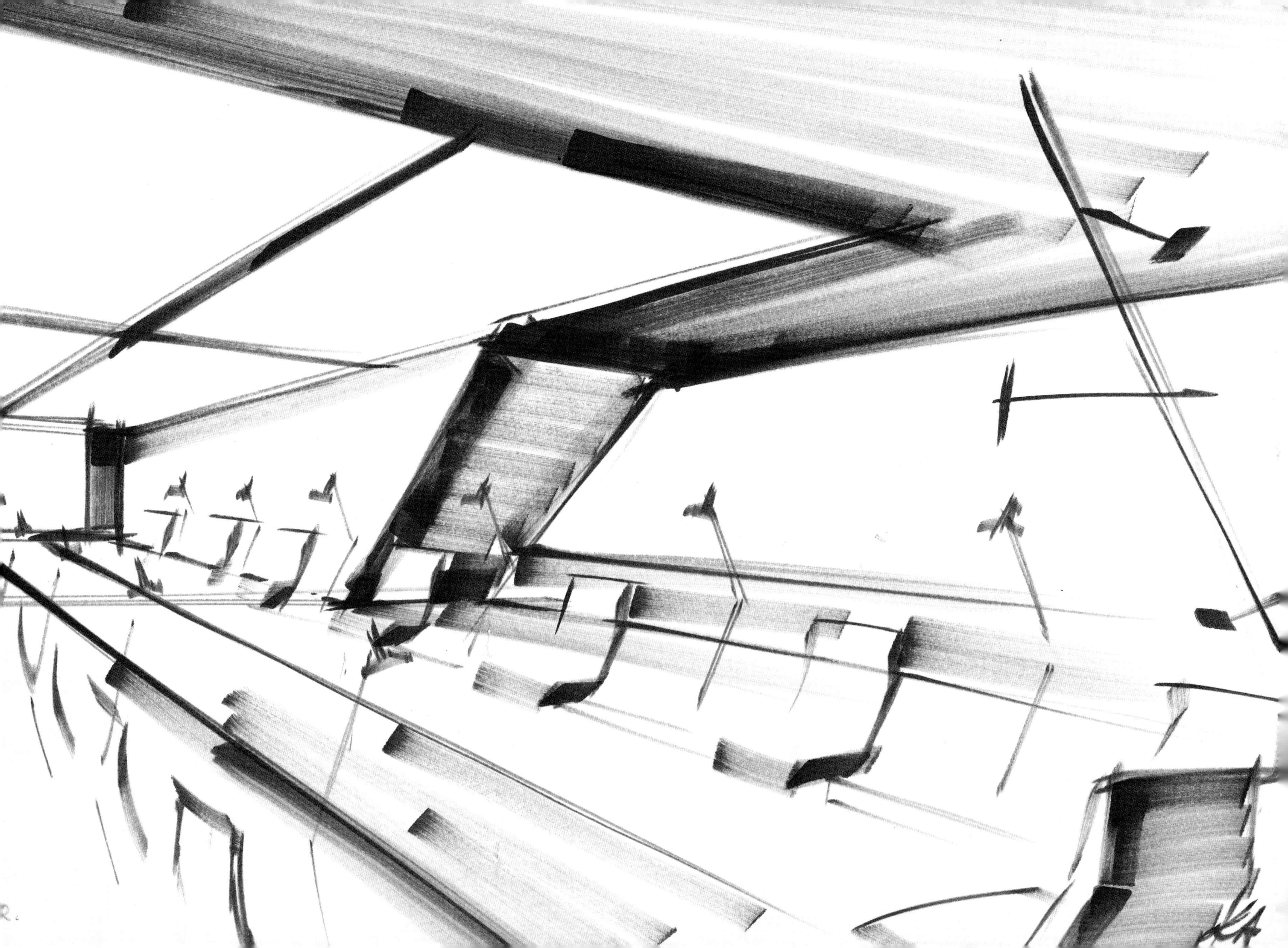

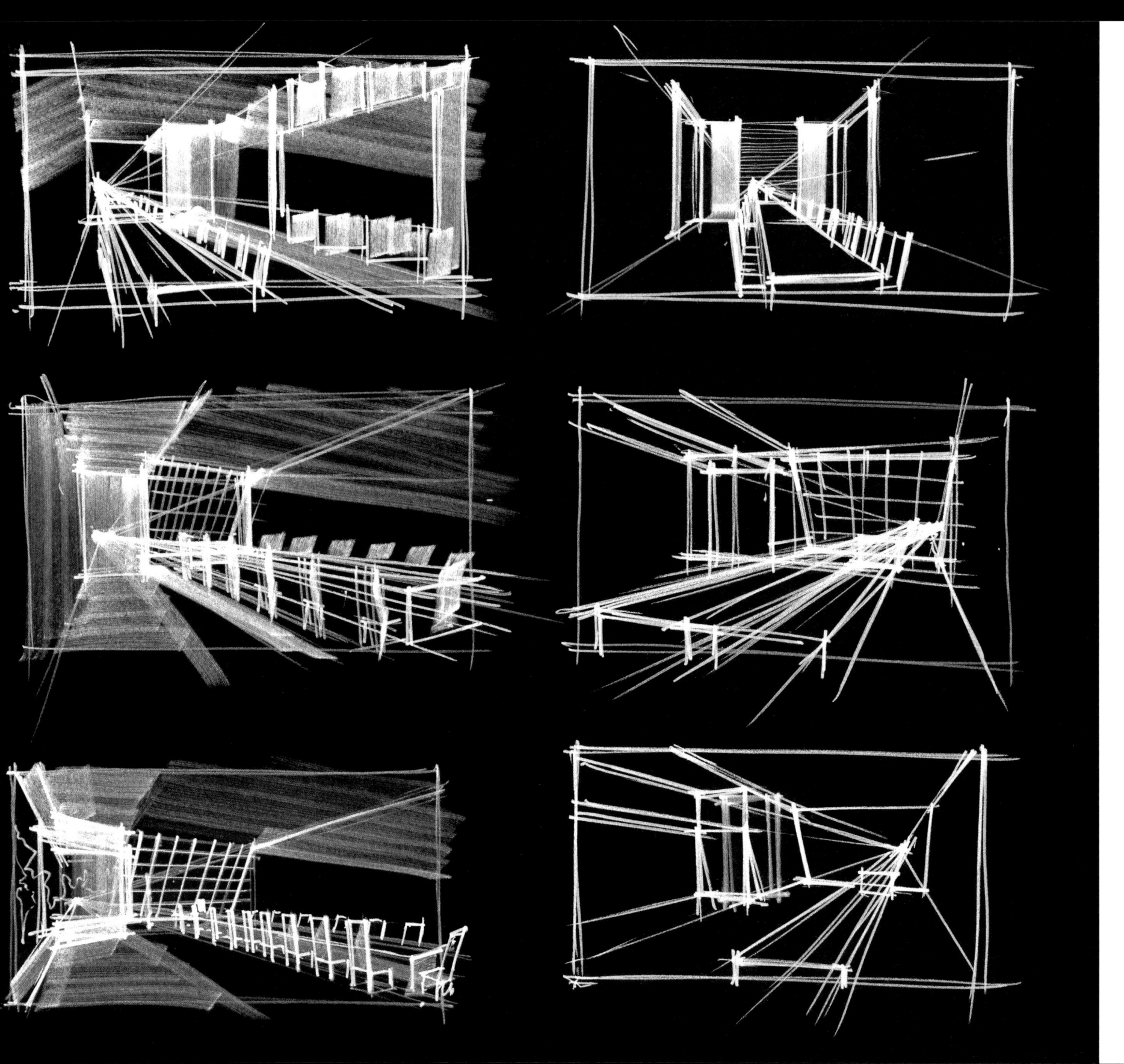

left **SPECTRE HEADQUARTERS**
Six drawings, showing the evolution of SPECTRE's headquarters from various Adam-style perspectives, 1964.

opposite above and below **WHITEHALL**
Set still and final concept drawing of the vast conference room at the Admiralty, with high-backed Vatican chairs and 40-foot-high and 60-foot-wide tapestries that lifted up to reveal various maps and charts, 1964.

'By this time I'd had boardroom after boardroom and I didn't know what to do with SPECTRE headquarters in Paris [opposite]. I decided not to have a board table, but to design every leather chair with its own control console and lighting, and a gangway down the centre – which also gave me the opportunity to have the chair in which the villain is electrocuted disappear into the floor and come up empty....'

THUNDERBALL
COLOUR AVAILABLE

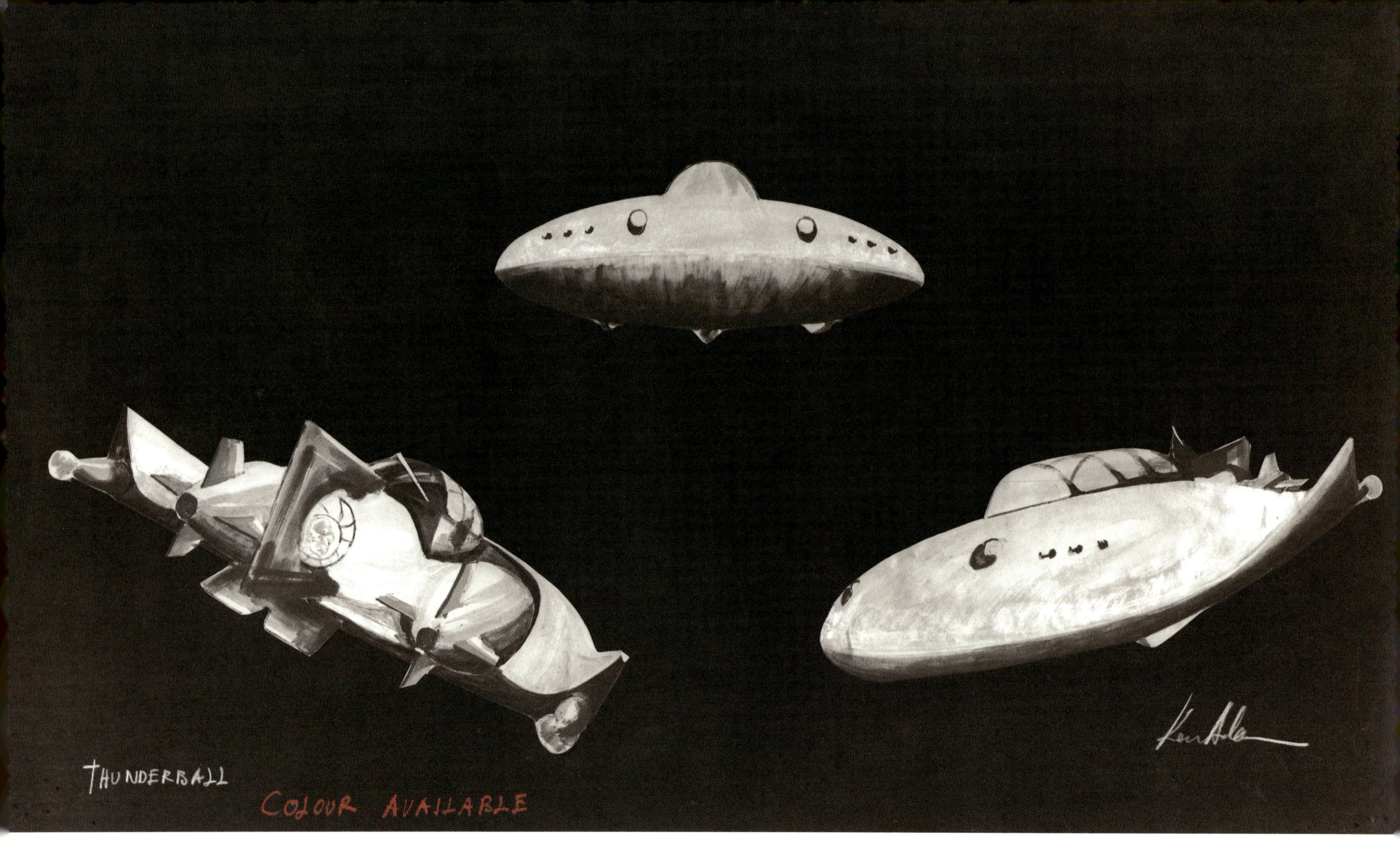

THE MINI-SUBMARINE Final concept of the underwater bomb-carrying mini-submarine, 1964.

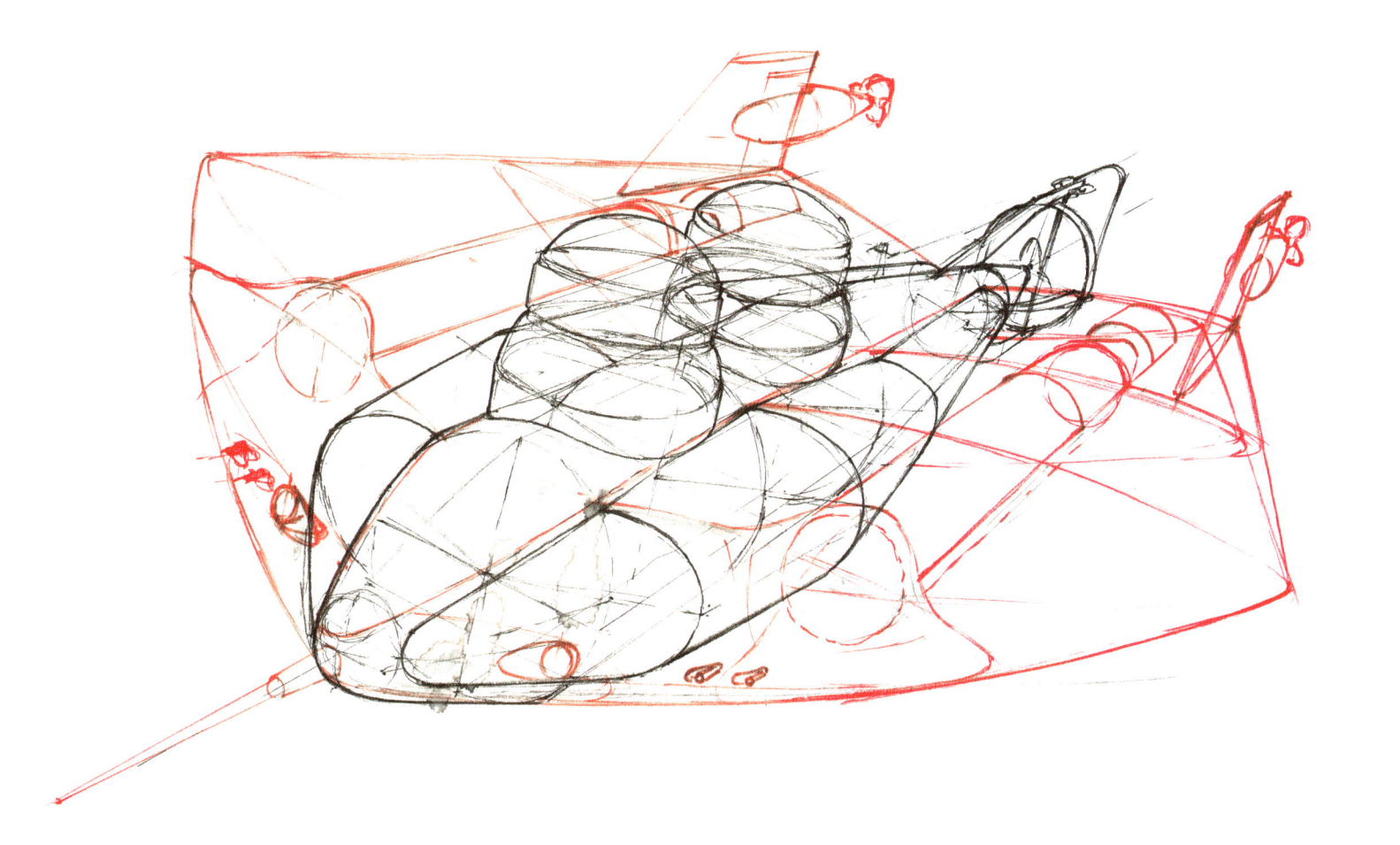

'For the underwater nuclear bomb carrier, I managed to find somebody in Miami who built mini-submarines, and I showed him my drawings. "Yeah, it should work," he said, "if you raise the engines for balance." I always found somebody who could make things work.'

above **THE MINI-SUBMARINE** Initial concept of the mini-submarine.

right **THE YACHT** Final concept drawing of Largo's *Disco Volante* yacht. This was constructed from an old hydrofoil with its length doubled by the addition of a catamaran-like structure around the rear. To prevent the two hulls breaking apart at speed, naval experts added two one-inch slip bolts on either side.

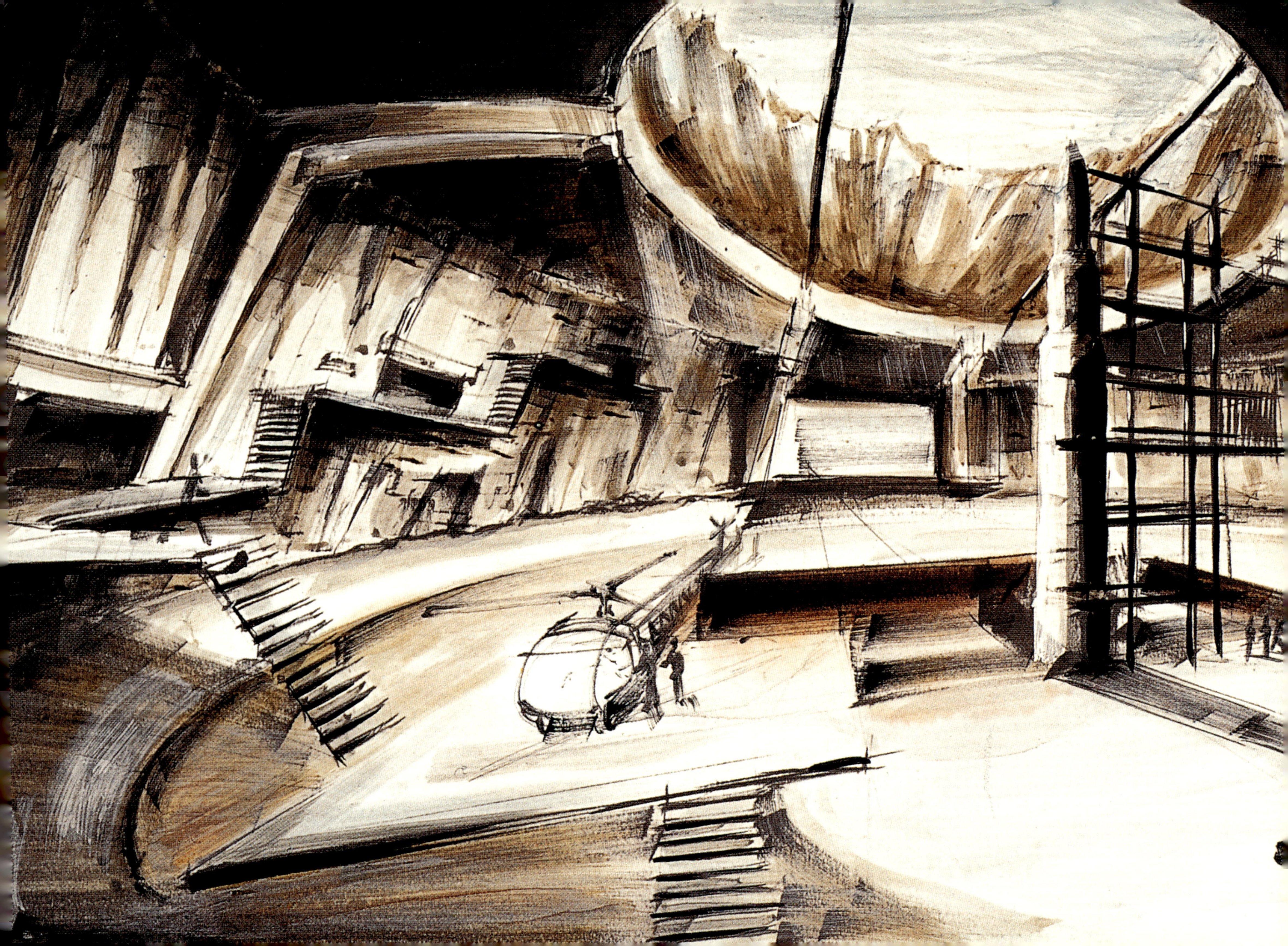

YOU ONLY LIVE TWICE [1967]

'Somewhat against the clock,' says Ken Adam, 'we decided that Ian Fleming had either never been to Japan or had not spent too much time there.' The most interesting designs Adam had to create included Tiger Tanaka's office, with two copper spheres for television sets and an aluminium chute; assorted Japanese domestic interiors, hotel rooms and bedrooms; and 'Little Nellie', the DB5 equivalent, a mini gyrocopter which is carried in a series of Italian-made crocodile-leather suitcases designed by Letizia Adam. But the most elaborate set, which cost more than the whole budget of *Dr. No*, was a volcano with a missile base hidden inside it. The exterior was shot near the island of Kyushu; the interior, built at Pinewood Studios, was some 130 feet high with a diameter of around 440 feet. It was topped with a sliding artificial lake and, in addition, a mobile heliport and a 110-foot space rocket. In the novel, the climax took place in a rather different setting — a castle with a poison garden. The volcano was one of many beautiful exotic locations in the Bond series which hide lethal technologies — the skull beneath the skin....

left and below **THE VOLCANO** Final concept of Blofeld's command centre inside a Japanese volcano, and corresponding set still at Pinewood, 1966.

'Ian Fleming had set *Twice* in Japan, but we found – after covering two-thirds of the country in two helicopters – that none of the locations he'd written about existed in reality. So we had to come up with our own ideas.'

below **PRE-CREDITS SEQUENCE**
Final design concept for the pre-credits Hong Kong bedroom sequence where Bond appears to be shot dead, 1966. The bed springs up into the wood-framed wall.

YOU ONLY LIVE TWICE

left and below **JAPANESE BEDROOM**
Still and design concept for the bedroom where Bond and agent Aki 'do everything Japanese style', and Aki is then mistakenly poisoned. Ken Adam's set — a simple, highly stylized Japanese interior, with the bed on the floor — was constructed at Pinewood.

chair with copper back
for Bond to activate
fluoroscope.

Gun with close circuit television camera
trained on Bond

rotating desk with
fluorescent screens
and Tape Decks.

INT. OSATO's OFFICE

Tabulating Machine with gun sight on monitor screen behind partition.

Swivel Safe set in stainless Steel Surround

'There is an enormous fight between Bond and one of the security guards, an all-in wrestler, so we had sliding paper screens that could be torn. I also introduced a lot of stainless steel around the bar, a tree, and a gun in the ceiling that follows Bond all the time. A modern version of the traditional Japanese idiom, inside a high-rise building.'

left and right: **OSATO'S OFFICE** Final design concept with written explanations, and corresponding film still, of the penthouse office of Osato Chemicals, 1966.

YOU ONLY LIVE TWICE

DESIGNING JAMES BOND

DIAMONDS ARE FOREVER [1971]

Originally to be filmed entirely in the USA without Sean Connery as Bond, *Diamonds Are Forever* ended up being filmed at Pinewood, with Connery cast in the lead role after all — his last appearance in an EON Bond film. Locations for this story about a worldwide diamond conspiracy included Las Vegas, Palm Springs and Santa Barbara. The most prominent designs were for reclusive millionaire Willard Whyte's penthouse (loosely based on Howard Hughes's equivalent, only 'more operatic, less realistic'); Bond's Las Vegas hotel suite, with a huge circular waterbed containing tropical fish; a moon buggy testing-ground filmed in a gypsum mine; and a diamond satellite that looked like a radar dish cum mobile sculpture. Ken Adam was present when producer Cubby Broccoli phoned his friend Howard Hughes, 'but I never actually met him'. Adam did, however, visit Hughes's ranch in Nevada, when the security guards asked him in all seriousness, 'Are you Mr. Hughes?' The colour schemes for the Vegas sequences, with deliberately kitschy pinks, were uncharacteristic of Adam's usually restrained palette — more Sodom and Gomorrah than Bond....

below and right **THE DIAMOND LABORATORY** Set still and final concept for the diamond laboratory, 1971.

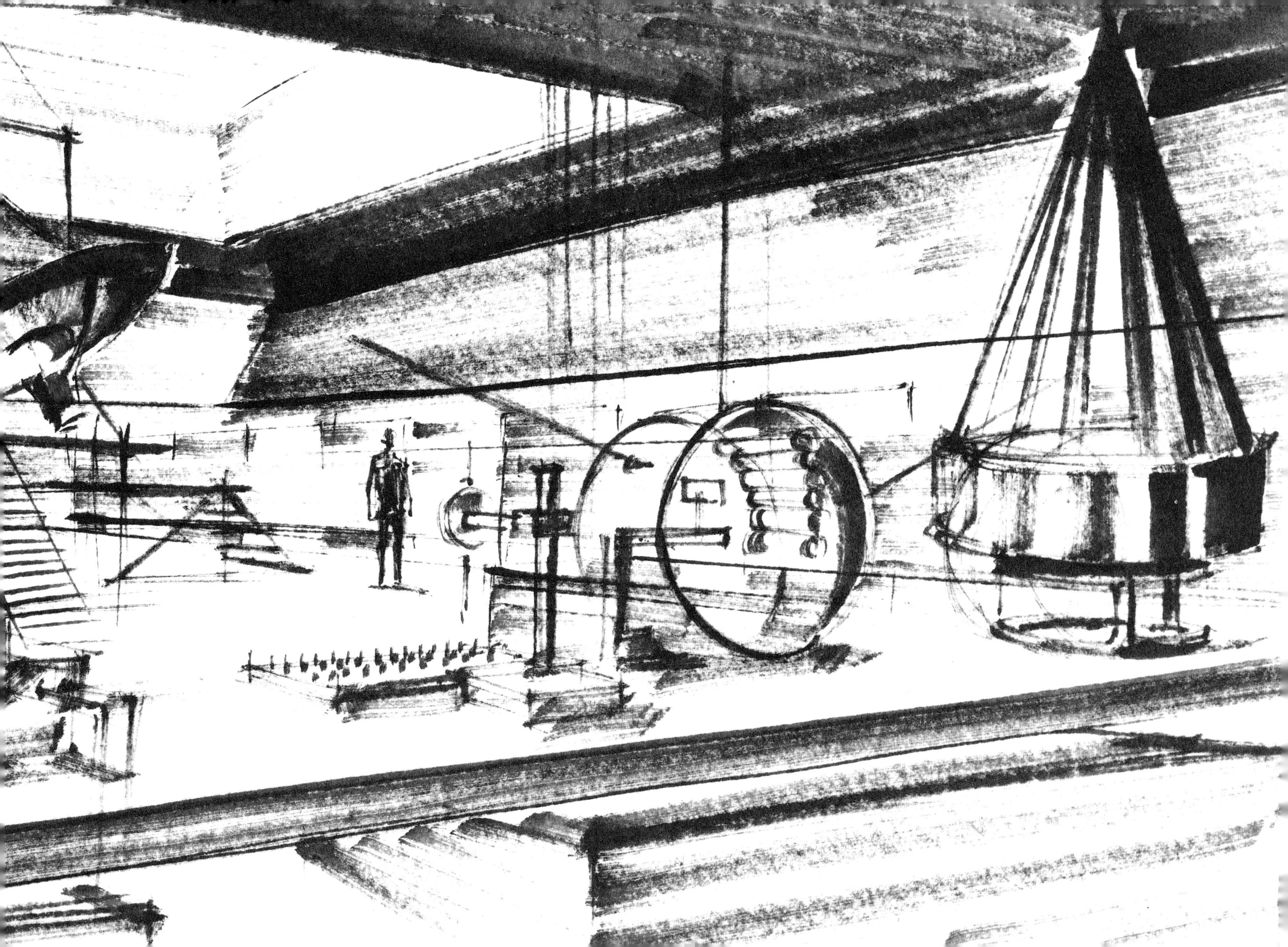

'It was Cubby Broccoli's idea to base Willard Whyte's character on Howard Hughes. I had to design or find a building that suited. Hughes was in those days living in a penthouse in Las Vegas. Eventually I came up with an existing building, which I enhanced to two or three times the height by putting something else on top of it – partly real building, partly painting. Albert Whitlock, the special-effects man, did a travelling matte shot of a car arriving at Whyte's place which then panned up to the sign on top: this had never been done before.'

opposite **THE DIAMOND SATELLITE**
Final design concept of the collapsible diamond satellite.

below **THE PENTHOUSE COMPLEX**
Three drawings of Willard Whyte's penthouse complex, which in the film was to be part-real (located in Las Vegas), part-matte painting, 1971.

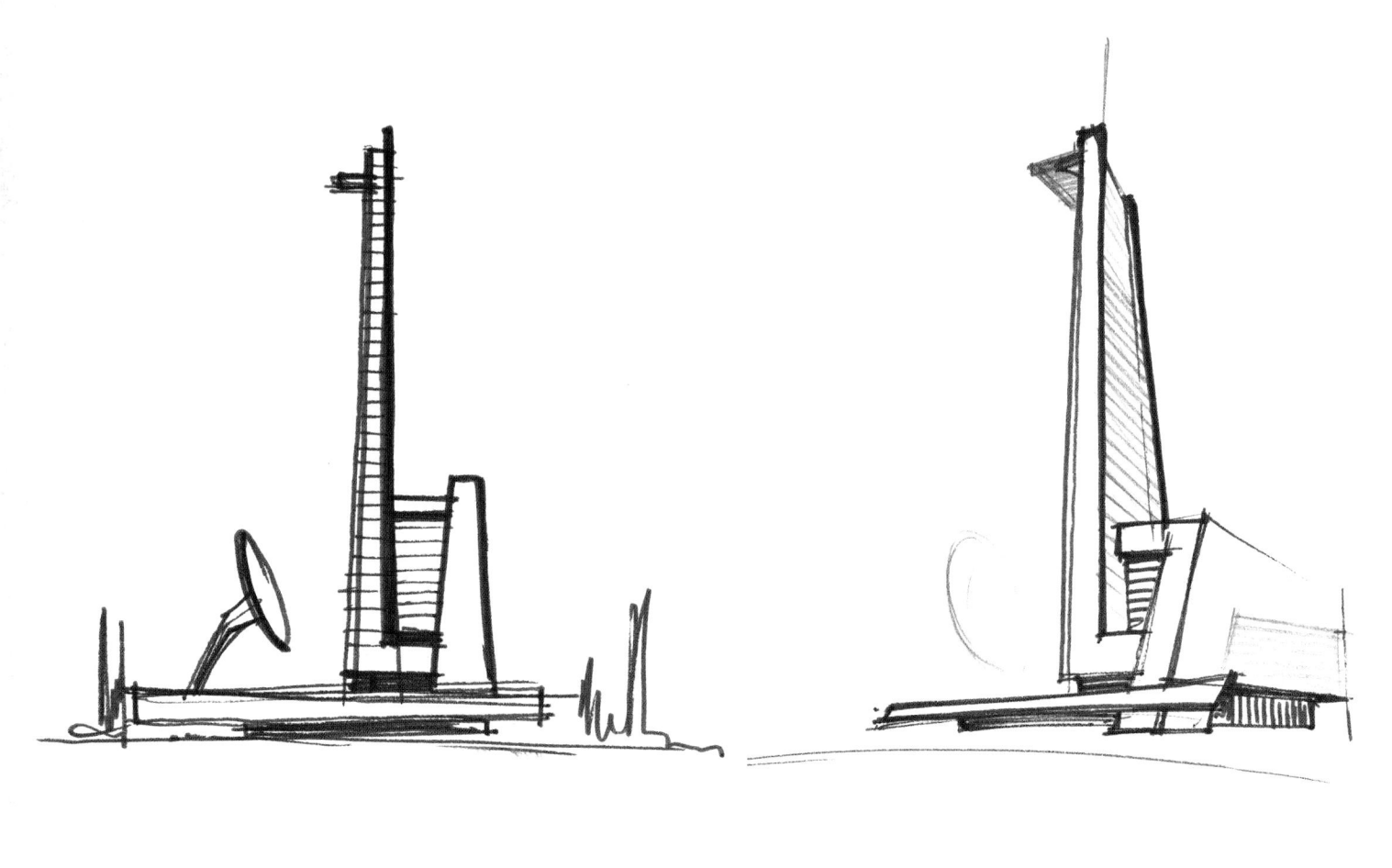

DIAMONDS ARE FOREVER

above **THE LAS VEGAS HOTEL SUITE**
Design for the hotel suite in Caesar's Palace, Las Vegas.

opposite and left **HOTEL WATERBED**
Initial design for the circular waterbed that would have tropical fish swimming around it, and corresponding film still.

DESIGNING JAMES BOND

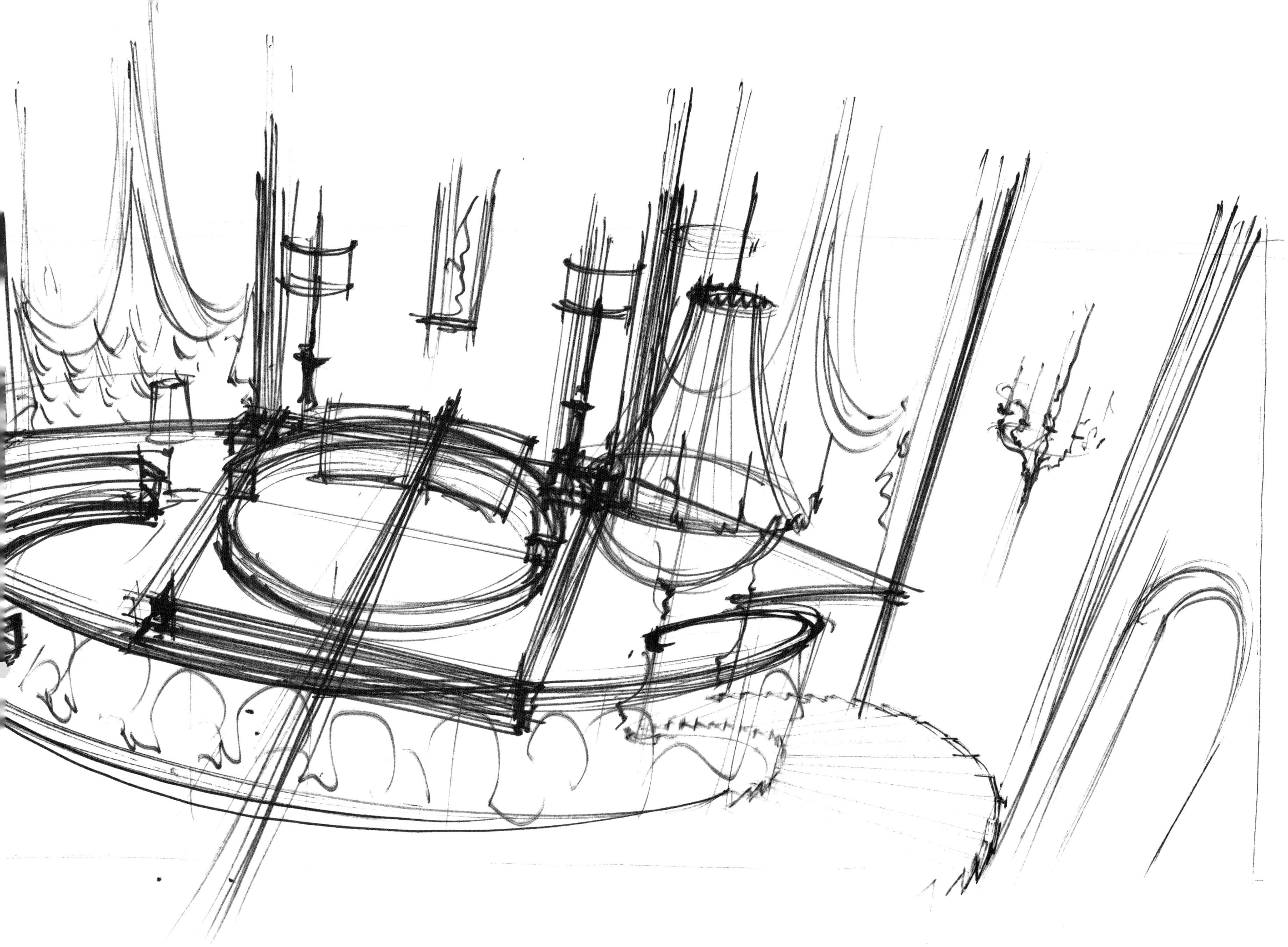

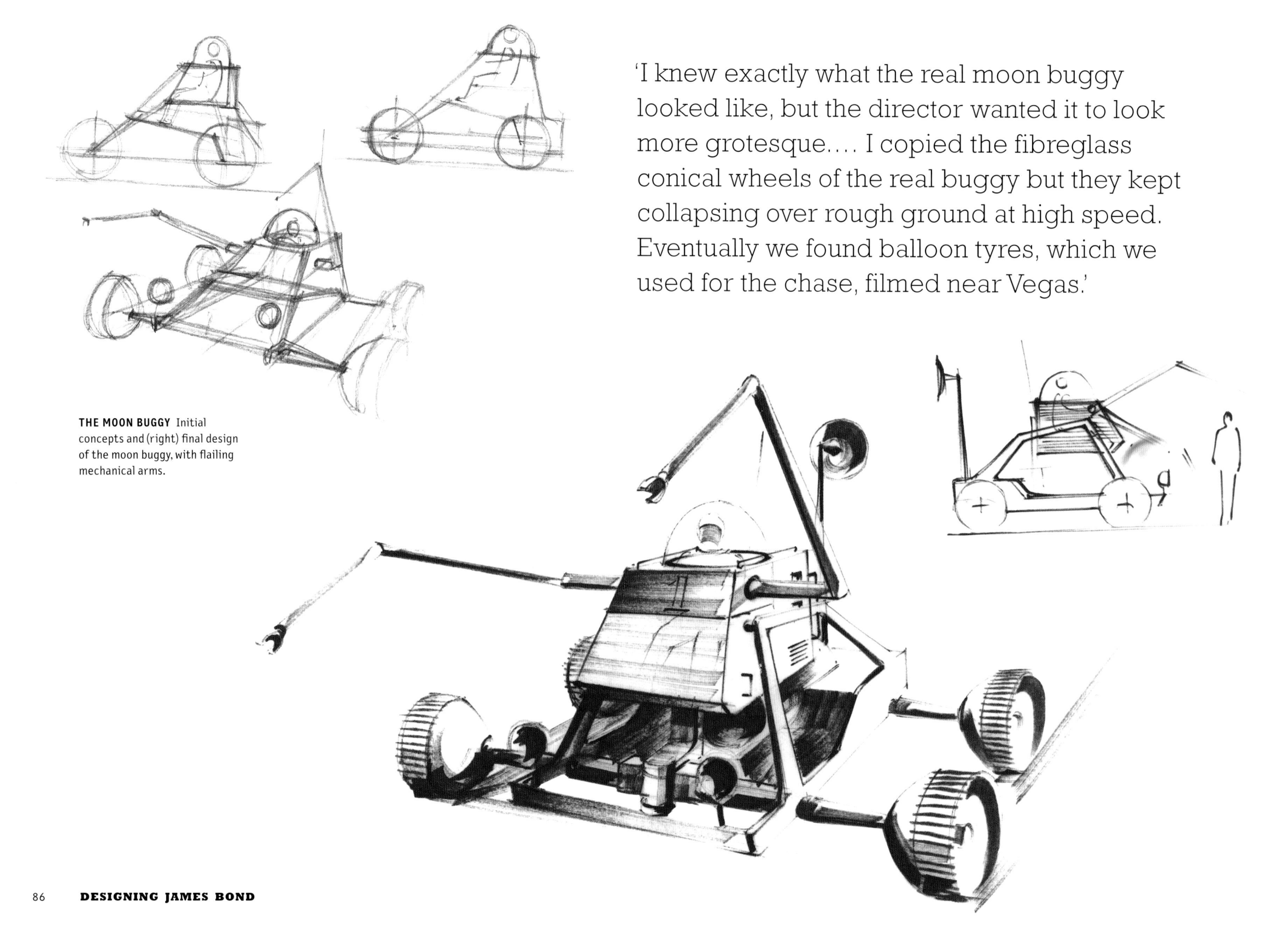

'I knew exactly what the real moon buggy looked like, but the director wanted it to look more grotesque.... I copied the fibreglass conical wheels of the real buggy but they kept collapsing over rough ground at high speed. Eventually we found balloon tyres, which we used for the chase, filmed near Vegas.'

THE MOON BUGGY Initial concepts and (right) final design of the moon buggy, with flailing mechanical arms.

86   DESIGNING JAMES BOND

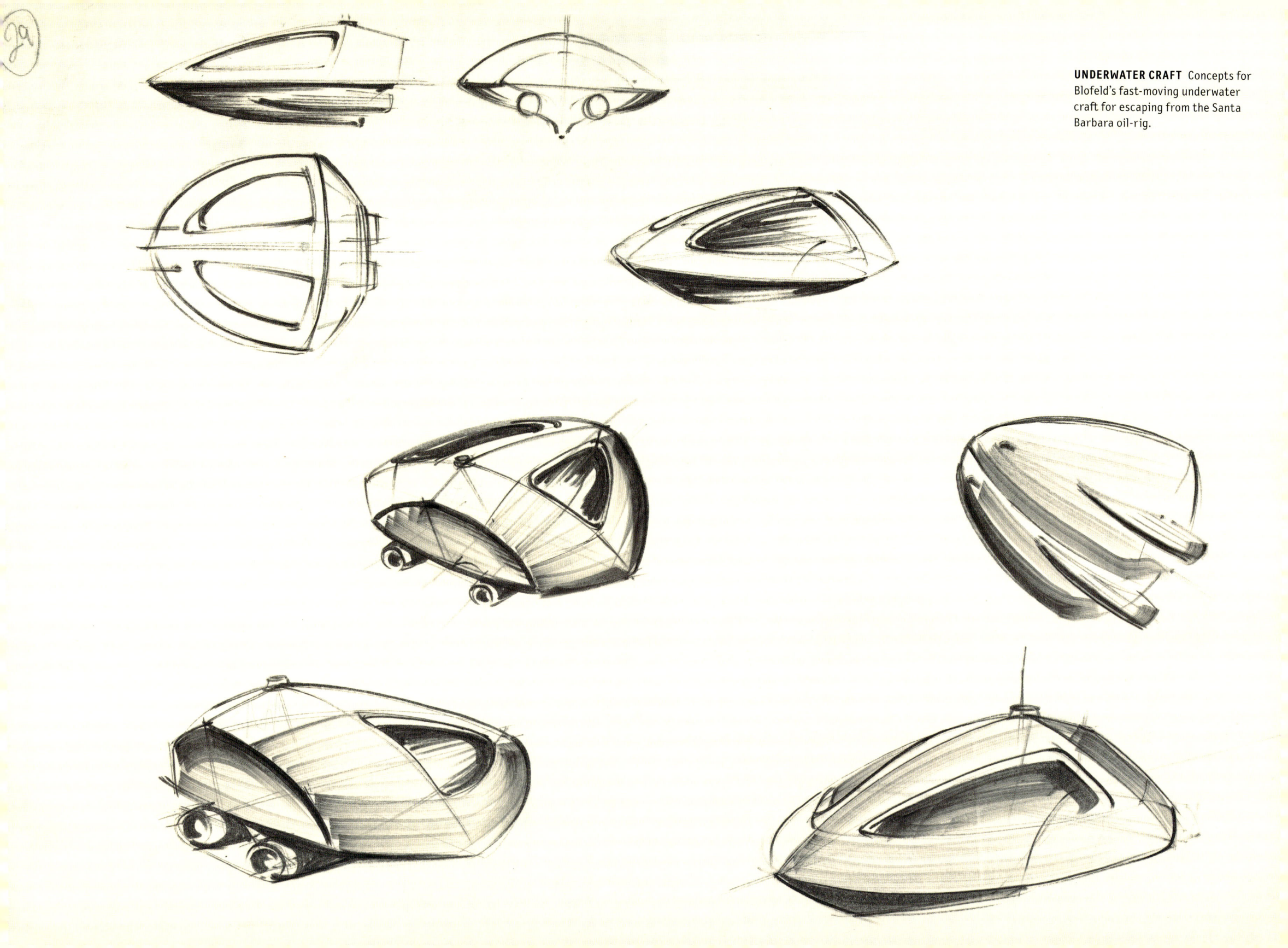

UNDERWATER CRAFT Concepts for Blofeld's fast-moving underwater craft for escaping from the Santa Barbara oil-rig.

THE SPY WHO LOVED ME [1977]

After a rest from the Bond series between 1971 and 1976, when Roger Moore took over the role of 007, Ken Adam returned for his largest-scale production design commission to date. In his will, Ian Fleming had specified that his 1961 novel, *The Spy Who Loved Me* — a love story, rather than a thriller — should not be filmed. So only the title was kept, with a new story about an arch-villain who hijacks NATO nuclear submarines inside a supertanker, and lives in an amphibious headquarters somewhere on the Mediterranean. Locations included St Moritz, Sardinia, Luxor, Aswan and Okinawa. The sets were built at Pinewood — the supertanker's docking bay for three nuclear submarines, as well as Stromberg's lair Atlantis, with its Renaissance palazzo dining room, complete with a Botticelli tapestry revealing a shark devouring Stromberg's secretary; even General Gogol's Soviet office was enormous and crypt-like — like a magnified scene from an Eisenstein film. 'With this project,' says Adam, 'once I started letting myself go, I kept on letting myself go.' *The Spy Who Loved Me* was the only Bond film to date to be nominated for an Academy Award for art direction.

right and below **STROMBERG'S QUARTERS** Final design concept for Stromberg's living quarters on the submersible Atlantis, and Ken Adam's Pinewood photograph of some of the furniture, 1976.

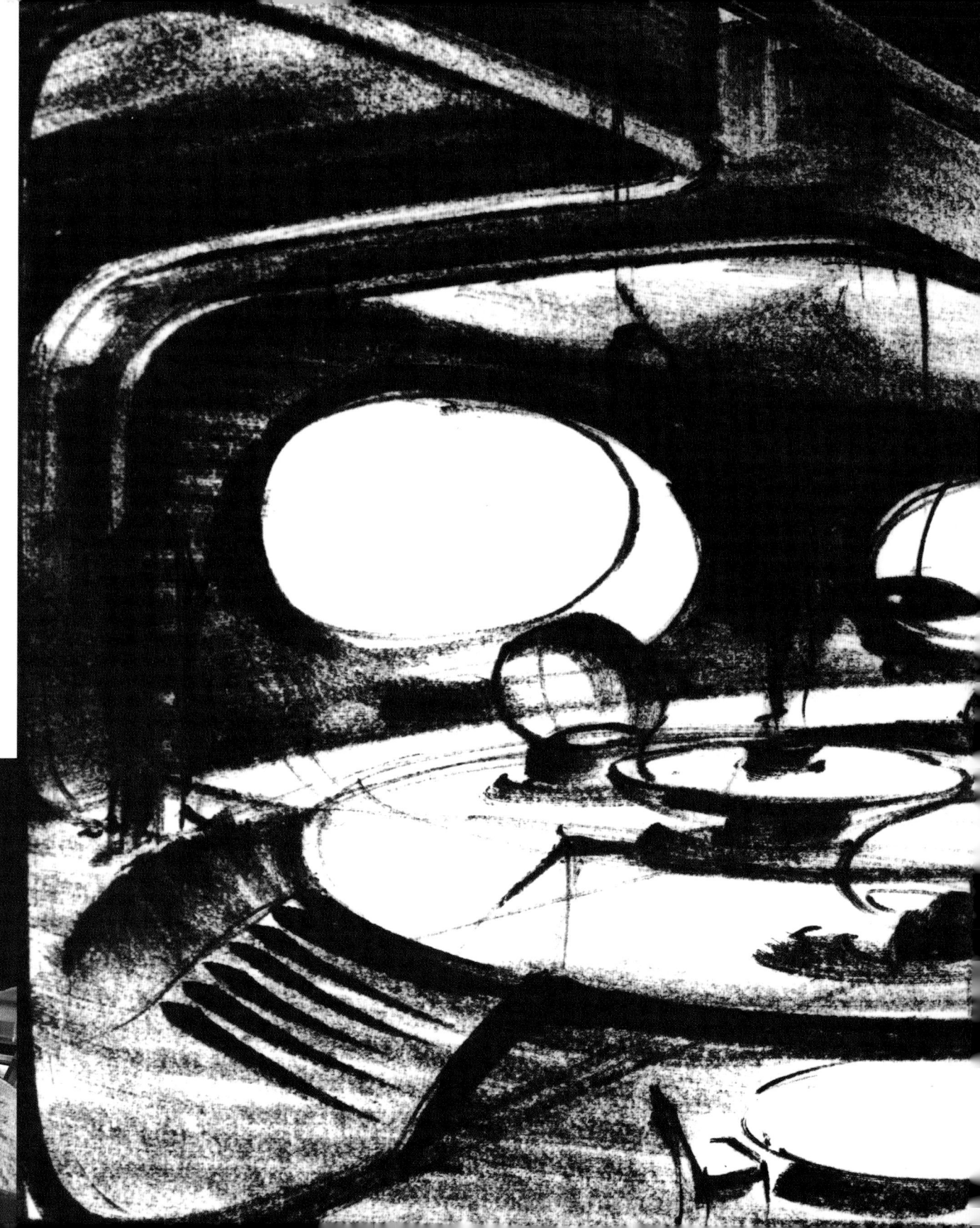

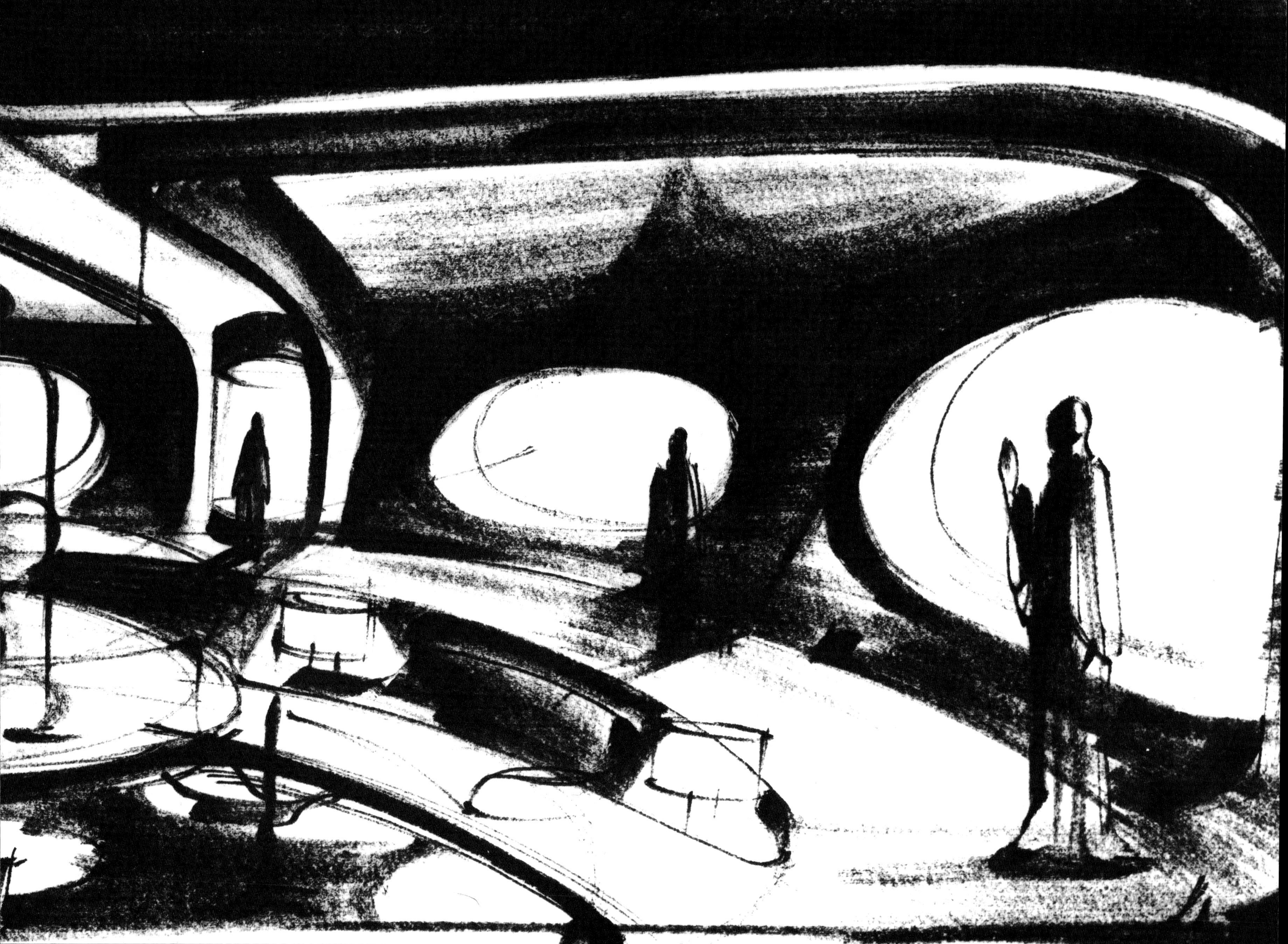

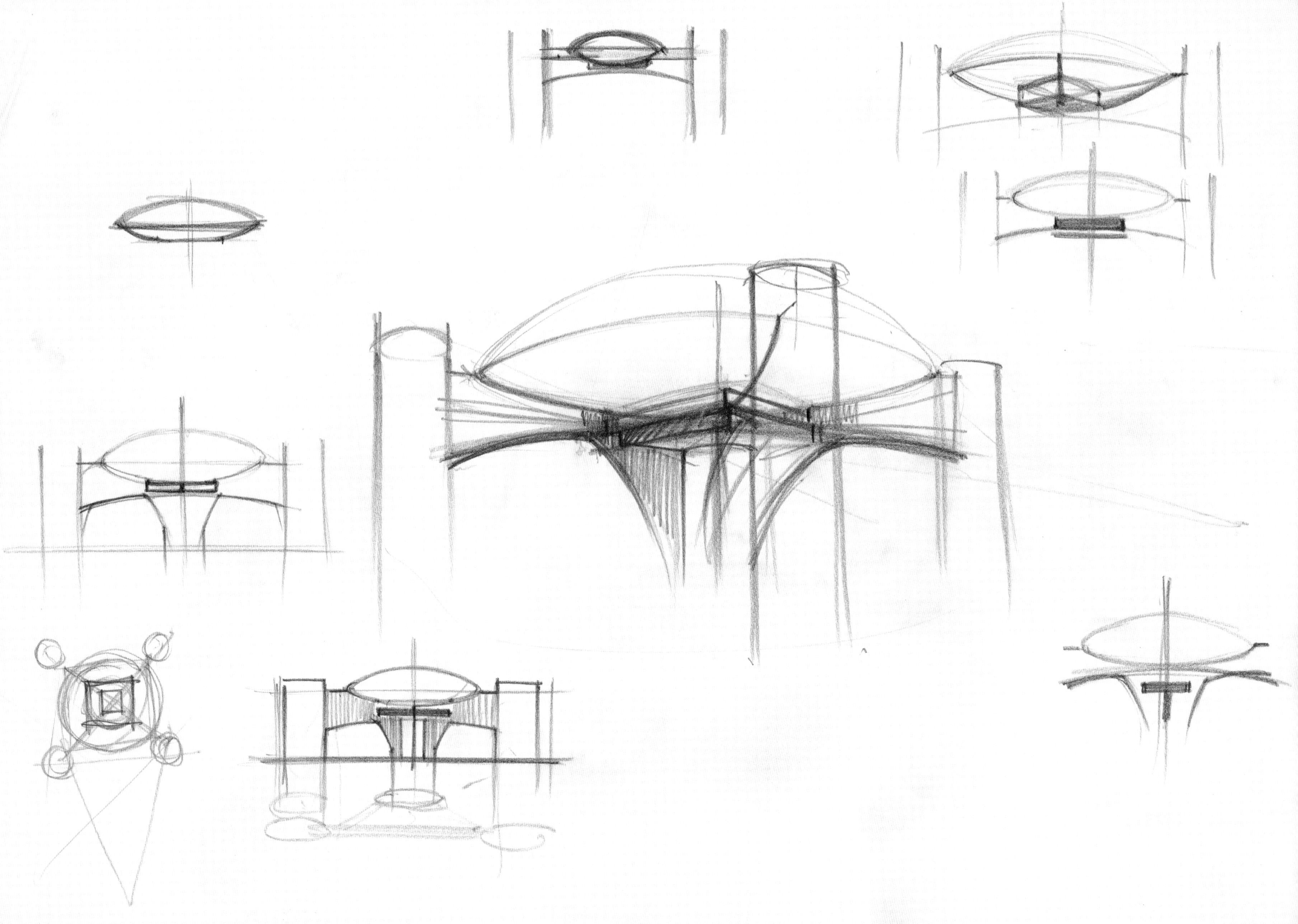

'Cubby's original idea was to base Atlantis on a floating city he'd heard about, built off the coast of Okinawa. But it was a disappointment, and looked more like a giant oil-rig. So back at Pinewood I had to come up with an original structure. I felt it was about time to start experimenting with curved surfaces instead of my usual linear design, and that's how the underwater structure of Atlantis was conceived.'

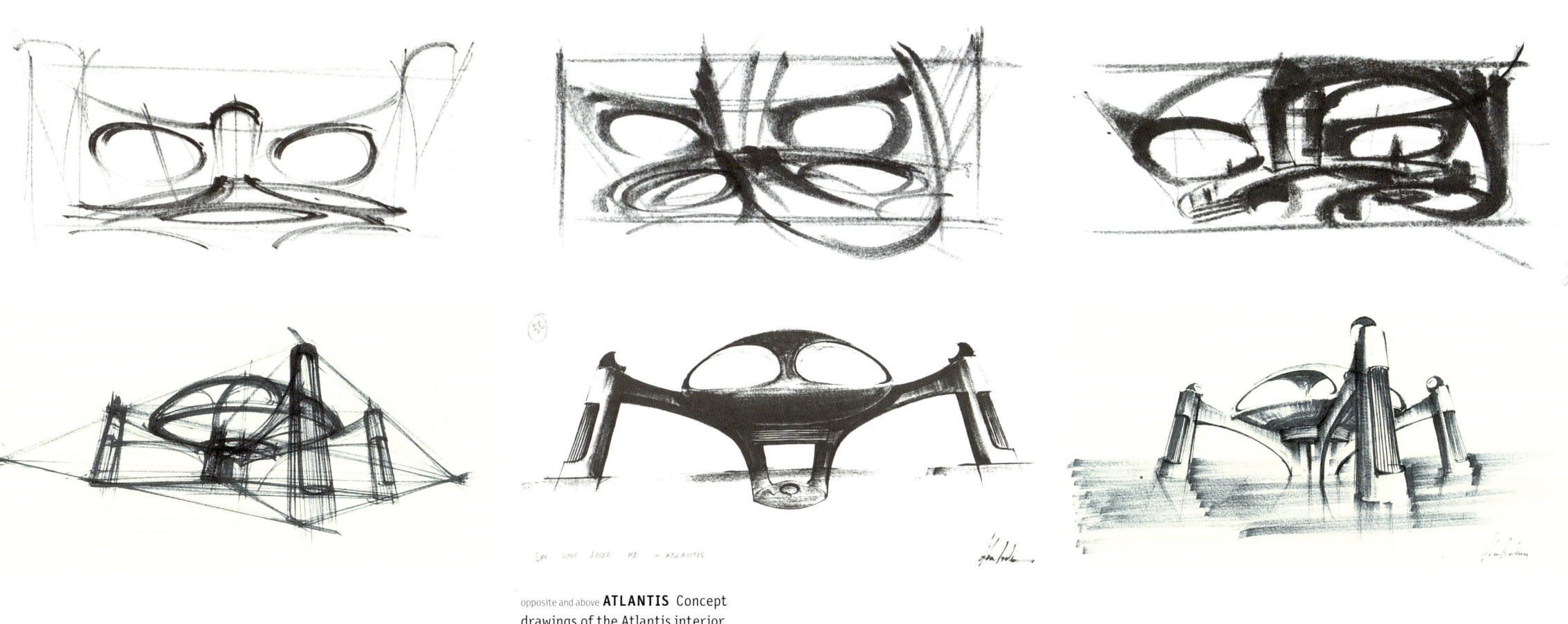

opposite and above **ATLANTIS** Concept drawings of the Atlantis interior and exterior, from various angles – a curved, spider-like structure rising from the sea.

DESIGNING JAMES BOND

this page **THE DOCKING BAY**
Three views of the submarine docking bay inside the supertanker *Liparus*: a still, and two visual studies, 1976. The Pinewood set was built over a tank, which Ken Adam enlarged to hold three nuclear submarines. Though of three-fifths actual size, the subs were still over 300 feet long, and a whole stage was constructed around them.

DESIGNING JAMES BOND

'Cubby had some friends who owned supertankers, but it was impractical to shoot on a ship. So I came up with one of the biggest sets ever built at Pinewood.'

above right **DOCKING BAY STRUCTURE**
Detail of the docking bay set, showing the exposed engineering.

right **THE SUPERTANKER BRIG**
Study for the brig on the supertanker. The real interior of a supertanker is divided up into smaller compartments. By leaving the construction as one vast compartment, and by accentuating the structural, engineering elements of the set, Ken Adam created a highly dramatic interior.

THE SPY WHO LOVED ME

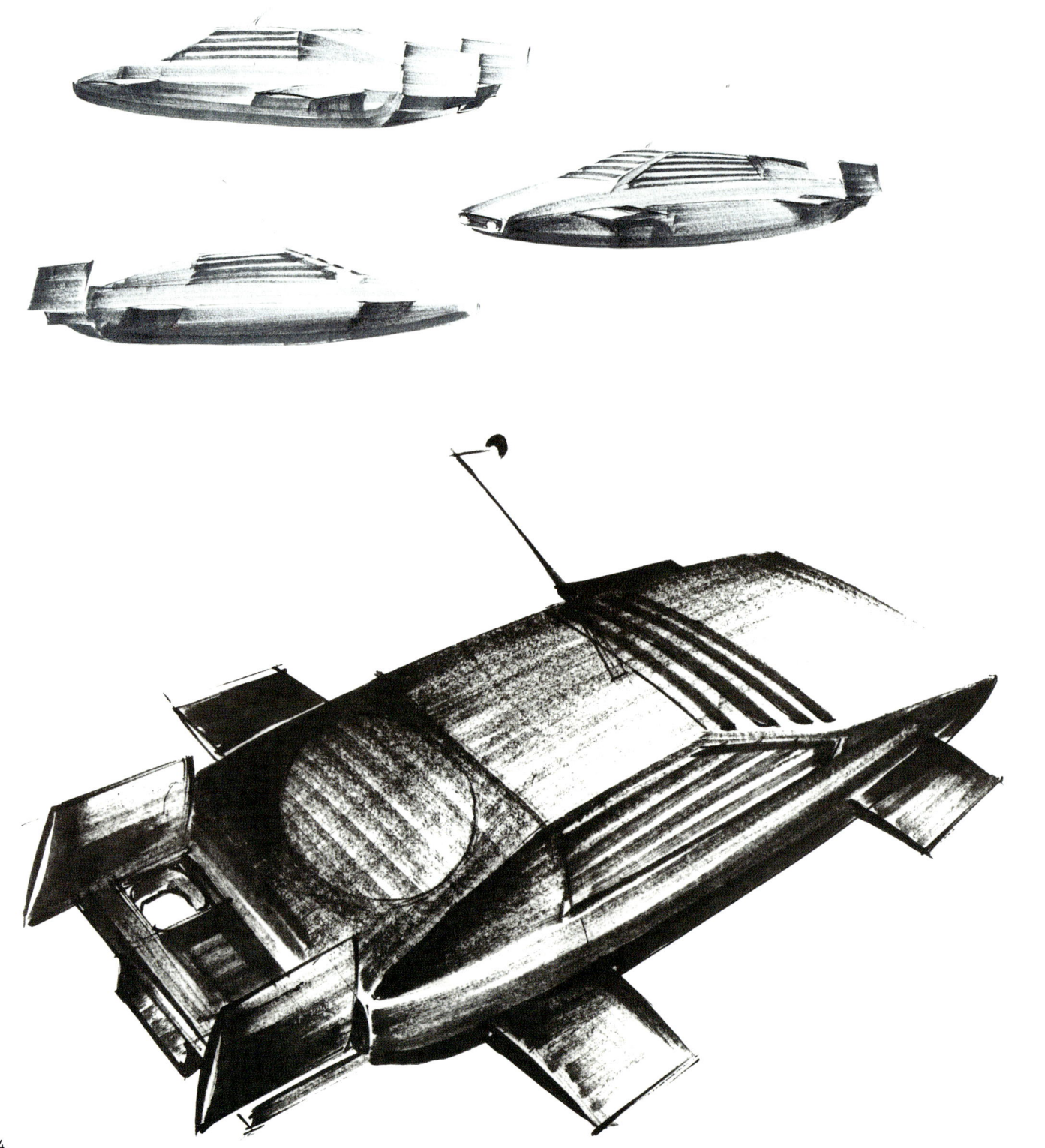

left and above **THE LOTUS ESPRIT**
Concepts for the underwater Lotus Esprit, and (above) the full-sized version in action.

'I loved the shape of the Lotus Esprit, and knew the designer Colin Chapman. It seemed to me ideal to convert into an underwater craft. In those days, we tried not to cheat the Bond audiences – and the Lotus actually did travel at seven knots to a depth of fifty feet. Obviously you had to have oxygen tanks to breathe in the car, but there was no codding up or anything….'

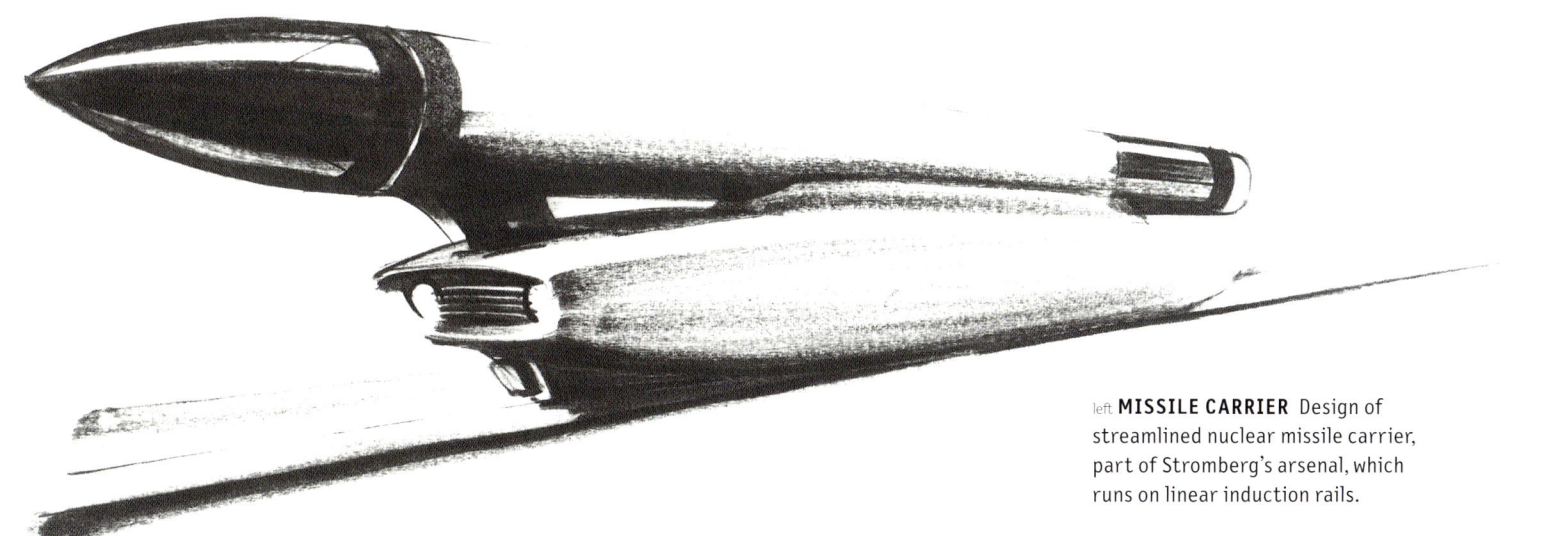

above and right **THE SPEEDBOAT** Final concept of the jet craft speedboat, and side and top views.

left **MISSILE CARRIER** Design of streamlined nuclear missile carrier, part of Stromberg's arsenal, which runs on linear induction rails.

DESIGNING JAMES BOND

MOONRAKER [1979]

Moonraker, the last of the James Bond films to be designed by Ken Adam, was filmed for tax reasons at three studios in Paris, and by five separate units 'shooting all over the world at once'. It was, says Adam, 'the biggest, most complex film I've ever worked on'. The megalomaniac Hugo Drax, a French neo-fascist, characteristically lives in an eighteenth-century French château immaculately transported from the Loire Valley to California, but next door runs a nuclear-armaments factory producing guided missiles — again, traditional and contemporary, private and public. His château was partly the real-life palace of Vaux-le-Vicomte and partly (for the interior) the Pompidou Centre. But the key to the film is the elaborate space station, on earth and in the sky, from which he aims to dominate world politics — complete with pyramid control room, centrifuge, space-shuttle launch complex and command centre. Ken Adam left the Bond franchise literally with a bang — blowing up the main set at Epinay. His explanation? 'I felt that, having gone into space, we'd gone as far as we could go. And the whole structure of making Bond movies had changed … and I also felt, rightly or wrongly, that the Bonds were a British expression of the 1960s and '70s that I could relate to.'

right and below **THE SPACE STATION** Initial concept for Hugo Drax's space-station interior, 1978, and corresponding still.

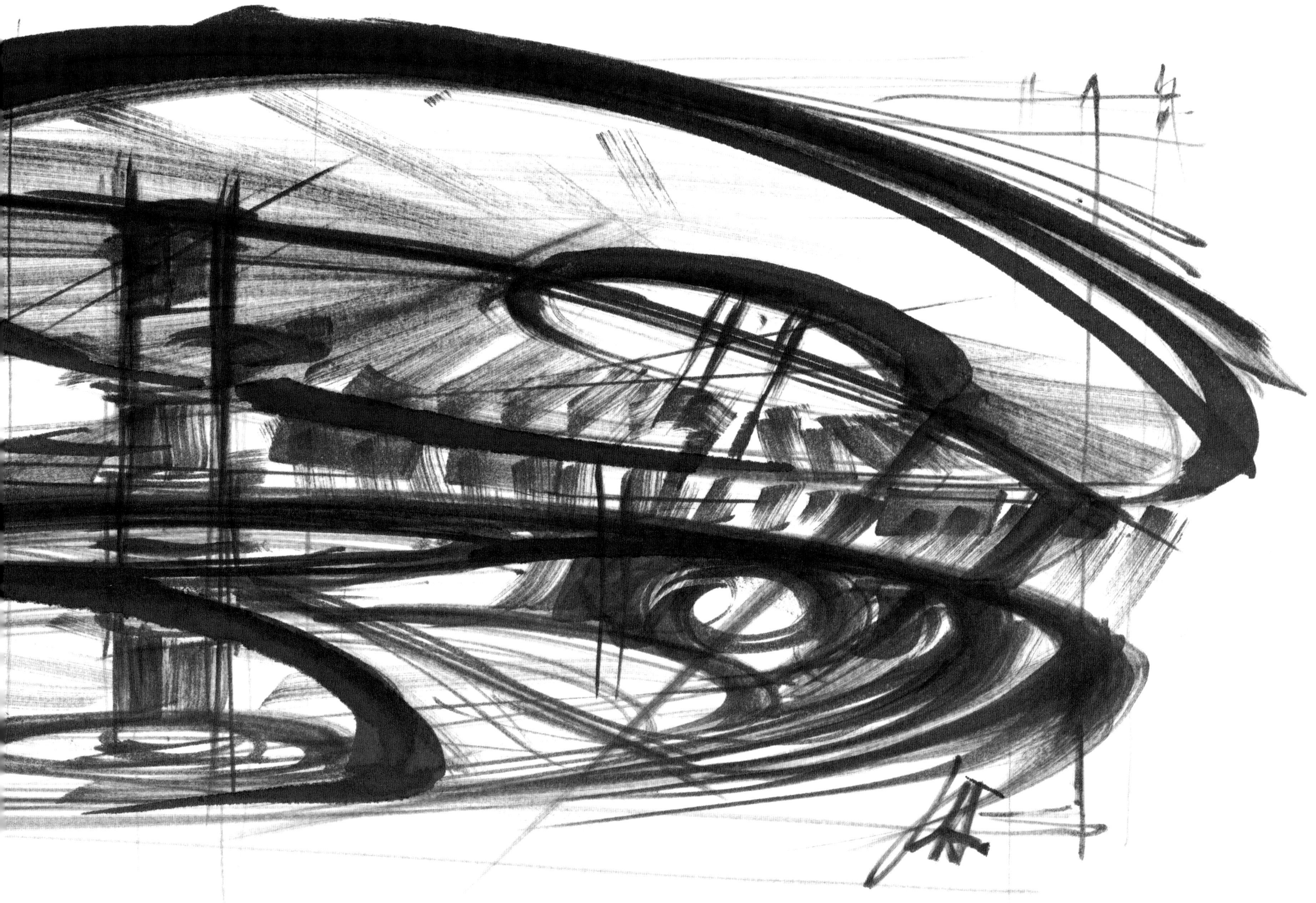

'Hugo Drax has this hidden launch complex for the Moonraker rockets concealed behind the Iguaçu waterfalls on the Brazil-Argentine border. There was a control room in the shape of a pyramid with an adjoining Great Hall in the Mayan style. I partly based this on Mayan art – in a contemporary setting….'

'There's also a shot of Bond in a speedboat, and the top of the boat becomes a hang-glider and he glides over the waterfalls. It was very dangerous for the stuntman because of the currents. He glided over the waterfalls and ended up in the South American jungle somewhere.'

above and right **THE EXHAUST CHAMBER** Photographed detail of the space-shuttle Exhaust Chamber set, and final design concept of the chamber with removable conference room beneath, 1978.

opposite above and below **THE GREAT CHAMBER** Final design concept of the Great Chamber, 1978, and still with Roger Moore in the foreground.

this page and opposite **PYRAMID CONTROL ROOM** Final concept drawing of Drax's pyramid control room, with details of the actual set, showing Mondrian-inspired colours.

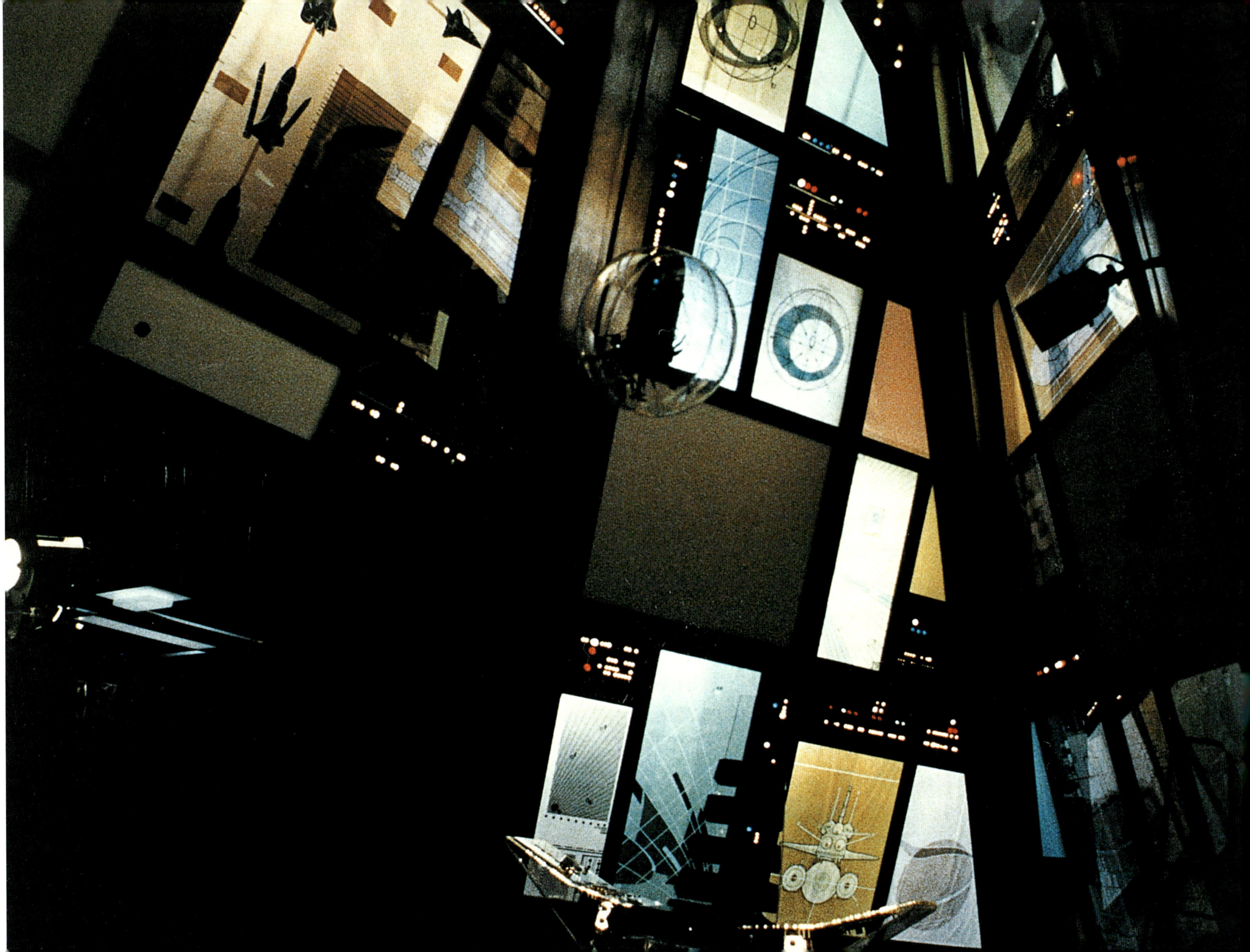

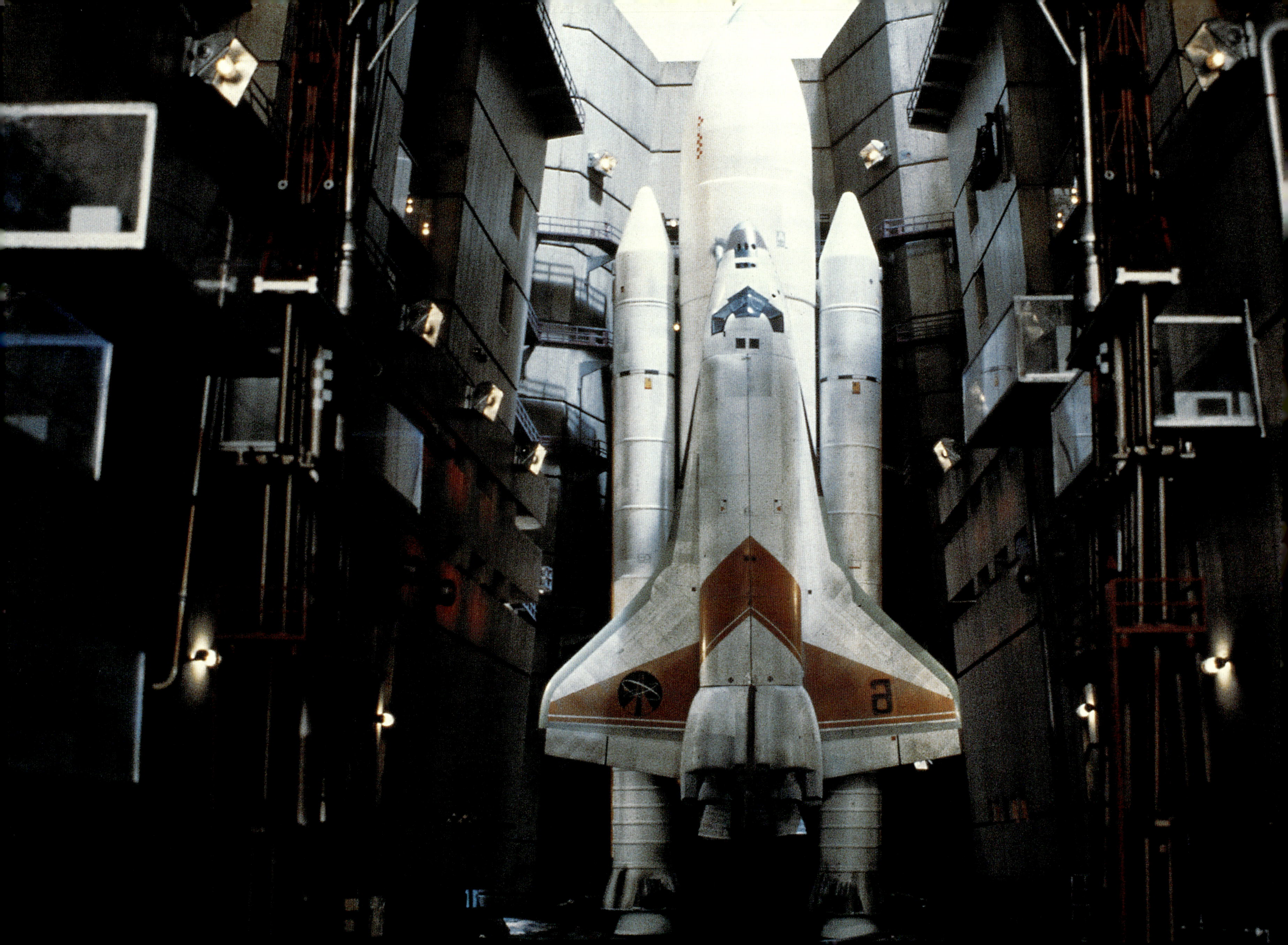

'The space-shuttle launch pad was over the Exhaust Chamber. It was a model, whereas the chamber – which doubled as a conference room with folding furniture – was built full-size. I tried several designs for the launch pad before I came up with control rooms that slid in and out, close to the blast-off. Of course the launch pad had to be buried underground as well.'

opposite and this page **THE LAUNCH PAD** Still of the space-shuttle launch pad – a model shot – with early concept drawing and final design.

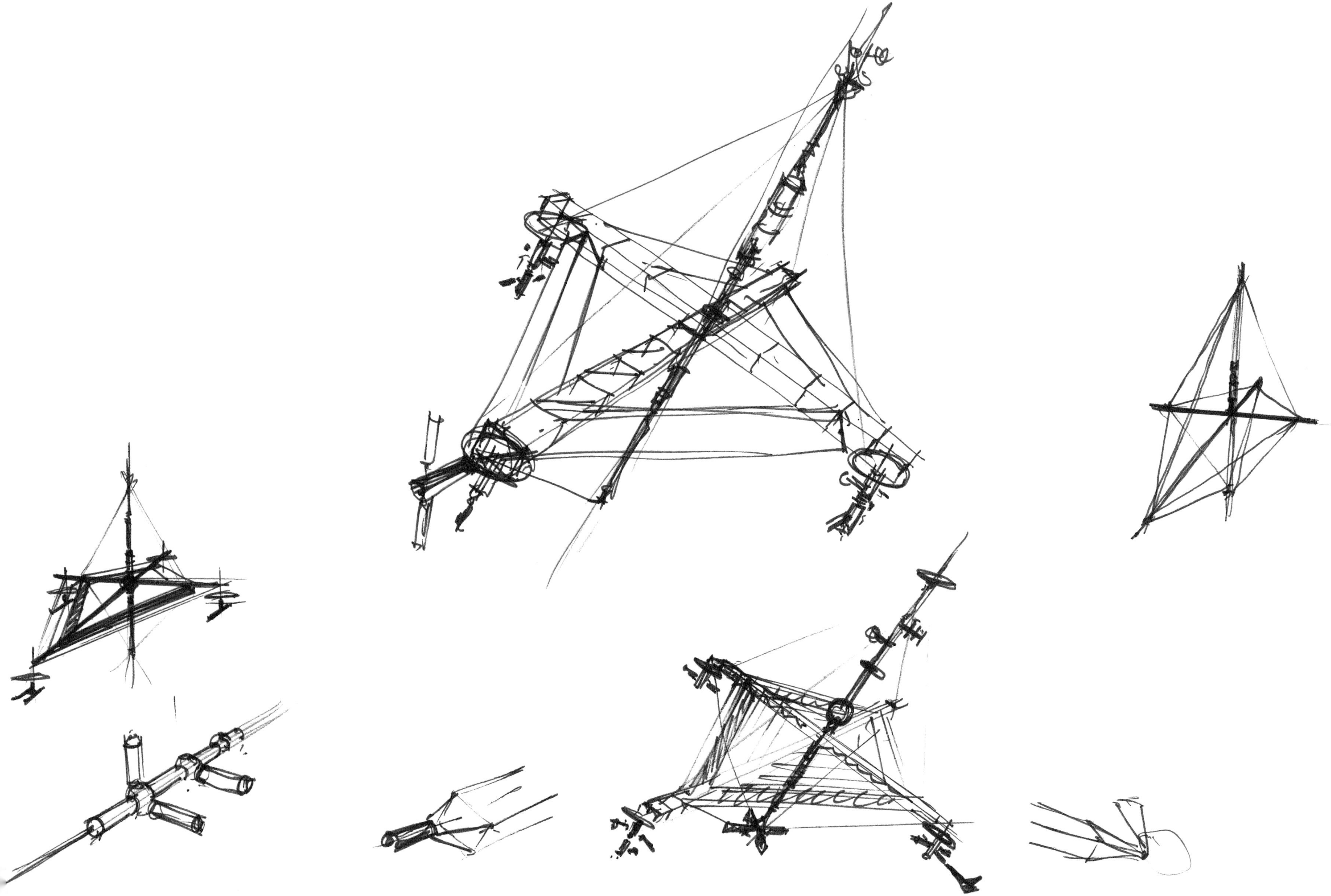

MOONRAKER

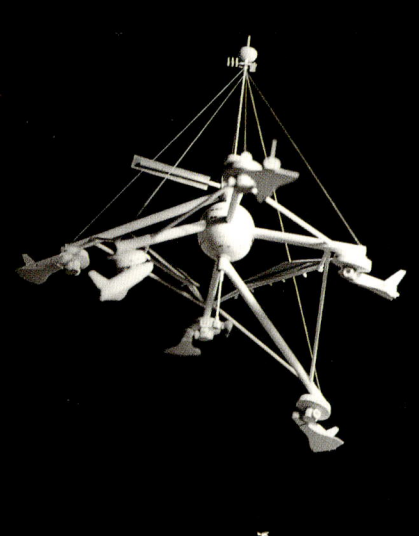

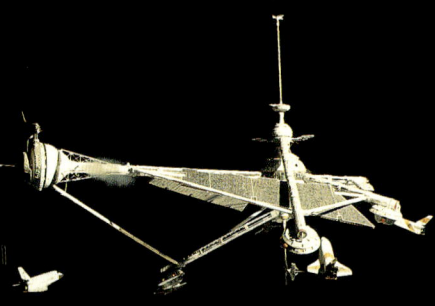

opposite and this page **THE SPACE STATION** 'Designed like a bolted-together mobile, in a completely irregular form which rotates': initial concepts, models, and one of Harry Lange's technical illustrations.

MOONRAKER" INT. COMMAND SATELLITE - SPACE STATION

left and opposite **THE COMMAND CENTRE** Final design concept for the space-station command centre interior, and still of the centre blowing up at Epinay Studio.

'I spent a couple of days at NASA in California and they showed me some of their very futuristic conceptual designs, but the actual space stations – the designs that were effective – didn't look very interesting to me. So we built our space station at Epinay Studio in Paris … and on nearly the last day of shooting we had to blow up the main set, as we always did!'

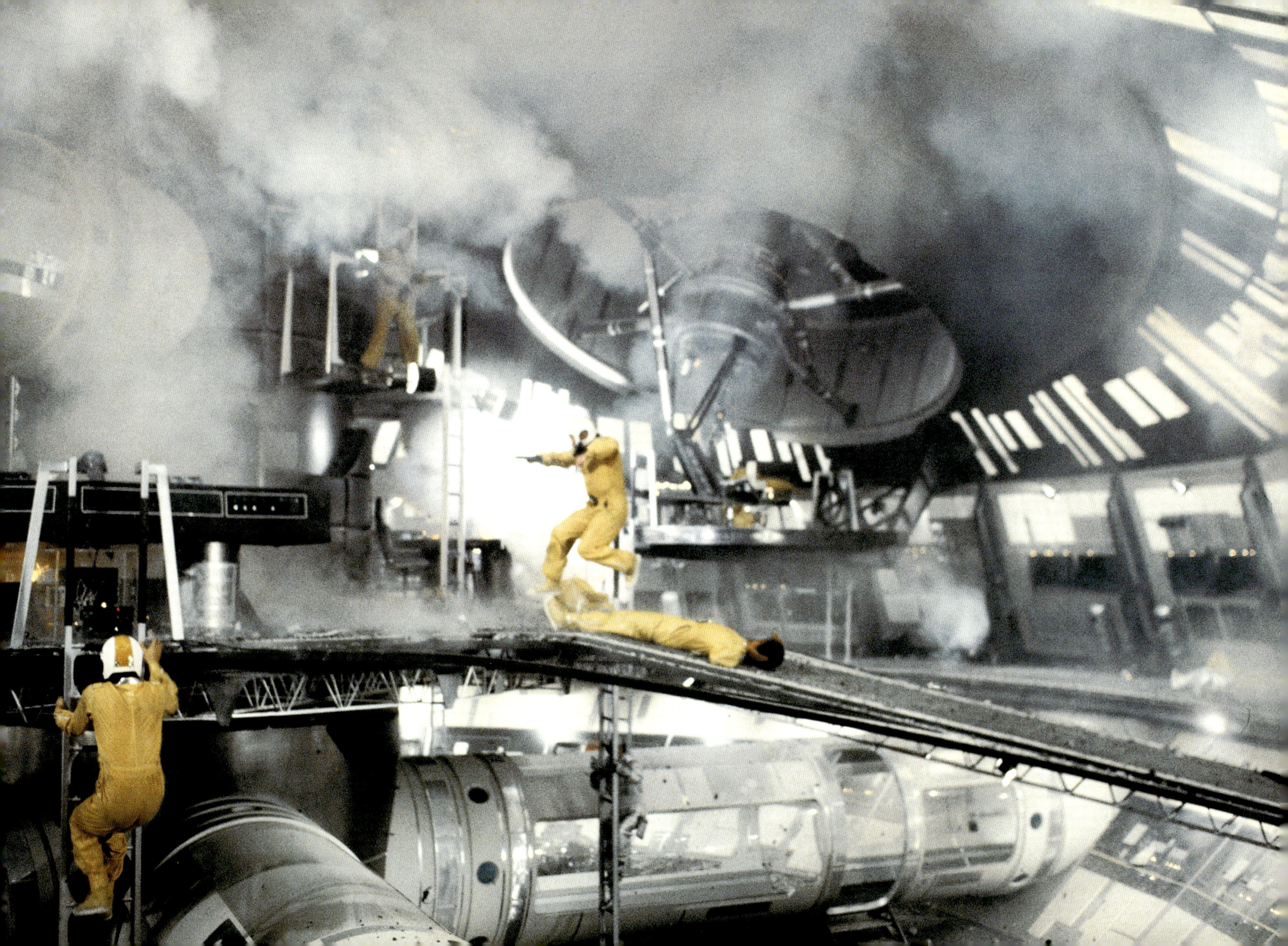

'We thought it would be fun to have a zero gravity chamber in the satellite, with people floating around. It was all designed and built, but we were so over schedule that they couldn't shoot it. But they did shoot the sequence with Bond and the girl in the lower half of the space shuttle on its return trip.'

right and above **THE ZERO GRAVITY SATELLITE** Final concept for the zero gravity satellite on the space station (never used), and a sketch of James Bond and Dr. Holly Goodhead embracing in zero gravity.

15 ZERO GRAVITY SATELLITE -

108   DESIGNING JAMES BOND

E. STATION

MOONRAKER

GOLDENEYE: ROGUE AGENT [video game, 2004]

In 2003–04 Ken Adam designed his first computer game – 'Goldeneye: Rogue Agent' – for Electronic Arts in Hollywood. The linking story was of an ex-British agent with a cybernetic eye, who seems to have defected and now works for Dr. No and Goldfinger – who, in turn, sometimes fight each other in a battle of the giants. The player becomes the James Bond figure, who has to negotiate and blast his way through this maze of loyalties. It was a chance to reinvent digitally some of Adam's classic Bond sets of the 1960s and '70s – Crab Key from *Dr. No*, Auric Enterprises and Fort Knox from *Goldfinger*, the conference room from *Thunderball*, the volcano headquarters from *You Only Live Twice*, the Las Vegas casino from *Diamonds Are Forever*; even an underwater resort called Octopus which resembles Atlantis in *The Spy Who Loved Me*. Adam designed the 'sets' for six separate sequences. At first he was reluctant to sign up, not wishing simply to recycle his work, but the multiple viewpoints of the game players, as distinct from the single viewpoint of the cinema audience, and the new geography of the sets that this demanded – plus the fact that the game could go on for up to twenty hours – made the project an interesting challenge, and a chance to develop some of his greatest hits.

'For the boardroom of Fort Knox, they added a round table and lighting ring as a homage to *Dr. Strangelove* – I didn't put that in! The design for Dr. No's headquarters was also changed. My first concept was too wild for them, too much like a shark or frightening animal, so I came up with a new design – which was still pretty sinister.'

opposite and this page **VIDEO-GAME SETTINGS** Three concept drawings for video-game settings, 2003–04: Dr. No's submersible headquarters at the Octopus Resort (opposite); initial concept of the boardroom in Fort Knox with Strangelove-style table (above); and initial concept of hangar with circular roof aperture and two rockets, hidden by Goldfinger beneath Auric Enterprises in Switzerland (right).

GOLDENEYE: ROGUE AGENT

"OCTOPUS RESORT" CONCEPT FOR REVERSE ANGLE OF GROTTO ROOM

Ken Adam
April 19/04

Opposite and this page **VIDEO-GAME SETTINGS** More concept drawings for video-game settings, 2003–04: the curved Grotto Room inside the Octopus Resort (opposite); the final concept of the sinister Shark Corridor in the resort (right); and the docking bay for Dr. No's boat, 'the equivalent of the submarine pen but smaller' (below).

"OCTOPUS" INT. DOCKING & SECURITY BAY

'Characters end up going through various interiors, meeting obstacles all the time. Designing a computer game is not like designing a single film, but like designing eight films at once.'

ANOTHER SPY

THE IPCRESS FILE [1965]

Conceived as 'an anti-Bond' spy film, with Michael Caine playing a soldier with a chip on his shoulder seconded to the Secret Service, much of Sidney J. Furie's *The Ipcress File* was filmed on location in a grey and gloomy London. The main set was the cell and programming room where Caine is held for brainwashing. The 'Brainbox' consisted of a suspended room in a warehouse with translucent walls and film projectors attached, projecting strange, subliminal images onto the wall surfaces. The office of Major Dalby, the MI5 chief played by Nigel Green, was the antithesis of M's palatial premises in the Bond series: in a sparse Edwardian interior somewhere near Victoria, a trestle table and a camp bed tell us all we need to know about this military character. This idea was controversial with producer Harry Saltzman, who still had Bond on his mind.

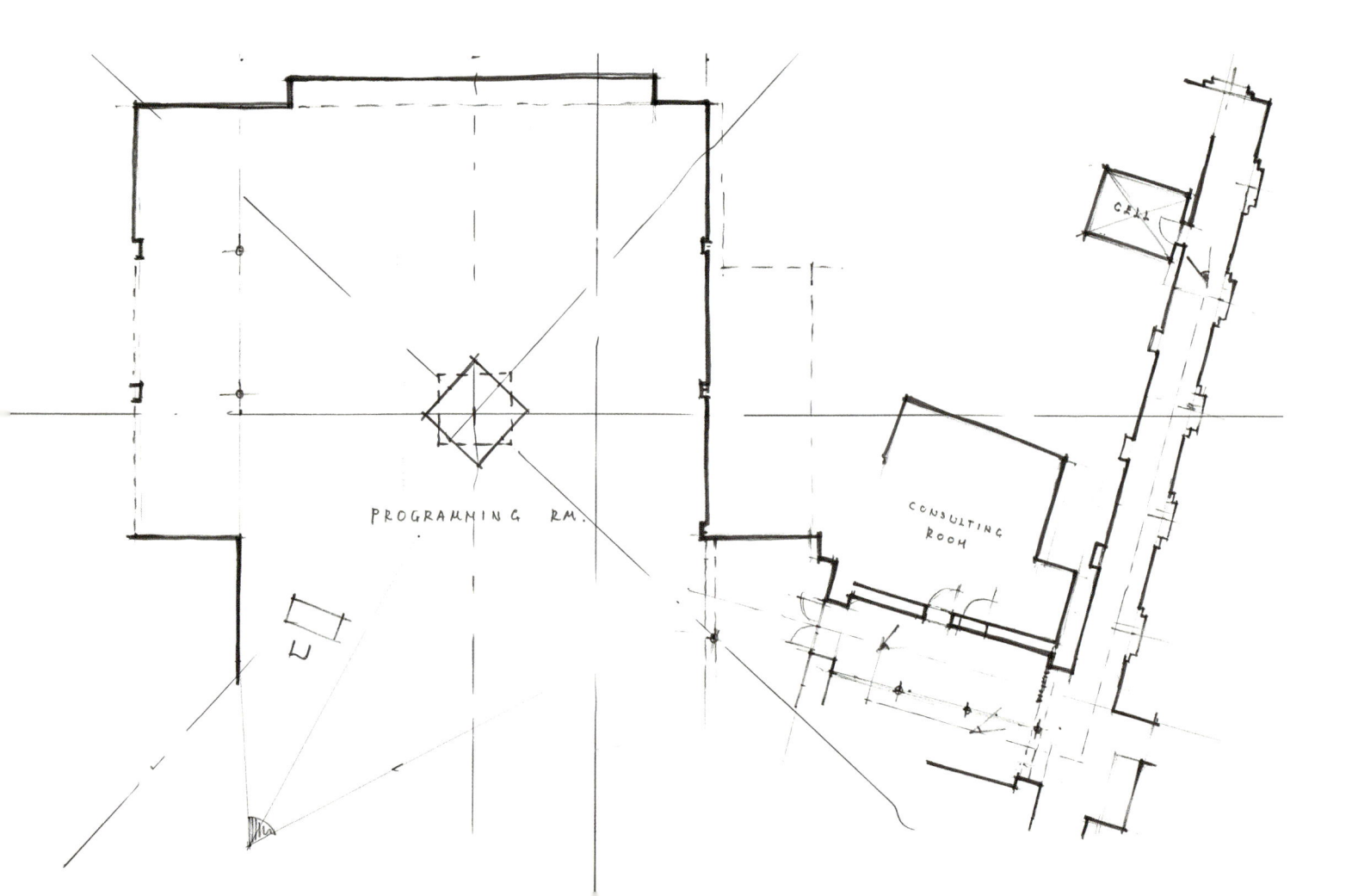

left and above **THE WAREHOUSE**
Technical floorplan of the warehouse with 'brainwashing machine', and main warehouse set as constructed at Pinewood, photographed from above.

'Nigel Green's room was a real room inside a Grosvenor Place building, and I loved it so much because of the three tall windows and just the fireplace. Harry Saltzman wanted to put computers and the latest gadgetry everywhere, but I kept it bare with a camp-bed, a trestle table and a bust of Wellington or Caesar.'

above right **MI5 OFFICE** Final interior concept of Major Dalby's military-style office at MI5.

right **PRISON CORRIDOR** Study for the prison corridor along which Harry Palmer (Michael Caine) is led.

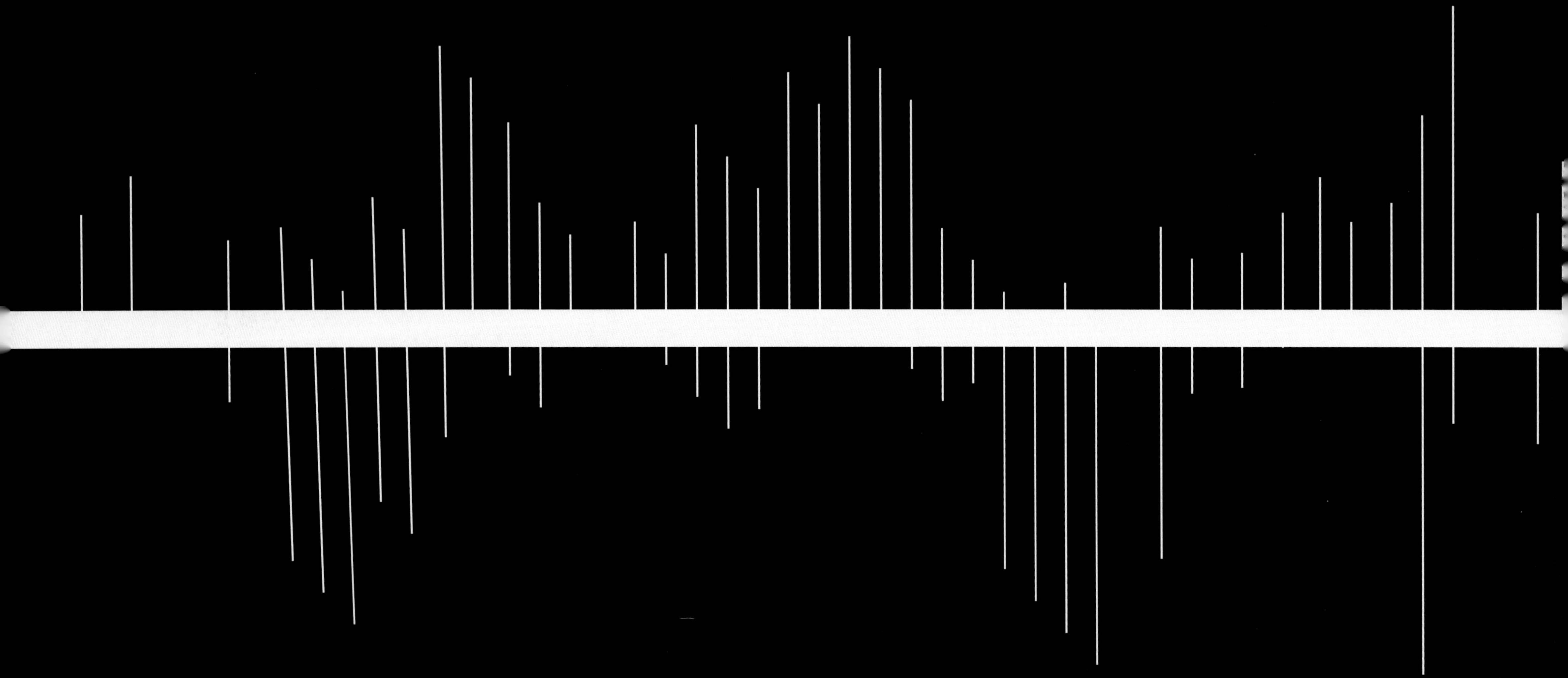

4 THE THEATRE OF HISTORY

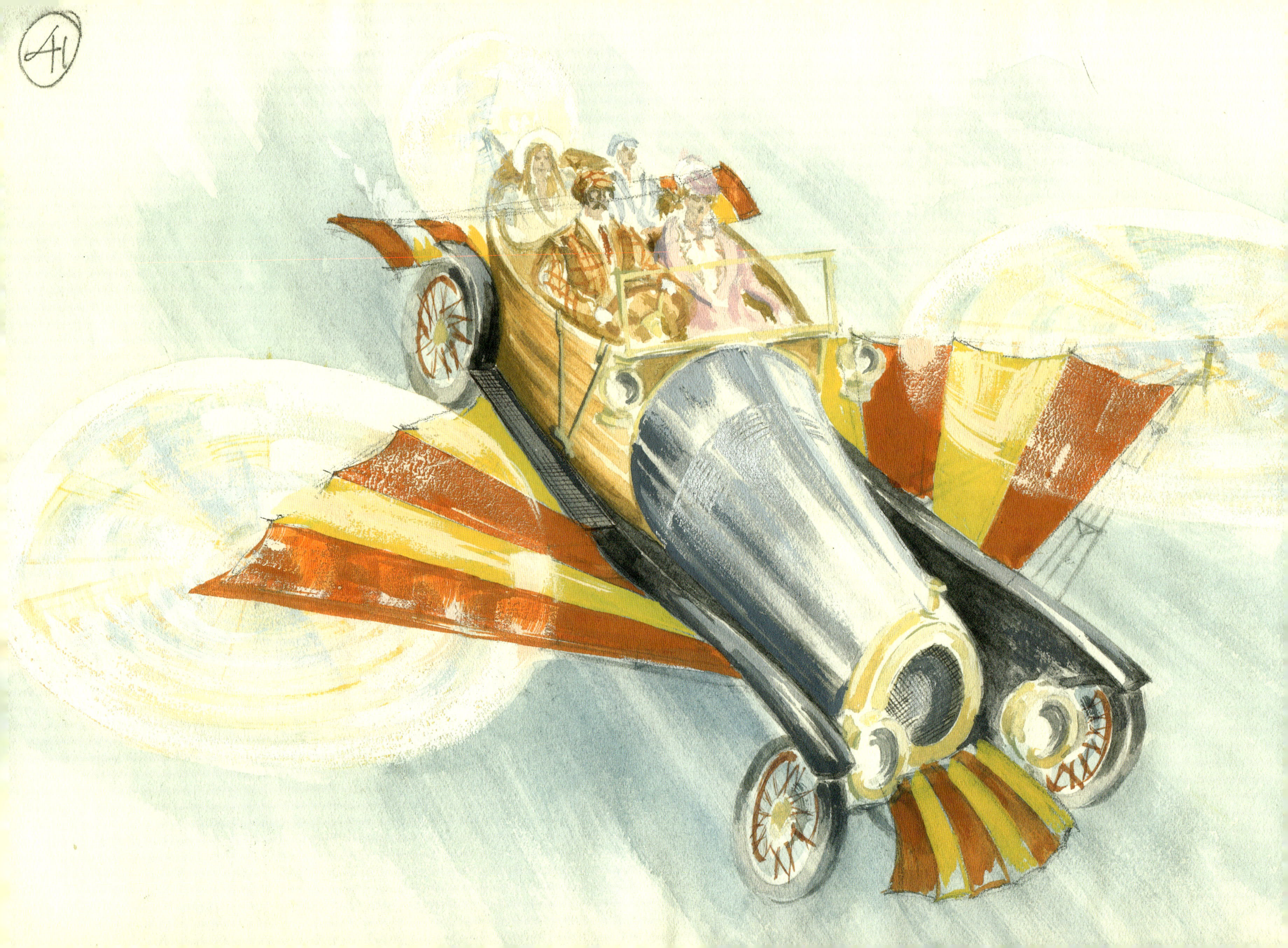
41

CHITTY CHITTY BANG BANG [1968]

Based on the children's book written by Ian Fleming while in hospital recuperating from a heart attack, and produced by the James Bond team, this 1968 family musical is set in Edwardian England and a fairytale Germany. Adam's storybook designs combined period gadgetry — the vintage racing car which can also fly and hover on the water, and Baron Bomburst's airship — with elaborate interiors, such as the sweet factory where everything is in black and white except for the brightly coloured sweets. The songs were composed by the Sherman brothers, who had written the hit film *Mary Poppins*; with these, plus the casting of Dick Van Dyke as Caractacus Potts, 'Cubby Broccoli was trying to repeat the success of that film'.

left and this page **VINTAGE CAR** Final concept of the flying Edwardian car (left), and three concept drawings, two of the car on its hovercraft base and one in flight, 1967 (right). Several examples of the car were built full size.

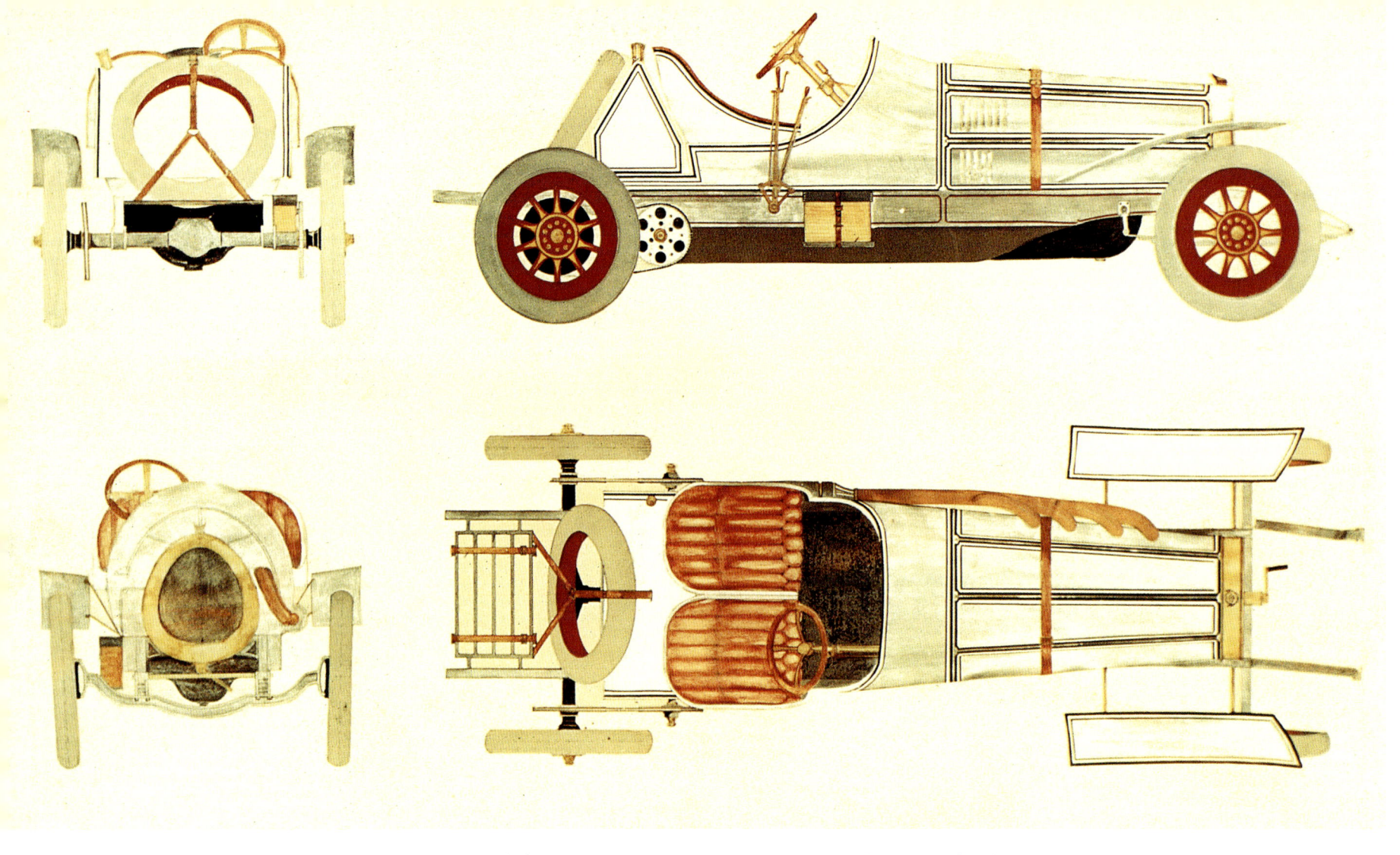

above and right **THE RACING CAR** Final designs of the racing car – Rolls-Royce body, Bugatti radiator and Mercedes bonnet strap, 1967.

far right **AT PINEWOOD** Ken Adam in his Pinewood office, designing the car.

'The Bugatti cars always fascinated me, and I loved the body of the classic old Rolls-Royces, so I combined them.... I had a shipbuilder construct the beautiful body in wood, and when the car arrived at Pinewood for the first time the whole studio stood still in admiration. It was really beautiful.'

THE THEATRE OF HISTORY

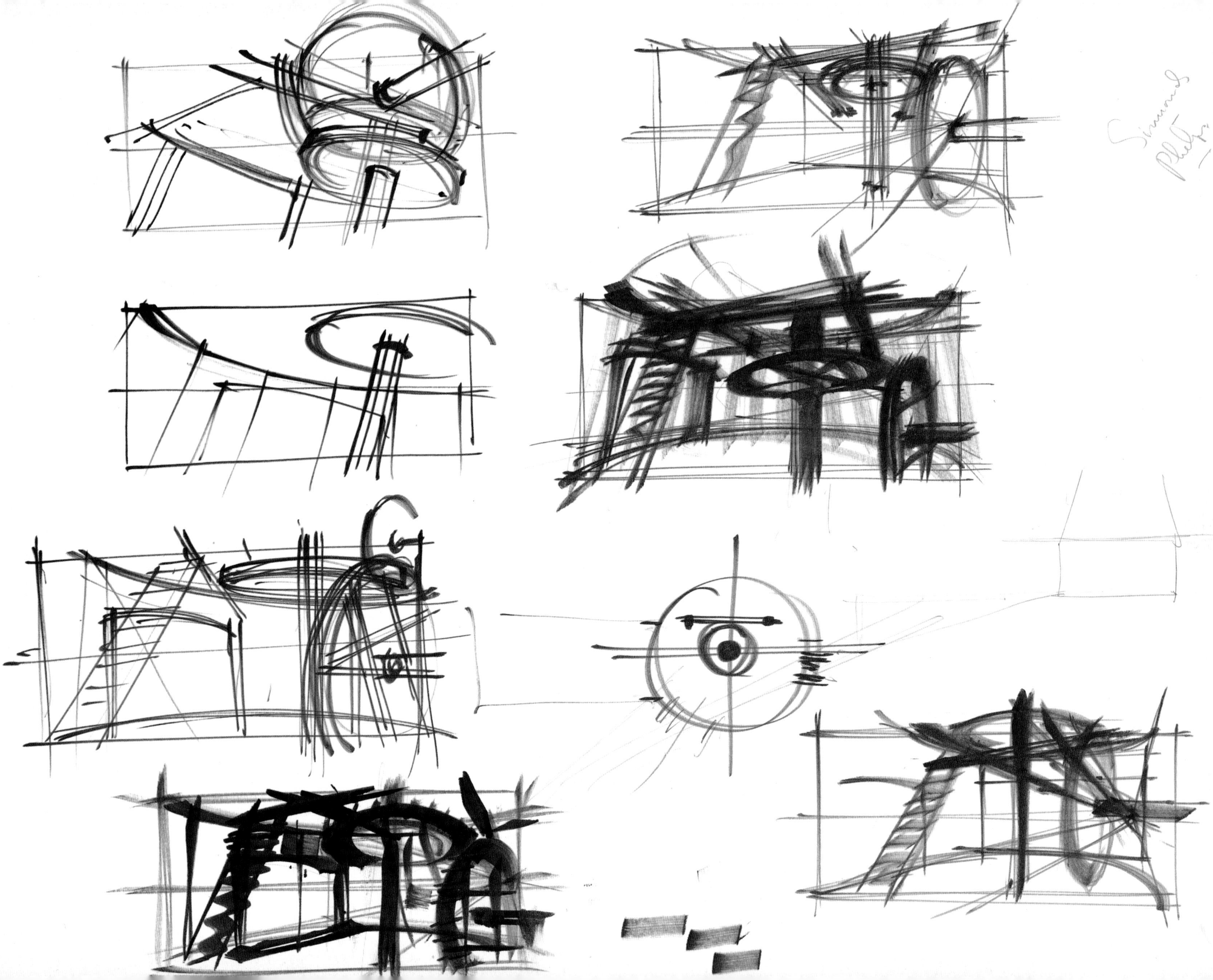

opposite and this page **THE WINDMILL** Early drawings of the mill-mechanism of Caractacus Potts's work room (opposite), and a series of concept designs of work-room details, including the windmill setting, 1967.

THE THEATRE OF HISTORY

THE AIRSHIP Final concept drawing of Baron Bomburst's airship, which was eventually built full-sized.

'The airship was originally to have been a model, but then two famous balloonists offered to build and fly it full-size, a 120-foot airship. I based my design on a French model called the Labaudier. Well, it turned out that the Labaudier never actually flew! One day the airship broke loose from its moorings and crashed into some high power-lines in Dorset, cutting off the electric supply to some angry farmers. But we got the footage.'

'The castle was the real Neuschwanstein Castle in Germany. It was like Disney. We also filmed in the nearby town of Rothenburg, which was quite frightening. Very *Dr. Caligari*, with narrow streets and gabled roofs.'

above **THE CASTLE** Final concept of the courtyard of the castle, built as a set at Pinewood.

left **THE PRISON** Detail of the children's prison in Baron Bomburst's Castle, 1967.

THE THEATRE OF HISTORY

GOODBYE, MR. CHIPS [1969]

Big musicals made in England and based on classic novels were fashionable with Hollywood in the mid- to late 1960s. This production—the second film version of the James Hilton novel (the first had been made in 1939 with Robert Donat)—was the start of Ken Adam's seven-film partnership with ex-choreographer Herbert Ross, which ended with *Boys on the Side* in 1994. Locations ranged from Sherborne School, Dorset, where Peter O'Toole played Arthur Chipping ('Mr. Chips'), the long-serving schoolmaster of Brookfield, to Positano and Pompeii, where he goes on a life-changing holiday with Katherine Bridges, a music-hall star played by Petula Clark. The production team visited many schools, including Eton and Winchester, but decided that Sherborne would be most easily manageable during filming, and also lent itself best to the famous quadrangle scene in which Mr. Chips roll-calls the schoolchildren. The cricket match (below) was not shot in the school grounds, however, and the interior of the school assembly hall was actually constructed at Elstree.

below **THE CRICKET MATCH** Final concept of Brookfield cricket pavilion and playing field, for the Speech Day sequence, 1968.

'Part of the film was on location at Sherborne, part reconstructed as sets – the Assembly Hall and so on. We also had a great time in Italy. In fact I tricked the director of photography, Ossie Morris, into shooting in Positano, because I loved it so much. It involved five thousand steps down to the harbour, and miles and miles of cabling. The associate producer thought we'd all gone mad.'

above **THE ASSEMBLY HALL** Concept drawing of the assembly hall in its school setting.

below **POSITANO** The waterfront at Positano, redecorated to stand in for Naples, where Arthur Chipping and Katherine Bridges fall in love, 1968.

SLEUTH [1972]

Sleuth was an adaptation of a successful stage play of 1970 by Anthony Shaffer, which was entirely set in the living room of a country house called Cloak Manor belonging to a crime writer. Ken Adam selected Athelhampton, near Dorchester, for the exterior, and then designed elaborate, linked, part-Gothic/part-1930s interiors to be built on the stages at Pinewood Studios. The challenge was to turn a very theatrical idea into a film, matching the wit and cleverness of the text with the sets and furnishings and game-playing. *Sleuth* was directed by Joseph L. Mankiewicz—his last film. When it was released, several location scouts wrote to Ken Adam, asking him where the interiors had been found, as they were convinced they were real. Perhaps for this reason, the film was not nominated for an Academy Award.

right **CLOAK MANOR** Final concept of Cloak Manor and grounds, including the maze, from a bird's eye view, 1972.

below **ON SET** Michael Caine and Laurence Olivier on Ken Adam's Cloak Manor set at Pinewood.

GUERITE'S BEDROOM WINDOW

ANDREW'S BEDROOM WINDOW

MILO WITH LADDER

BIRD'S EYE VIEW · CLOAK MANOR

SLEUTH 1972

'I had meetings with Joe Mankiewicz for nearly two weeks, and right at the start he said this famous thing: "If the film is a success, as director I will take all the credit; if it's a flop, I can always put the blame on you." He was so cynical about it. Then he went through every single aspect of the play.'

above **ATHELHAMPTON MANOR**
The original slide of Athelhampton Manor, near Dorchester — after much searching, the exterior location for the film.

THE THEATRE OF HISTORY 129

above and opposite **THE GREAT HALL**
Final concept of the Great Hall of Cloak Manor, and an overhead still of the hall (with stand-ins) as constructed on the big stage at Pinewood, 1972.

THE THEATRE OF HISTORY

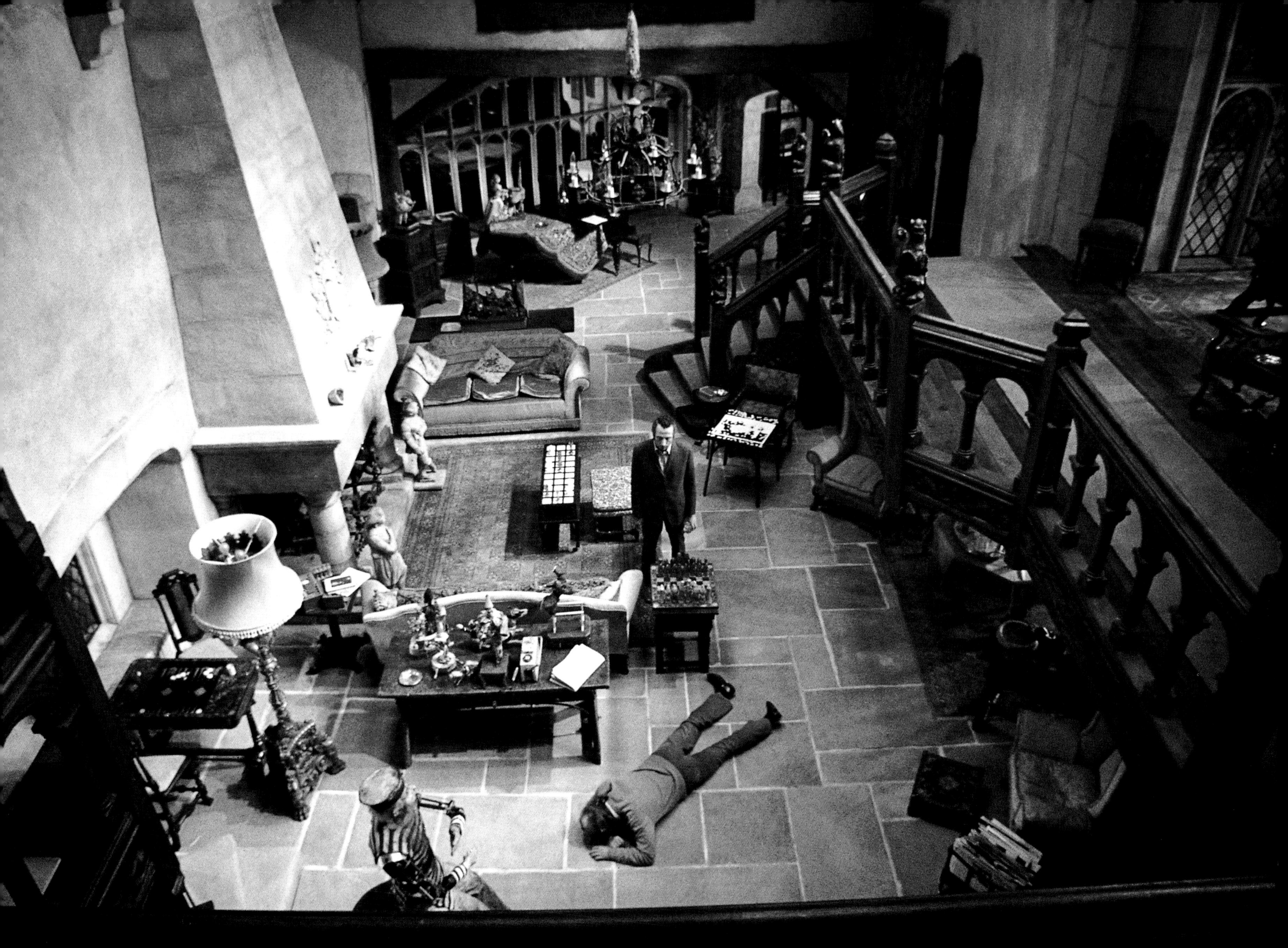

THE SEVEN-PER-CENT SOLUTION [1976]

The fourth filmed collaboration between Ken Adam and Herbert Ross was an adaptation by Nicholas Meyer from his own novel. The story was a pastiche Sherlock Holmes, in which the great detective (Nicol Williamson) is a cocaine addict who has a fixation on Professor Moriarty (Laurence Olivier), which Sigmund Freud (Alan Arkin) tries to cure through the new science of psychoanalysis. The film was shot at Pinewood, with locations in Vienna and on a railway in the Severn Valley. The main sets included the Watsons' cosy home; a distorted 221b Baker Street, as seen through the eyes of a drug addict; Freud's art nouveau consulting room; and a Lipizzaner riding academy where Holmes and Freud are nearly trampled to death. A conscious attempt to get away from traditional Holmesian settings — and in particular from Alexandre Trauner's very detailed reconstruction for Billy Wilder's *The Private Life of Sherlock Holmes* — as Adam says, 'This certainly wasn't the normally accepted design.'

below left and right **221B BAKER STREET** Two studies of the interior of 221b Baker Street: the hallway and staircase, and the great detective's living room. Note the slightly sloping walls, indicating that all is not well in Holmes's head.

right **THE DREAM SEQUENCE** Final design concept for the dream sequence of Gothic stairway and entrance in Vienna, 1975.

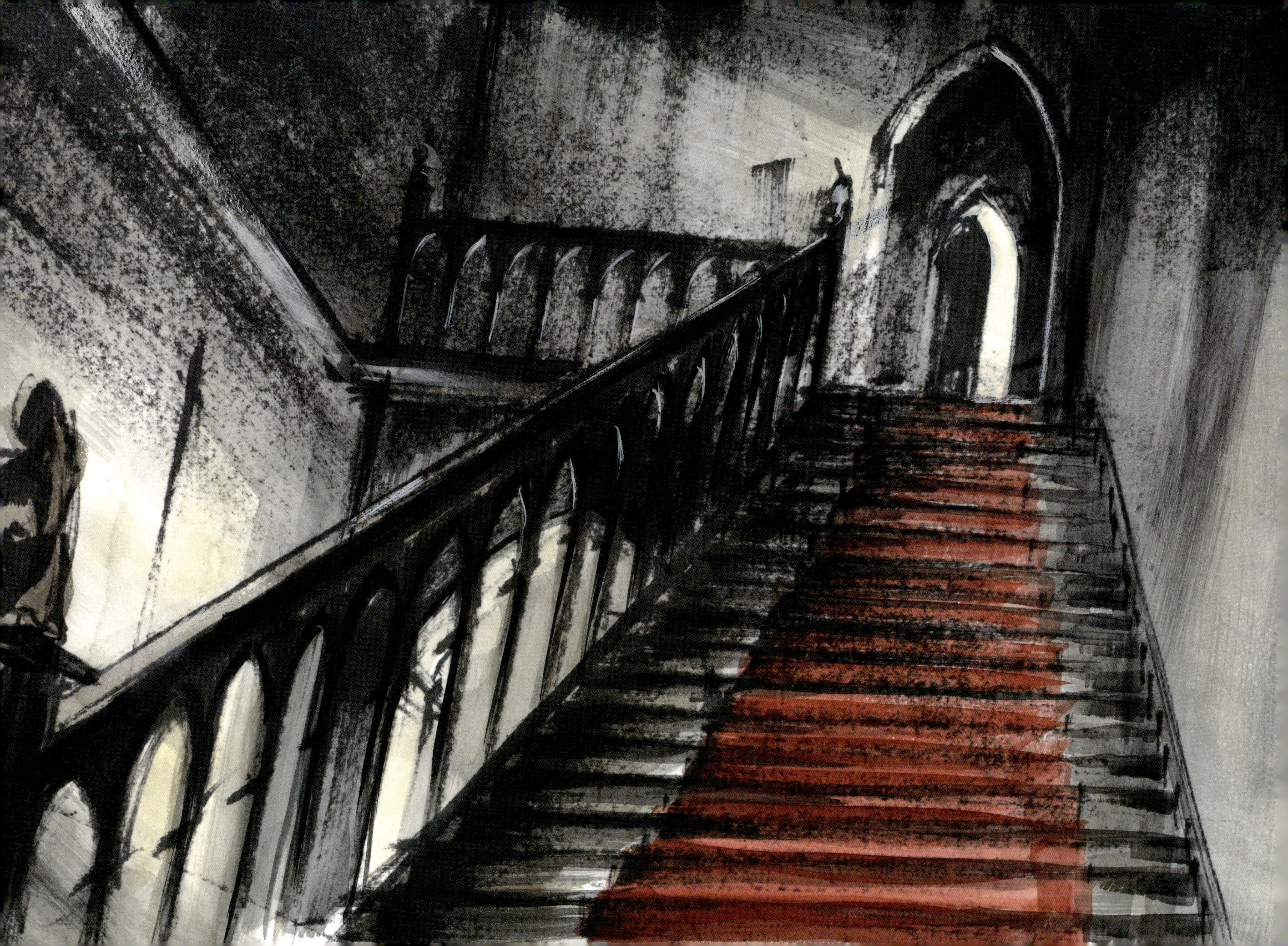

SALON KITTY

THE NAZI OFFICE Final design concept for the vast, high-ceilinged Nazi office, complete with marble floor along which an officer roller-skates.

THE BROTHEL The Berlin brothel interior during its art nouveau phase. Later, for the Nazi period, the brothel will have an art deco makeover.

THE THEATRE OF HISTORY

SALON KITTY [1976]

Recovering from his gruelling time on *Barry Lyndon*, Ken Adam worked with larger-than-life Italian director Tinto Brass on *Salon Kitty*. 'He realized I had been through absolute purgatory, and was very understanding about it.' Because of the film's extreme subject matter — it was a soft-porn excursion into *Cabaret* territory — and because of accusations of very bad taste, *Salon Kitty* is still probably the most undervalued of all Adam's production designs. The main setting is a brothel in which specially trained German girls test the loyalty of high-ranking Nazis — a scenario in fact based on a true story. Adam's designs contrast an art nouveau Berlin brothel of the 1920s (school of Klimt) with the art deco makeover it was given during the Nazi period 'to accentuate the difference between them'. Research was done at the Pension Schmidt off the Kurfürstendamm, where the original Gestapo cellar — 'in which they overheard all the conversations' — still existed. In the film, there is also a Speer-like Nazi office in which every feature is exaggerated and larger than life-sized. Having designed several Führer bunkers in Bond films, here at last was the real thing....

THE BROTHEL SET Cast photo on the art deco brothel set of *Salon Kitty*, known in the United States as *Madam Kitty*.

PENNIES FROM HEAVEN [1981]

Pennies From Heaven was based on Dennis Potter's eight-hour BBC TV serial screened in 1978. It was set in Depression England and full of cockney dreams mimed to evoke 1930s records. The film version, directed by Herbert Ross, was transposed to Chicago but set in the same period and starred Steve Martin in the role originally played by Bob Hoskins. The initial idea was to film on location, but eventually Ken Adam's sets were built on the large soundstages of three different Hollywood studios. The sets included the 'El' street intersection, which had an elevated railway built across the middle of it, together with rows of shops, a speakeasy, a bank and a pool hall (models were made after the drawing stage to test proportions and lighting effects); also the basement of the speakeasy where Christopher Walken performs his dance for Bernadette Peters; and the famous 'Nighthawks' bar. The film was to be the last of the big Hollywood studio-based musicals – one with a sad and important message. Adam was on the credits both as 'visual consultant' and 'associate producer'.

THE 'EL' STREET INTERSECTION Final design concept for the 'El' street intersection, Chicago, 1980.

PENNIES FROM HEAVEN

THE 'EL' STREET INTERSECTION
Three rough studies of the 'El'
street intersection, 1980.

'My problem was what to put in the Chicago street, and that's when I came up with the idea of using American painters for some of the exteriors. I used Hopper's *Nighthawks* on the corner. Also his *New York Movie* for the usherette, Reginald Marsh for the girls modelling furs, and an enormous collage of Walker Evans's Depression photos for the 60-foot backing outside the diner. It became a jigsaw puzzle of various artists of the period.'

left and right **THE 'NIGHTHAWKS' BAR**
The set of the 'Nighthawks' bar (based on the 1942 Hopper painting), constructed as part of a Chicago streetscape on the big stage at MGM (left), and a model of the bar in its Chicago setting (right).

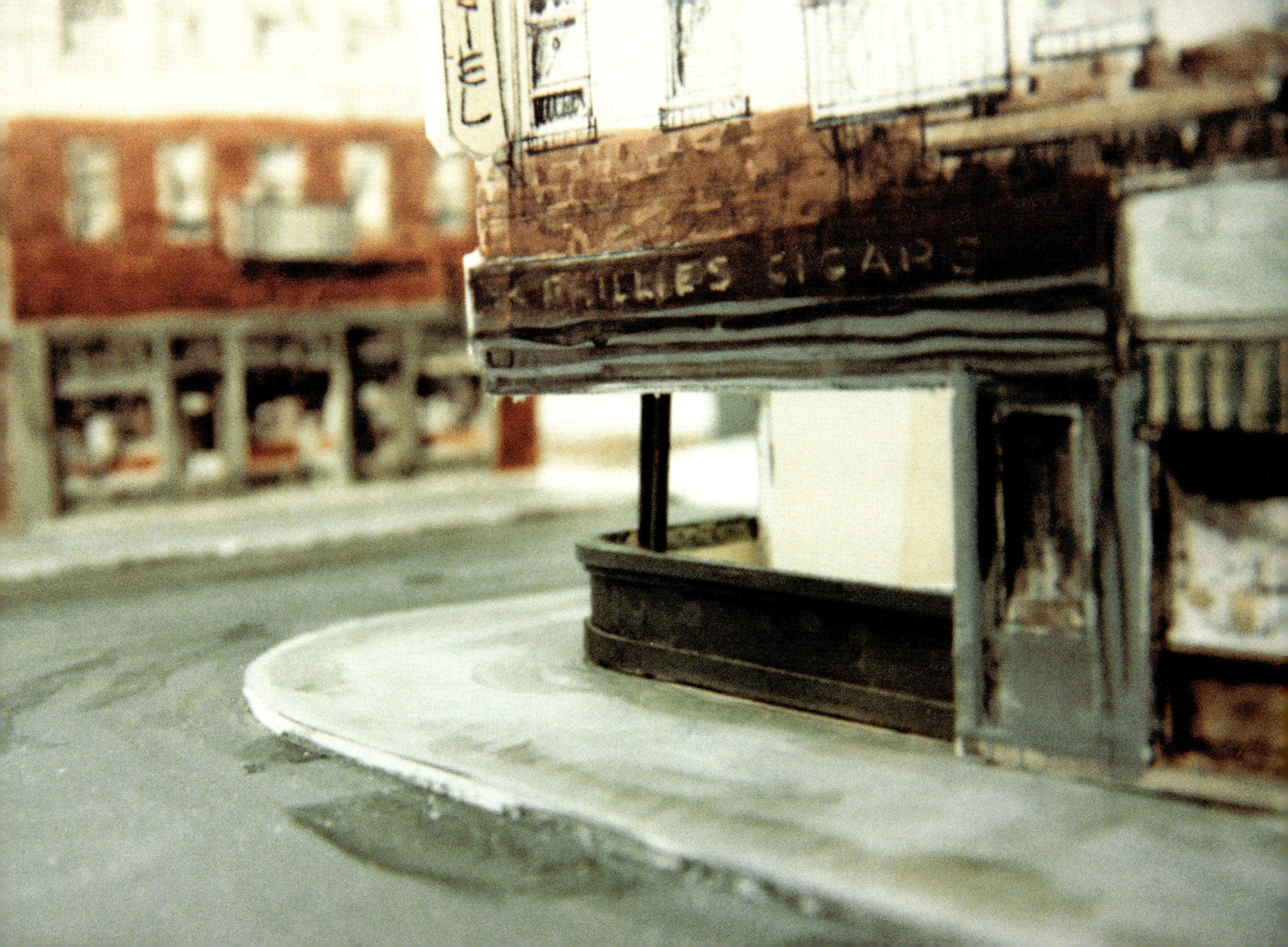

140 **THE THEATRE OF HISTORY**

opposite and above **THE MOVIE THEATRE**
Final design concept of the Chicago
movie theatre frontage, and
photograph of the completed set.

THE THEATRE OF HISTORY 141

THE BANK INTERIOR Four studies
of the huge art deco bank interior,

THE BANK FANTASY SEQUENCE Final concept of the bank fantasy, 1981.

'We had two banks – the actual art deco bank and the bank that had to be a transformation after everything goes crazy with the music and the fantasy. But I'd run out of money so we couldn't do a complete transformation. In the end we did it using my original art deco structure, just changing the stairs and creating a platform for a Busby Berkeley-style musical.'

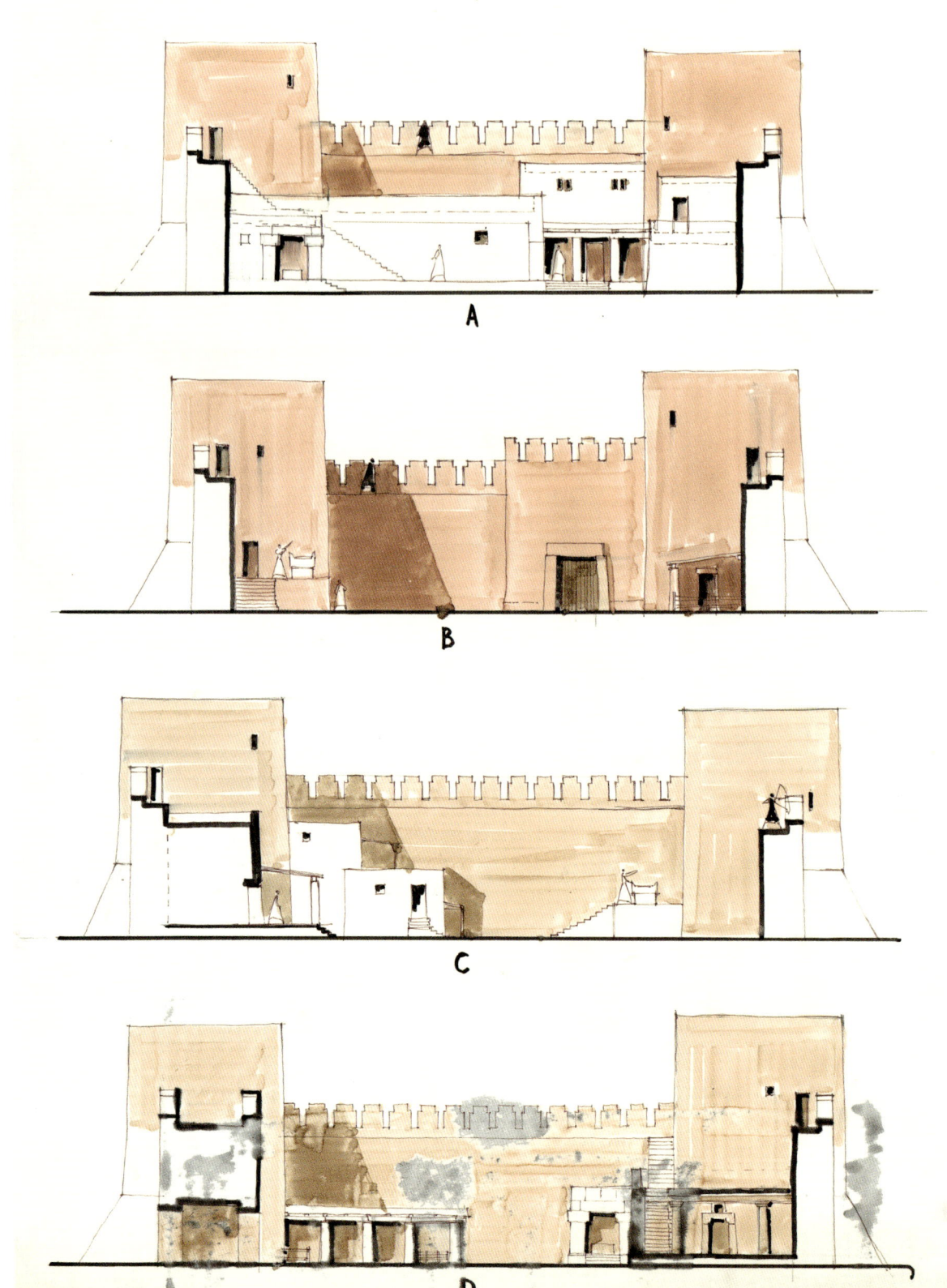

KING DAVID [1985]

Filmed at Pinewood and on location in Italy, Bruce Beresford's *King David* tried to get away from 'the Biblical pictures we'd become used to – with all that glamour' and instead opted for smaller-scale, more primitive-looking dwellings and cities of 1000 BC. The walls and towers of Jerusalem, as well as David's palace and the Tabernacle, were constructed amongst actual buildings at Matera in Puglia (a village built into a canyon in southern Italy, previously used by Pasolini for *The Gospel According to St. Matthew*). Saul's citadel was built outside Rome, David and Goliath fought in the Abruzzi mountains, and David's village was in Sardinia. The film told the story of David (an ill-at-ease Richard Gere) from shepherd boy to King of Israel, and – like *Sodom and Gomorrah* – it conjured up a convincing ancient world from almost non-existent research materials.

right and opposite above **SAUL'S CITADEL** Four cutaway views of Saul's Citadel, constructed at Cesano outside Rome, 1984, and final design concept for the citadel, with troops marching past.

'The village of Matera worked beautifully because it is one of the oldest habitations in the world – six thousand years old – and it goes through all these periods of history built into the side of a canyon. Just over the other side is a modern city, which is ghastly.'

below left and right **MATERA**
Photograph of Matera in southern Italy, with a drawing of its conversion into the city of Jerusalem, and David's Palace in the centre.

AGNES OF GOD [1985]

Based on a play set almost entirely in a Montreal convent, *Agnes of God* was filmed mainly at a disused school near Toronto. Ken Adam adapted the square building into the convent, adding a bell-tower and a chapel (filming actually took place inside and on top of the bell-tower). Sets for the convent interiors—corridors, cells and so on—were built at Kleinburg. Locations in and around Montreal were also used. The film had a bleak, wintry look, thanks in part to the cinematography by Sven Nykvist, and it has been called 'a companion piece to Alfred Hitchcock's *I Confess*', this time with the protagonists played by Jane Fonda (the psychiatrist), Anne Bancroft (the Mother Superior) and Meg Tilly (the novice Sister Agnes, accused of strangling her newborn baby).

THE CONVENT Final design concept for the conversion of a disused school near Toronto into a Montreal convent, complete with bell-tower and cloisters, 1984.

'We shot the grounds, the tower, the cloisters and all that on location. For six weeks Annie Bancroft and Meg Tilly were dressed up as nuns, with the liturgical music and the Latin Mass and the ambience, and they almost came to believe they were nuns. We couldn't accept them in modern clothes, and in some ways they couldn't either.'

above right **CONVENT CORRIDOR** Final concept of convent corridor, 1984.

right **CONVENT ROOM** Rough study for convent room, with sloping roof.

THE LAST EMPEROR [1985]

Despite working on Bernardo Bertolucci's *The Last Emperor* for nearly a year in 1985, Ken Adam was replaced by Ferdinando Scarfiotti during pre-production, the only time this had happened in his long career. Before leaving the project, Adam had visited the Forbidden City with the surviving brother of Emperor Pu-Yi (Adam's group were 'the first film people ever to be allowed into the City'). He had also been to Harbin in Manchuria, visited the Palace of Pu-Yi in Changchun, and set up an art department in Rome. His designs included the puppet coronation in Manchuria, the corridors and rooms and apartments of the Imperial Palace, and a vast storage chamber. These concepts experimented with 'traditional Chinese meets art deco', and Bertolucci seemed well pleased with them at the time. Looking back, however, Adam now says, 'I could never relate much to Chinese art.'

PALACE INTERIOR Long-shot concept of Pu-Yi visiting the dying Dowager Empress, 1985.

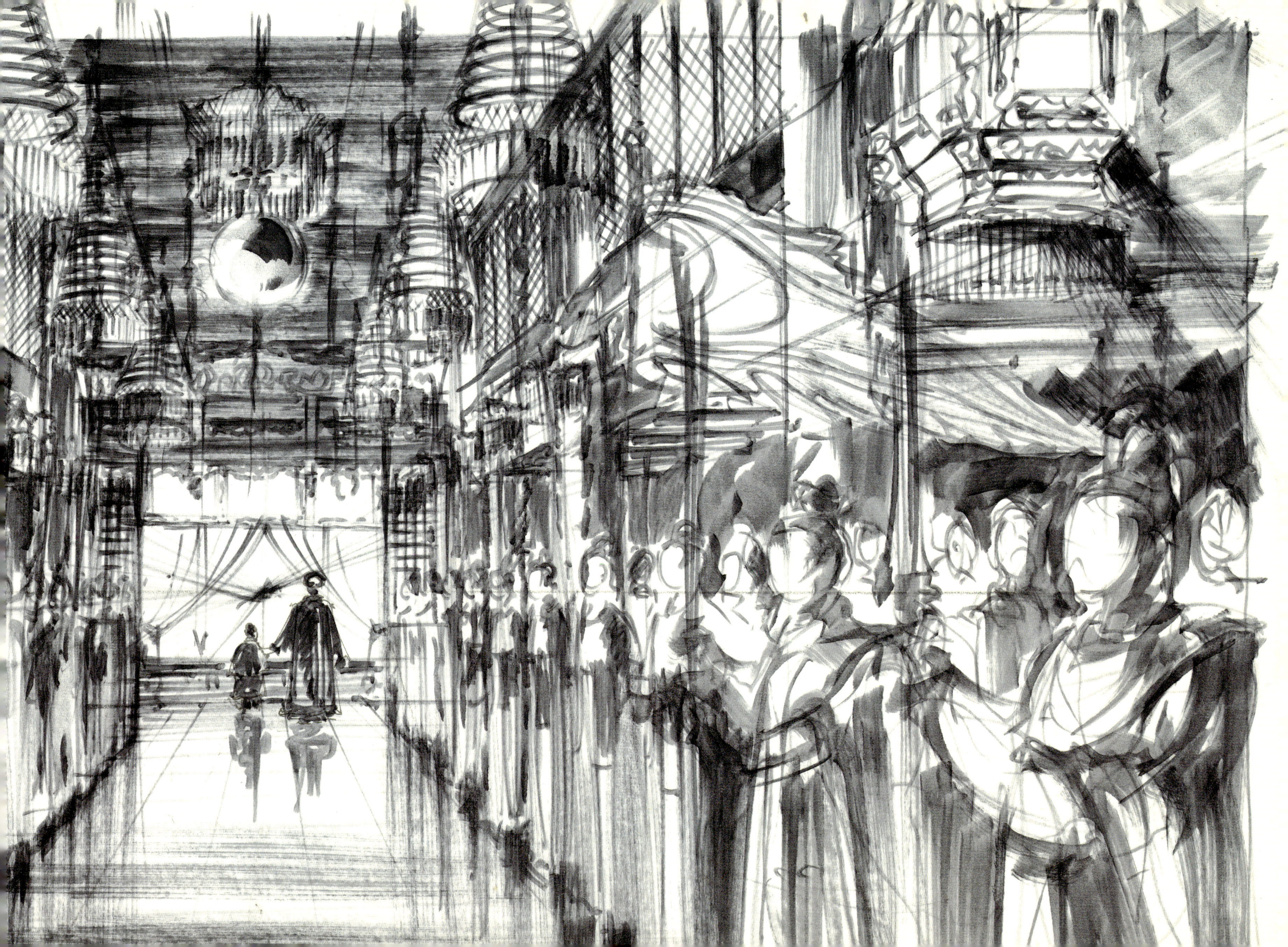

PALACE INTERIOR
Closer design concept of
Pu-Yi visiting the dying
Dowager Empress, 1985.

'For all the Manchurian sequences, where Pu-Yi becomes a puppet emperor, I used art deco. Most of the Imperial Palace they shot for real, except for some scenes which were sets built in Italy. I always had a problem with Chinese architecture, so I tried to repeat certain elements that I like – the grilles and circular openings and awnings.'

STORAGE CHAMBER Design concept for a storage chamber in the 'Forbidden City', 1985.

CRIMES OF THE HEART [1986]

Crimes of the Heart was an adaptation of Beth Henley's Pulitzer Prize-winning play, and—like *King David* of the previous year—it was directed by Bruce Beresford. Ken Adam adapted a derelict period dwelling at Southport in North Carolina, half an hour away from the studios of producer Dino De Laurentiis. Adam altered the design of the house, adding porticoes, towers and porches. He also gutted the interior and created designs room by room. The style he chose was a mixture of American Queen Anne and Eastlake, and, unusually, both the exterior and the interior were re-designed in this way. The project went on to attract attention in the architectural press, including the New York *Architectural Digest*. The film was a three-hander, between Diane Keaton, Jessica Lange and Sissy Spacek. At the end of filming, De Laurentiis sold the house and, as Adam said, 'made more money than I ever spent on adapting it!'

below and right **THE HOUSE** Photograph of the house at Southport, North Carolina, which Ken Adam converted into a folly, with (right) one of the bedroom interiors.

CRIMES OF THE HEART

OLD FRONT ELEVATION

NEW FRONT ELEVATION

'The house had absolutely no character, but it had a basic shell, and my idea was to turn it into a place that looked kooky – the girls were kooky, you see – so I completely altered the design. We didn't use any studio at all. It was the first time I'd done that, and it worked pretty well.'

OLD REAR ELEVATION

NEW REAR ELEVATION

THE HOUSE EXTERIOR Four elevations of the house, with final design concepts of its setting, 1986.

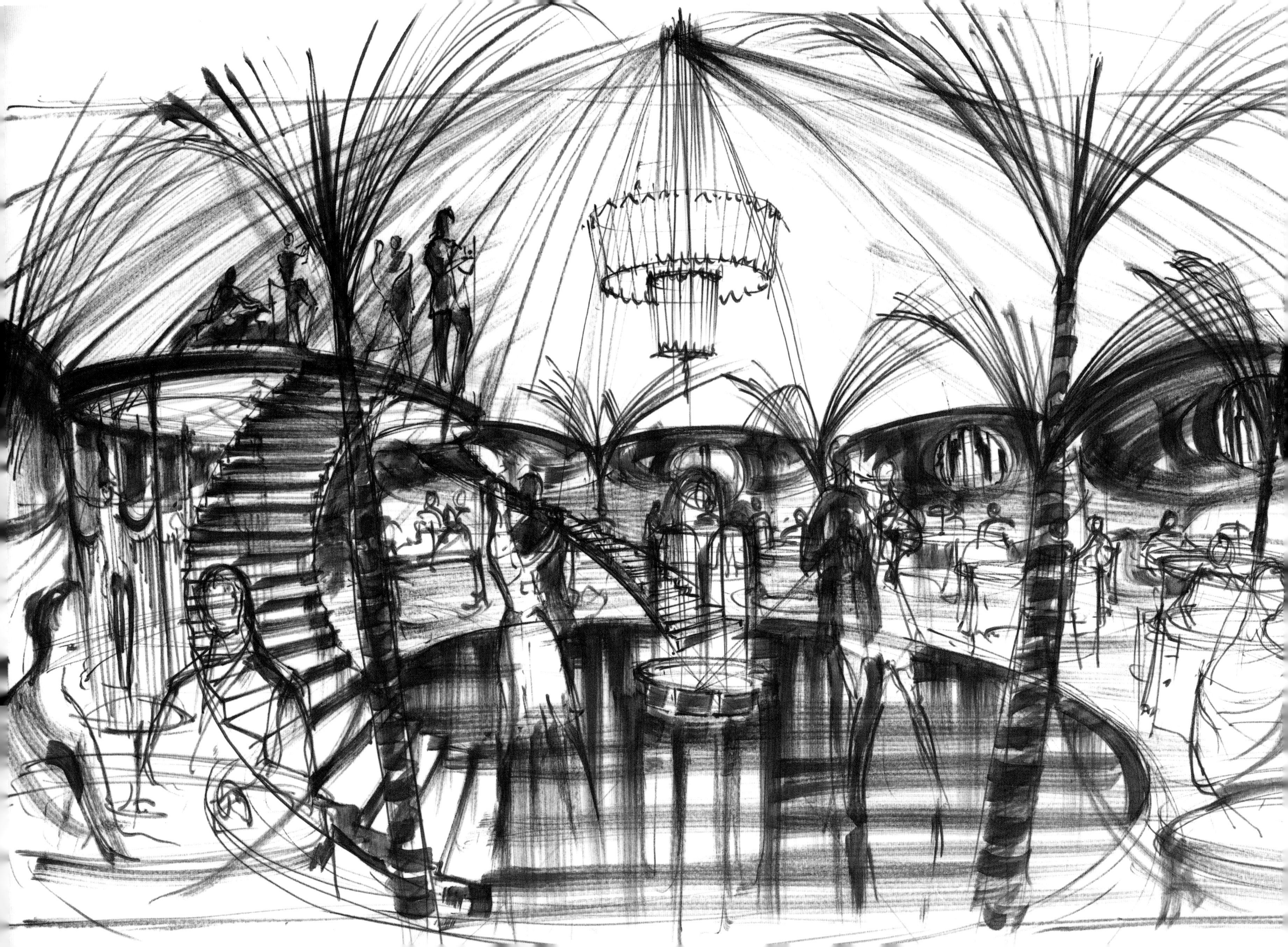

THE FRESHMAN [1990]

The Freshman was a comedy mainly set in and around New York's Little Italy, but interiors were shot in Toronto with locations in New York and Toronto (the railway station standing in for Grand Central). It was the story, written and directed by Andrew Bergman, of a Mafia boss – Marlon Brando parodying his own performance in *The Godfather* – who hires a naïve film student (Matthew Broderick) to run errands for him. Key sets included the 'old world social club' – built in false perspective to emphasize Brando's physical presence – and the restaurant where endangered species are cooked (Adam added two huge surgical lights to enhance the macabre atmosphere). Brando liked the set so much he gave an end-of-production party in it.

left **THE RESTAURANT** The final design concept of the 'temporary' deco restaurant in a tent, which might have to be dismantled at any moment.

'I decided it would be fun to design the restaurant as very chic and way out – but it had also to be a temporary place, because it was a place to eat endangered species, illegal like a speakeasy – and to treat it like an elegant art deco tent with a platform in the centre, a shiny black floor and deco details.'

above and below **THE RESTAURANT** Art deco details for the restaurant set.

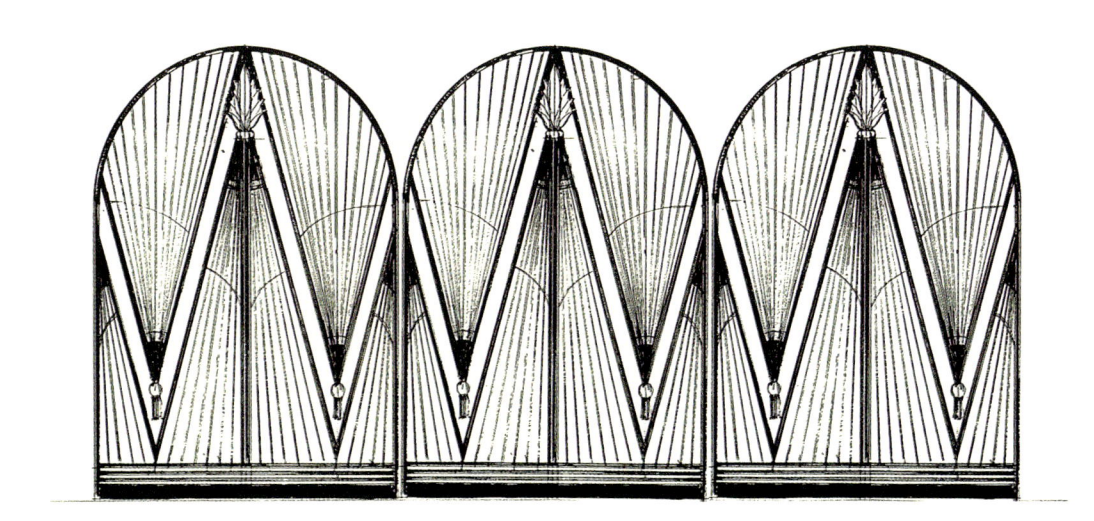

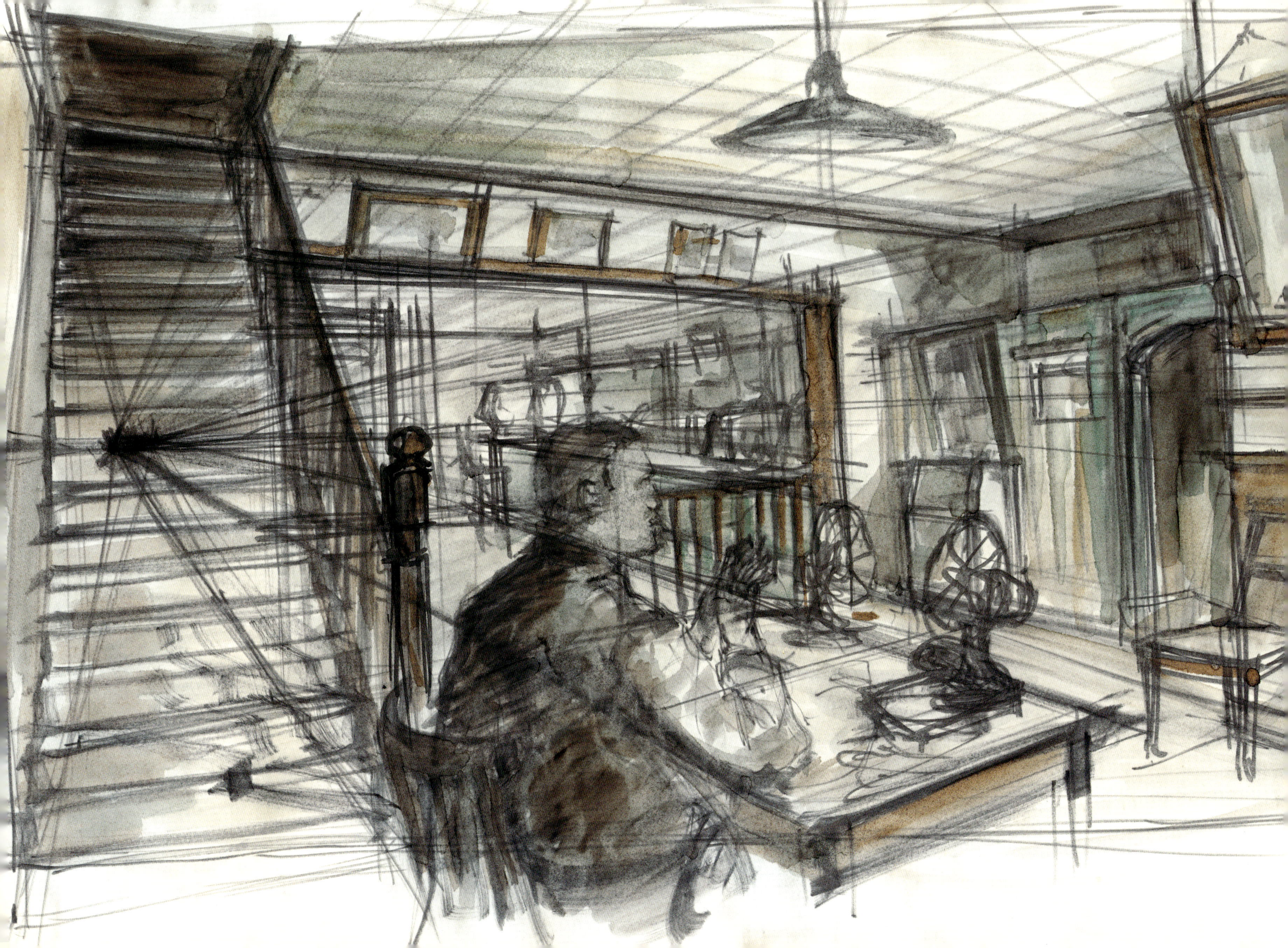

'I tried to look at some Italian social clubs in New York, but they wouldn't let me anywhere near them. Eventually we had the support of a Mafia boss, on condition that we ate in one of his restaurants, which served the worst pasta ever! I was finally allowed to glance at one of the clubs – and that gave me enough atmosphere.'

left **THE ITALIAN SOCIAL CLUB** Final design concept for the Italian Social Club, based on a glimpse of the real thing in Little Italy, New York, 1989.

above **THE KITCHEN** Final design concept for the gourmet kitchen, with 'operating table' and two surgical lamps.

THE THEATRE OF HISTORY

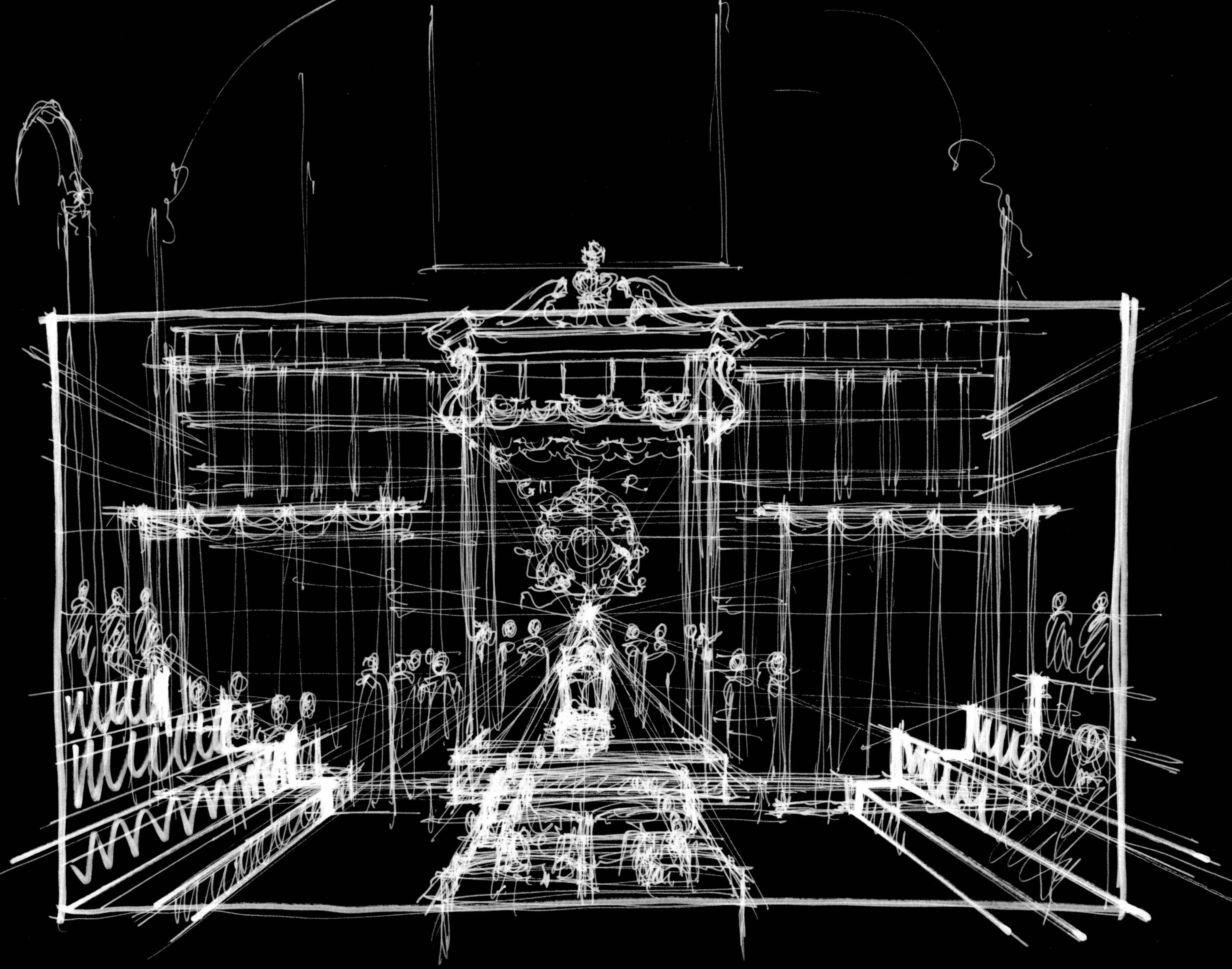

'*Madness* was the way I would have designed *Barry Lyndon* if it had been left to me twenty years before. You use the most spectacular existing locations and make them work for you by combining them with sets.'

opposite and this page **THE HOUSE OF LORDS**
Rough drawing of the House of Lords set, showing the camera angle (opposite); and (this page) the final design concept, 1994.

THE MADNESS OF KING GEORGE [1994]

Adapted by Alan Bennett from his hit play *The Madness of George III*, and directed by Nicholas Hytner (his first film), *The Madness of King George* was set in 1788 England, where the King's insanity almost provokes a constitutional crisis. The film was shot partly on location (Eton College for the Houses of Parliament; the Double Cube Room at Wilton House; Thame Park for Kew Palace; the roof of Arundel Castle with extra tall chimneys) and partly at Shepperton Studios (the Royal Apartments and surroundings; the interior of the House of Lords). Ken Adam's designs were a long way away from the grandiose 'documentary' ambitions of *Barry Lyndon*, and he won his second Academy Award for his work.

left **THE ROOF** The sequence on the roof of Arundel Castle, standing in for Windsor.

opposite **THE ROYAL APARTMENT** Four studies for the studio-built corridor and back stairs outside the Royal Apartment, Windsor, 1994.

'I was so impressed with the roof at Arundel and all those chimneys that I added some more to make it look like a Greek temple almost – the setting for a Greek tragedy. That's what production design is really about. The King collects the children from the nursery – a set at Shepperton. They go up an unbelievable spiral staircase – St. Paul's Cathedral. And they go through a door at the top... and arrive on the roof at Arundel.'

Outside the King's Apartments.

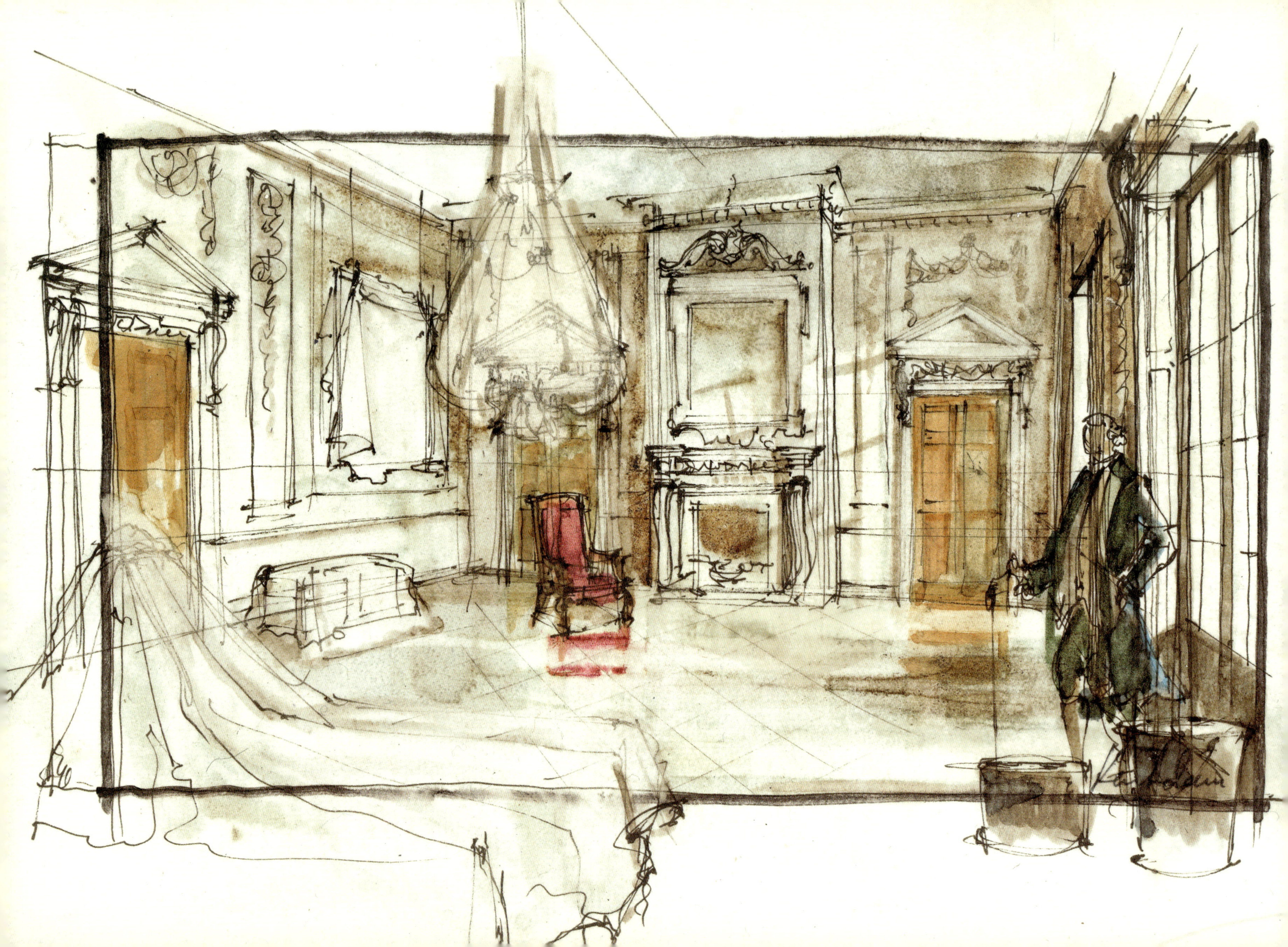

opposite **KEW PALACE** Study of the entrance hall, Kew Palace.

right and below **KEW PALACE** Final design concepts for the living room, looking towards the fireplace (right), and the dining room (below).

KEW – LIVING ROOM – TOWARDS FIRE PLACE

Dining Room. Kew.

'We used Thame Park, a derelict Georgian mansion, for Kew Palace – a palace that doesn't exist anymore. We re-dressed the mansion as Kew, where King George has his medical treatment. I decided to use only a few key pieces of set-dressing to make my point. A kind of exaggeration in simplicity, I like to think.'

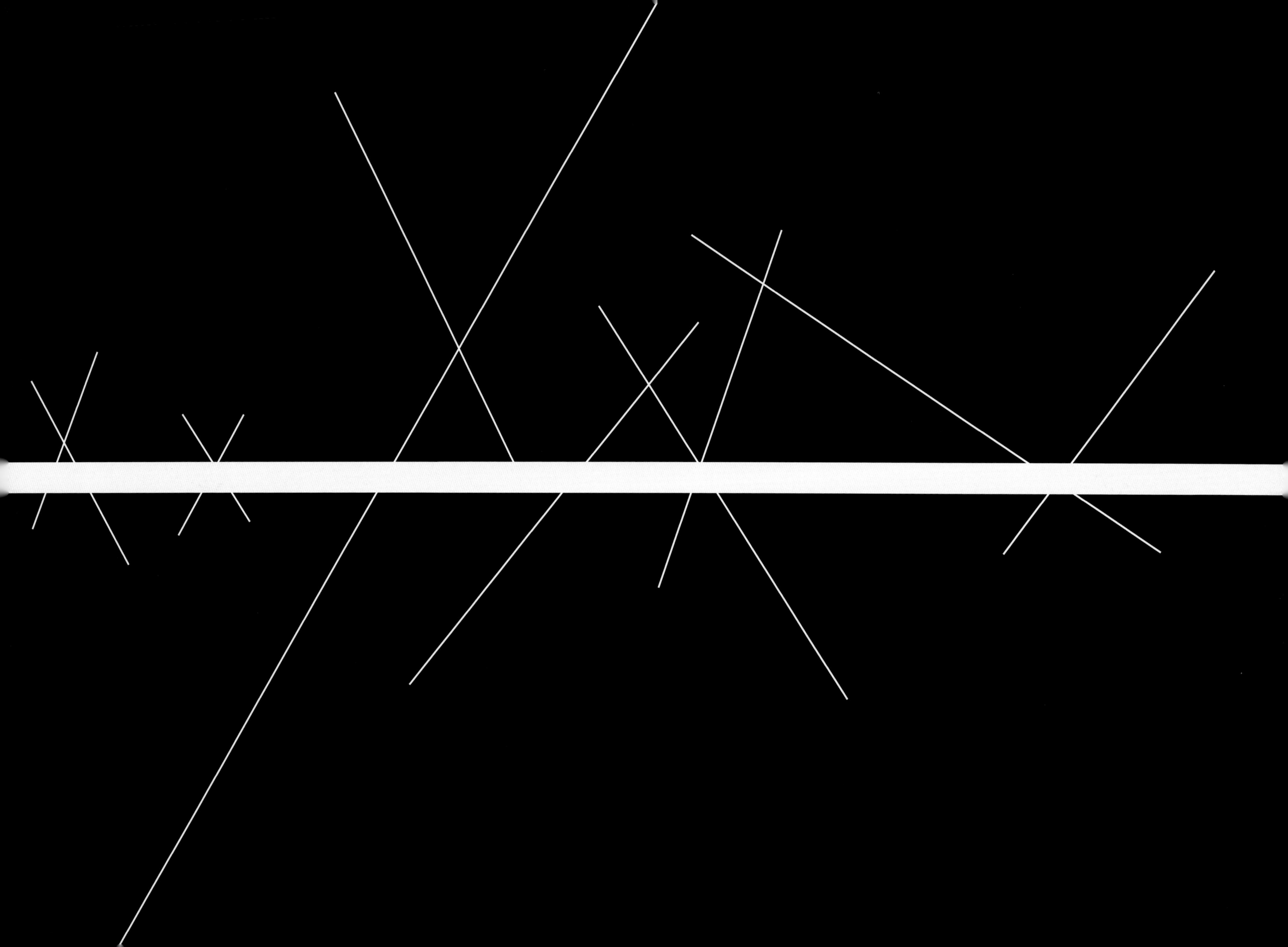

5
TWO OPERAS

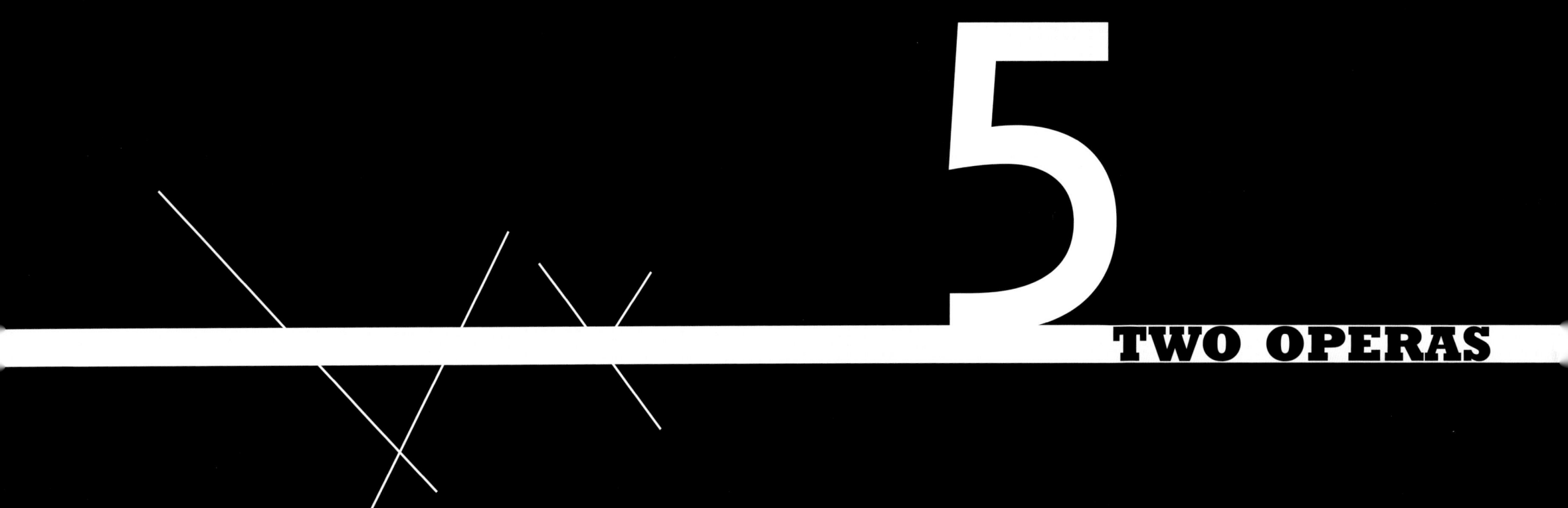

THE GIRL OF THE GOLDEN WEST [1977]

Ken Adam designed Puccini's *La Fanciulla del West* (*The Girl of the Golden West*) at the Royal Opera House Covent Garden in 1977, directed by Piero Faggioni and revived in 2005. He designed a new version, directed in 1985 by Bruce Beresford for the Spoleto Festival in Italy and in Charleston, South Carolina. Puccini set his opera in 1850, just after the Gold Rush, so Adam based his designs on 'hundreds of archive photographs' of ramshackle Gold Rush saloon bars, cabins and mines, with an emphasis on raw wood construction. Act Three — at the mine itself — included a full-sized water-wheel and a wooden bridge that was so long that 'they ran out of Puccini'. Adam took Stanley Kubrick to the 1977 production — followed by a behind-the-scenes tour of the house — and Kubrick was intrigued by the mechanics of scene-changing.

right **THE MINING CAMP** Early rough drawing for Act III, The California Mining Camp (in the libretto 'the Forest'), Covent Garden production, 1977.

opposite **THE MINING CAMP** Design concept for Act III, The Mining Camp, USA production, 1985.

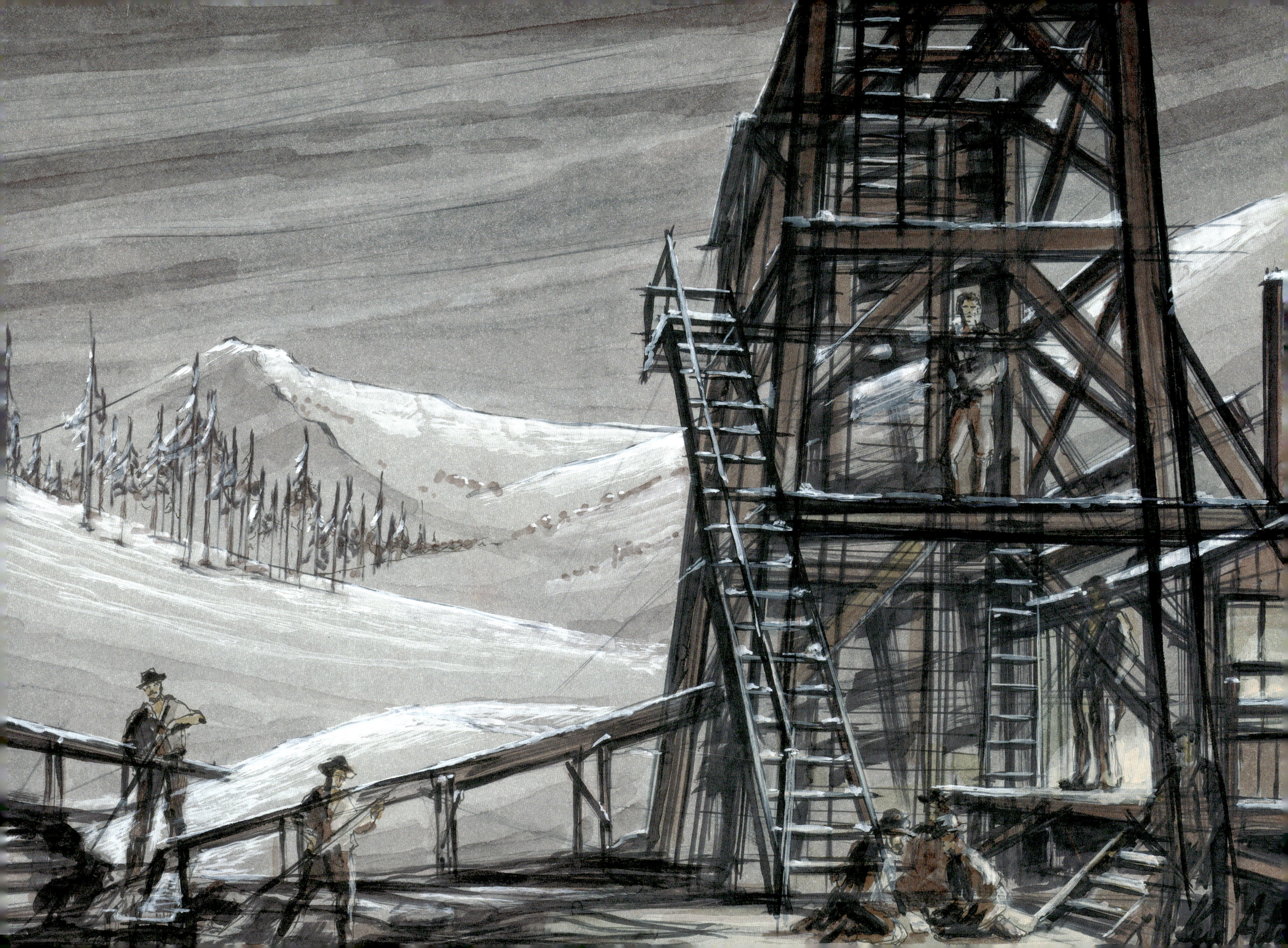

THE POLKA SALOON Interior of the vast Polka Saloon, for Act I of the Covent Garden production, 1977.

168   **TWO OPERAS**

MINNIE'S LOG CABIN Design concept for Act II, Minnie's Log Cabin, USA production, 1985, 'with trees and snow this time'.

TWO OPERAS

MINNIE'S LOG CABIN Design concept for Act II, Minnie's Log Cabin, Covent Garden production, 1977.

'I had never worked in opera before, and it was amazing how I got the job – via Hollywood. The conductor Zubin Mehta had mentioned at a dinner that he wanted the production to seem filmic, and Lew Wasserman and the supervising art director at Universal, Alex Golitzen, both said, "Well, the person you should use is Ken Adam." And that's how it happened.'

THE MINING CAMP Early studies of the Mining Camp, with its waterwheel and rickety wooden bridge, for Act III of the Covent Garden production, 1977.

WOZZECK [UNREALIZED, 1997]

In 1997 Ken Adam designed Alban Berg's *Wozzeck*, set just after the First World War, to be directed by William Friedkin at the Maggio Fiorentino in Florence. Preliminary studies included the lodging-house in the street, the doctor's consulting room and laboratory, the factory, the grain field and the garden festival. In the end, however, the production did not use Adam's designs.

MARIE'S LODGINGS Four studies of Marie's lodgings at different times of day, in a Caligari-like street setting, 1997.

'I designed *Wozzeck* in London, setting it in the period when Alban Berg wrote it – the 1920s; German Expressionism. William Friedkin loved the sketches, but then there were arguments with the opera house and the production got postponed, and then I was no longer available – so somehow it didn't happen.'

THE DOCTOR'S CONSULTING ROOM
Three studies, in Expressionist style, for Wozzeck's appointment with the doctor in his consulting room.

THE DOCTOR'S LABORATORY The doctor's experimental laboratory, where Wozzeck agrees to become a guinea pig.

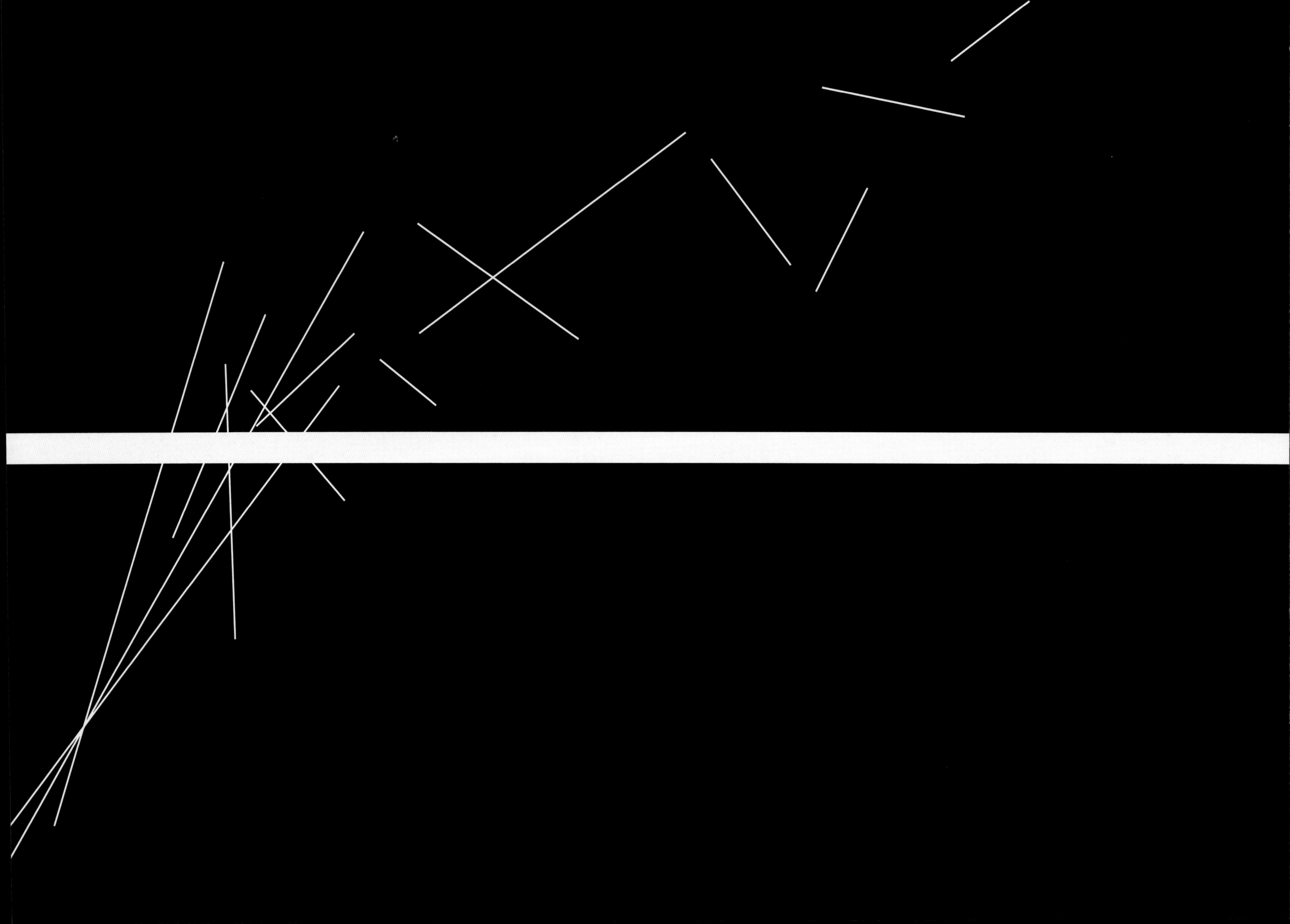

6

DRAWINGS COME TO LIFE

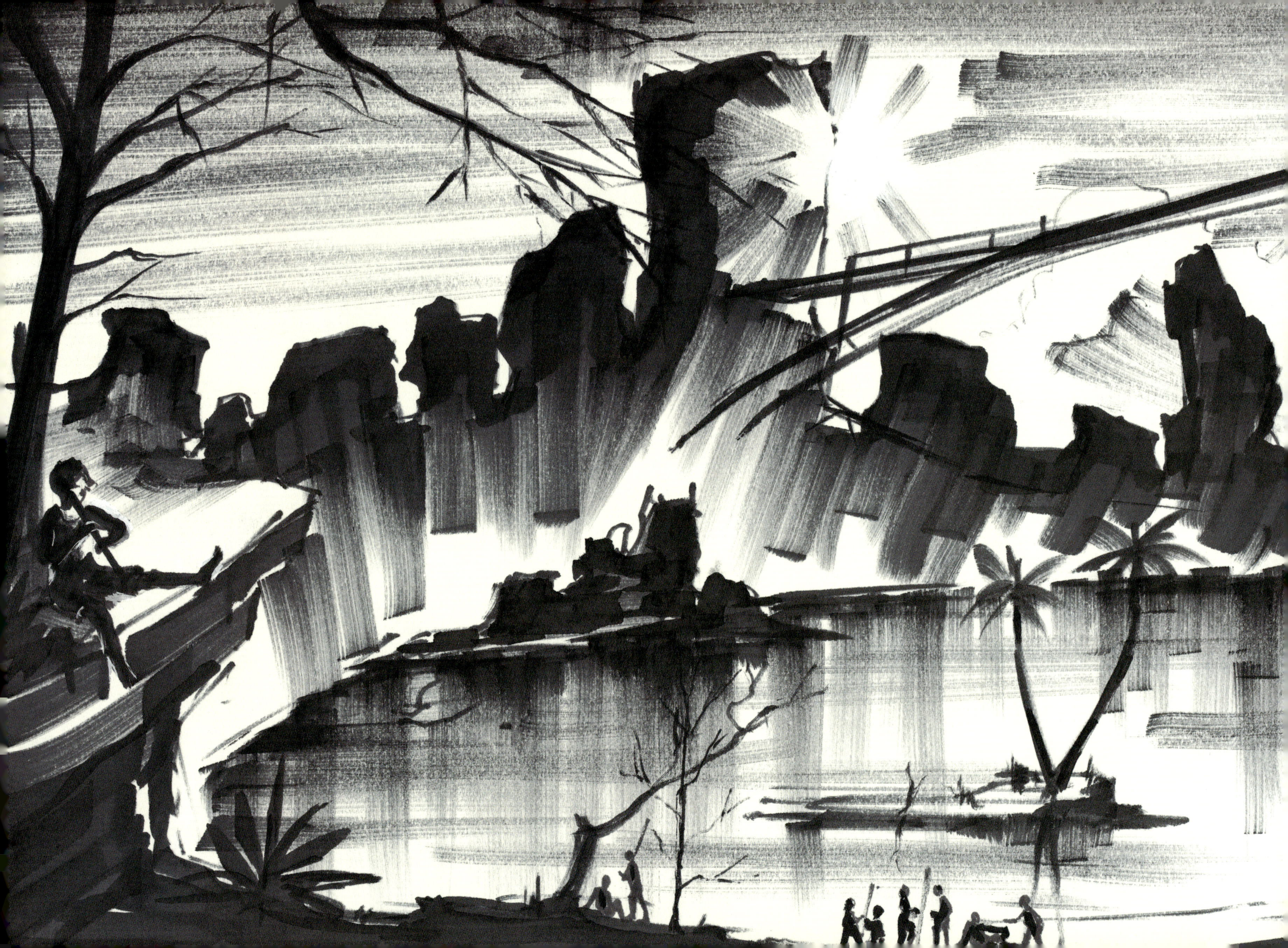

PETER PAN [1970]

Ken Adam worked on this project with Herbert Ross in 1969, shortly after completing *Goodbye, Mr. Chips*. It was to have been a musical version, with Mia Farrow in the lead and Mel Ferrer producing. Adam worked from Pinewood, 'designing the whole overall concept', including Never Never Land, the Pirate Ship, the Lost Boys' seven trees, and Peter's house. Ivor Beddoes, who was working with Adam and was a trained ballet dancer, sketched out the balletic flying sequences to Never Never Land. The film was never made, though Adam later learned that Universal recycled the designs on another film.

THE LAGOON Initial concept drawing of the lagoon in Never Never Land, 1969.

'*Peter Pan* was to use all studio sets, and there were thousands of sketches. But the picture didn't materialize. The sketches were sent to Universal, because they owned them and, when later on I came to work there on *Diamonds Are Forever*, the supervising art director said with a guilty face, "I have to confess we used your sketches for another film!" I still don't know which one it was.'

PETER PAN

FIRST IDEA - ENTRANCE TO PETER'S HOUSE

PETER PAN

PETER'S HOUSE Initial drawing of the entrance to Peter Pan's house.

178 **DRAWINGS COME TO LIFE**

FIRST IDEA FOR ENTRANCES TO SEVEN TREES

PETER PAN

SEVEN TREES Initial drawing of the entrances to 'the seven trees', where the Lost Boys live.

ADDAMS FAMILY VALUES [1993]

Designed and built in eight weeks flat, *Addams Family Values* was an affectionate tribute to the Charles Addams cartoons in *The New Yorker*, only in three dimensions. Ken Adam was attracted by Addams's drawings 'for their morbid sense of humour and their distorted perspective'. In this, the second big screen adaptation, Morticia and Gomez are tricked into sending their difficult children to summer camp in the mountains. Sets included the Family Mansion, complete with palatial mock-Expressionist interiors and a cemetery in the garden, as well as the Harmony Hut and Totem Pole of the summer camp where Wednesday Addams, played by Christina Ricci, enacts her own subversive version of the Pocahontas story. The film was an ambitious one, 'only to be compared with some of the Bonds', and 95 per cent of it was shot on several soundstages at once.

left **THE FAMILY MANSION ELEVATION** Elevation of the Addams family mansion, from two angles, 1992.

opposite **THE FAMILY MANSION** An overhead drawing of the house inspired by a Charles Addams cartoon in *The New Yorker*.

DRAWINGS COME TO LIFE

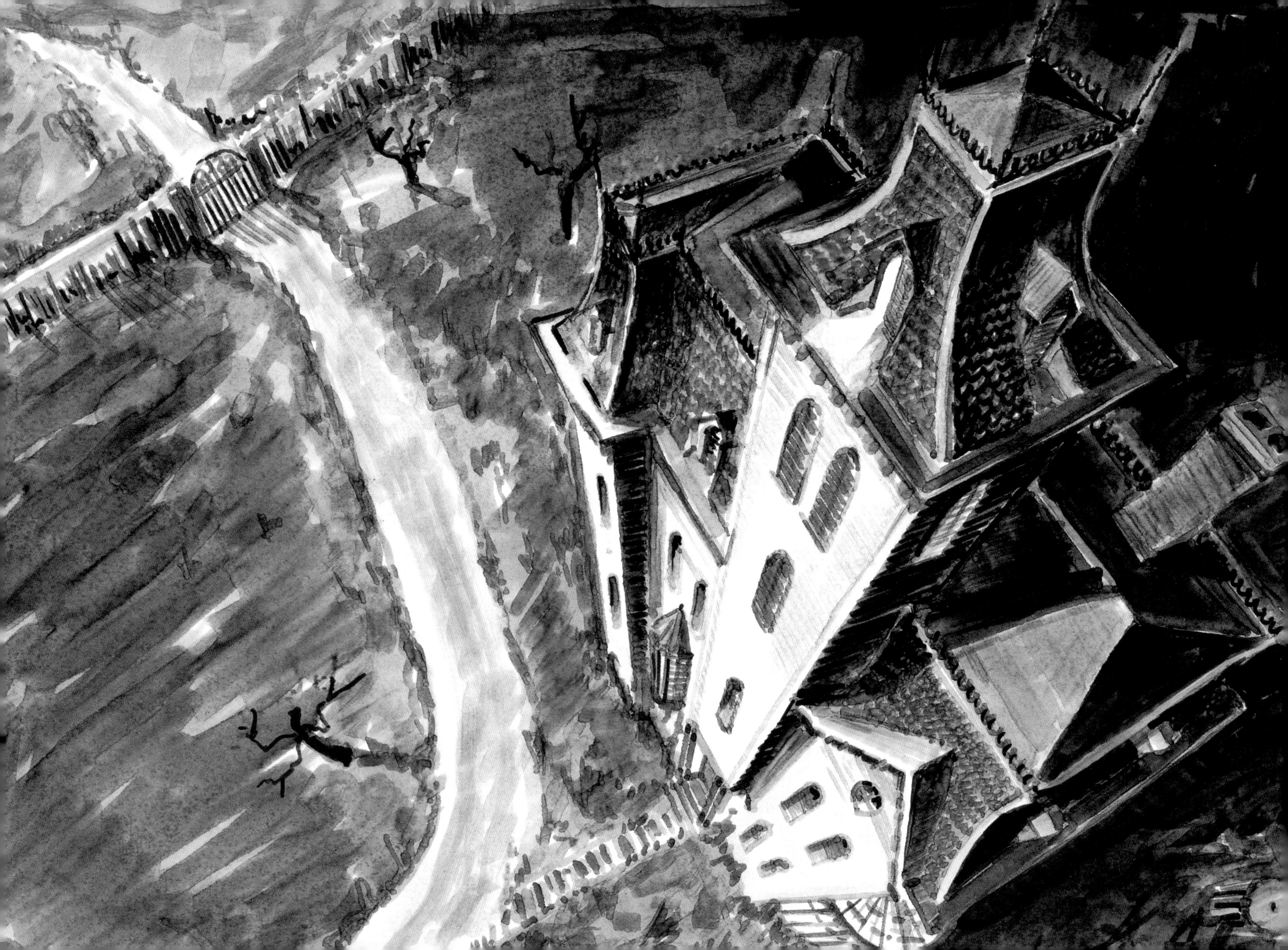

'I wanted to do the film as a tribute to Charles Addams, and I thought it would be interesting to translate his cartoon drawings into three-dimensional settings; to get more Addams into it, with his false perspective, mixed with true perspective, and no straight walls.'

above right **MORTICIA'S BEDROOM** Morticia Addams's bedroom, complete with wallpaper designed by Ken Adam.

right **THE NURSERY** The Addams nursery, pre-makeover, with cradle.

ADDAMS FAMILY VALUES

above **THE SUMMER CAMP** The Lakeside Summer Camp, where Wednesday and Pugsley Addams are sent.

left **THE TOTEM POLE** Totem pole detail for the Summer Camp sequence.

'We built the Summer Camp on location by a lake – a camp was already there. This was where Christina Ricci disrupts everything. It was a particular kind of log-cabin kitsch, and highly coloured.'

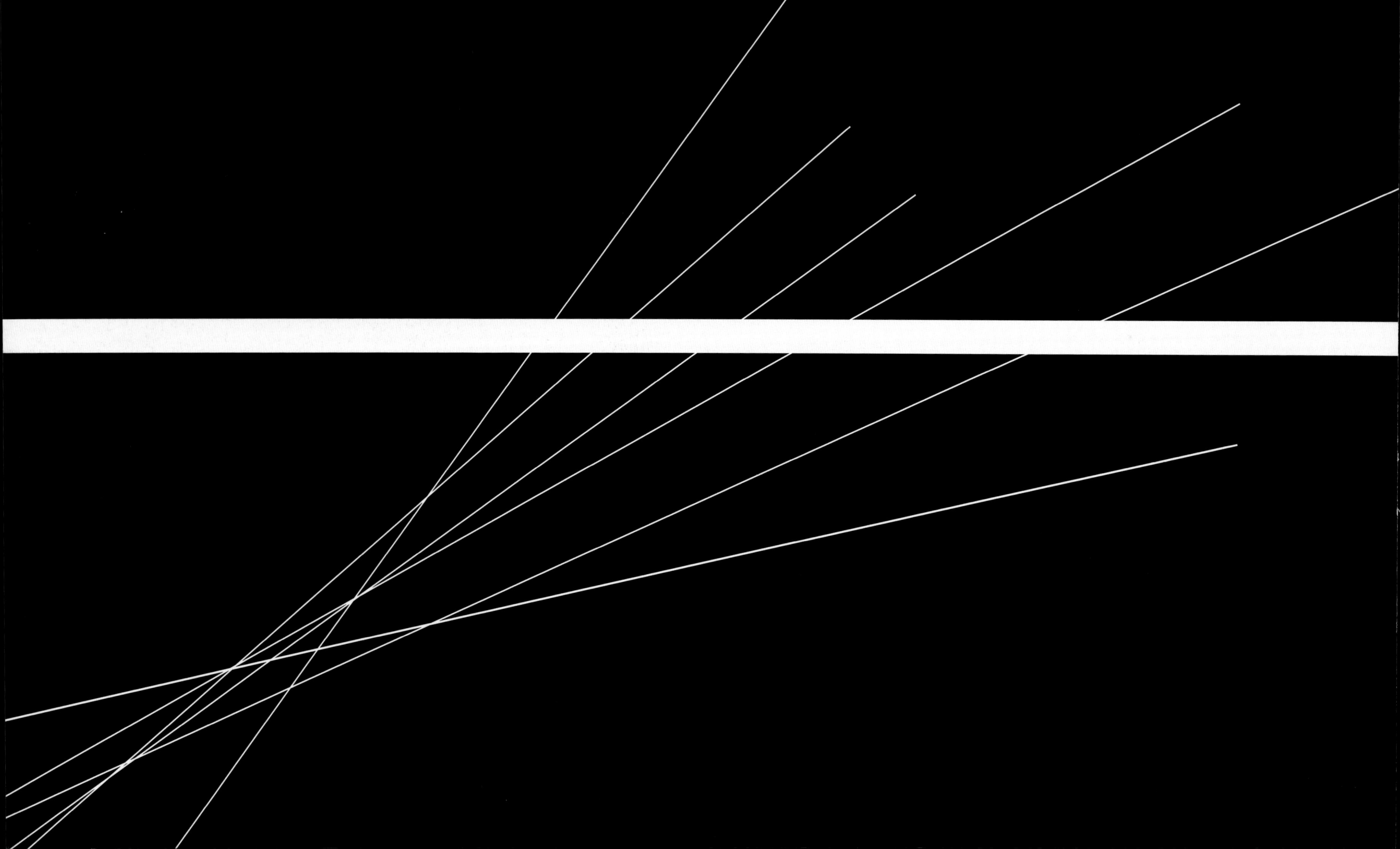

7 DESIGNING THE FUTURE

LORD L [1969]

In the late 1960s, Ken Adam went into partnership with the prolific Italian screenwriter Ennio De Concini on various development projects: Adam would produce and design, De Concini would write and direct. The most controversial of their story ideas was 'Lord L', about God becoming fed up with the way things are going in the counter-cultural 1960s. In the film there were to be meetings with Karl Marx and Sigmund Freud, a version of the Last Supper, and Sean Connery on a bicycle with a transistor radio waiting for the good news to come from the heavens. Universal was interested – this was the heyday of Hollywood investment in far-out projects in Britain – but insisted on another director and a tiny budget so the film was shelved.

'I was going to produce and design *Lord L*, which was a very original story by Ennio De Concini – a politically quite dangerous script about superstition and organized religion. There was to be a big hangar in the middle of nowhere, where Lord L has his meetings. Most of the film happens in the hangar. In the end, Lord L floats up to the heavens in a balloon that bursts. Remember it was the 1960s!'

above right **THE DEBATING CHAMBER** Concept for the debating chamber, to be used by characters such as Karl Marx and Joseph Stalin.

right **THE LAST SUPPER** Concept for an interior: a Last Supper, from above, as Leonardo didn't envisage it.

opposite **THE HANGAR** Study for the hangar, in the middle of nowhere, where Lord L has various encounters with remarkable men, 1969.

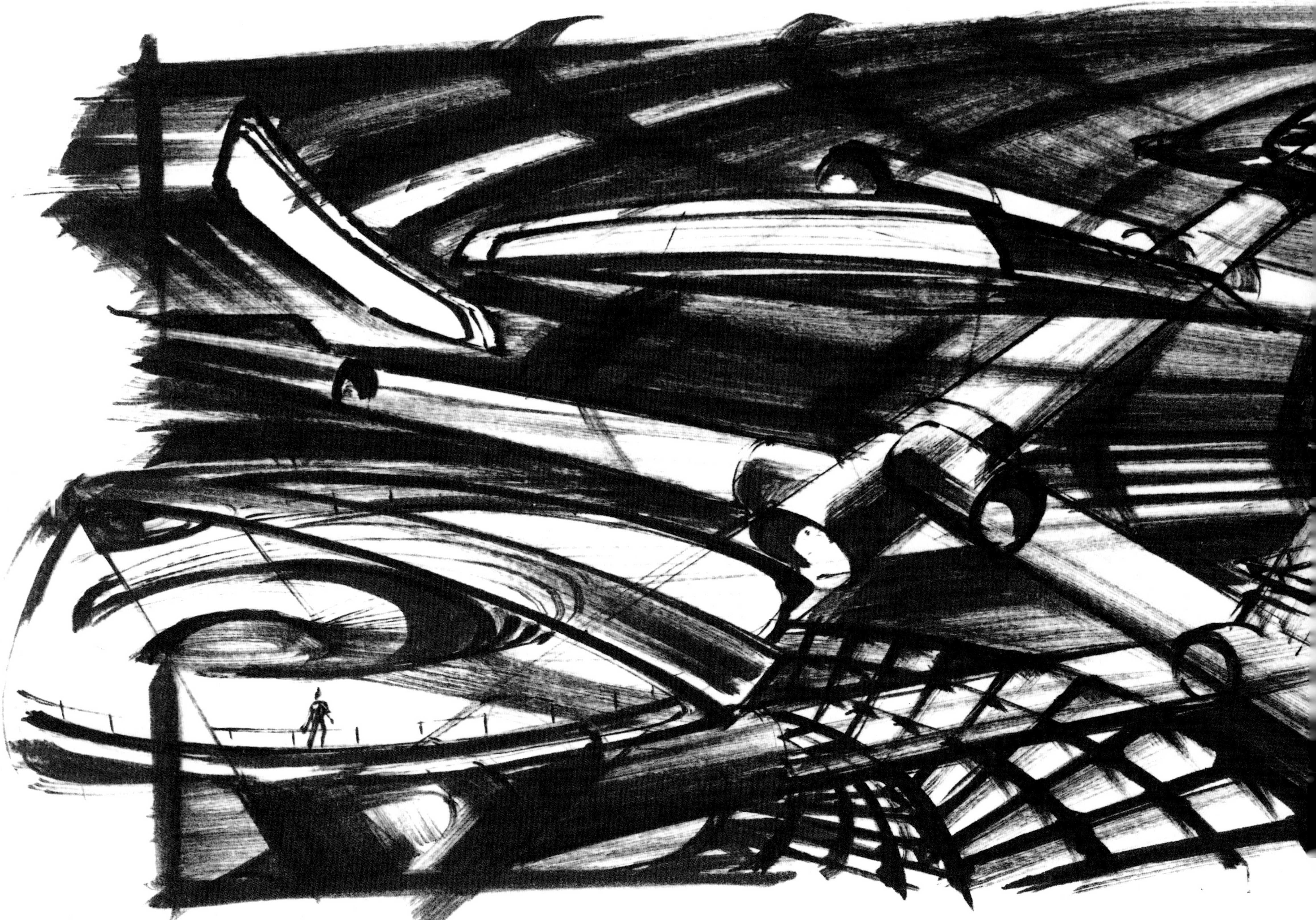

STAR TREK – THE MOTION PICTURE [1977]

For three months in 1977 Ken Adam worked on this first big-screen version of the mid-1960s television series. Gene Roddenberry was the producer, and Philip Kaufman the director and writer. The story was set in 2400 AD, and it involved a 'Super Brain', a huge 'Meditation Chamber' and, of course, the Starship Enterprise itself. Stanley Kubrick, thinking of the extra-terrestrials that would have to be designed, warned Adam off, saying, 'Forget it.' Paramount eventually cancelled the project, but then revived it eighteen months later with Robert Wise directing Nicholas Meyer's new script.

THE STARSHIP ENTERPRISE Concept for the interior of the Enterprise, including the control centre and bridge, 1977.

'I was approached by Gene Roddenberry, and we got on like a house on fire. The story was set in 2400 AD, which didn't worry me too much, except that we had to come up with a lot of concepts – an alien planet environment, space technology, even what the Earth might look like a thousand years or so from now.'

'This is my concept for the "Super Brain" – like a giant machine on an alien planet. You can see the scale by the size of the humans. I did so much on that project. I redesigned the Starship Enterprise, and I created a huge Meditation Chamber with another tiny figure in it. *Star Trek* was really science fiction and way out.'

STAR TREK – THE MOTION PICTURE

this page **THE STARSHIP ENTERPRISE** Concept drawings of the Starship Enterprise, from various angles.

opposite **THE SUPER BRAIN** Study for the Super Brain, 'a giant machine on an alien planet'.

DESIGNING THE FUTURE

STAR TREK – THE MOTION PICTURE

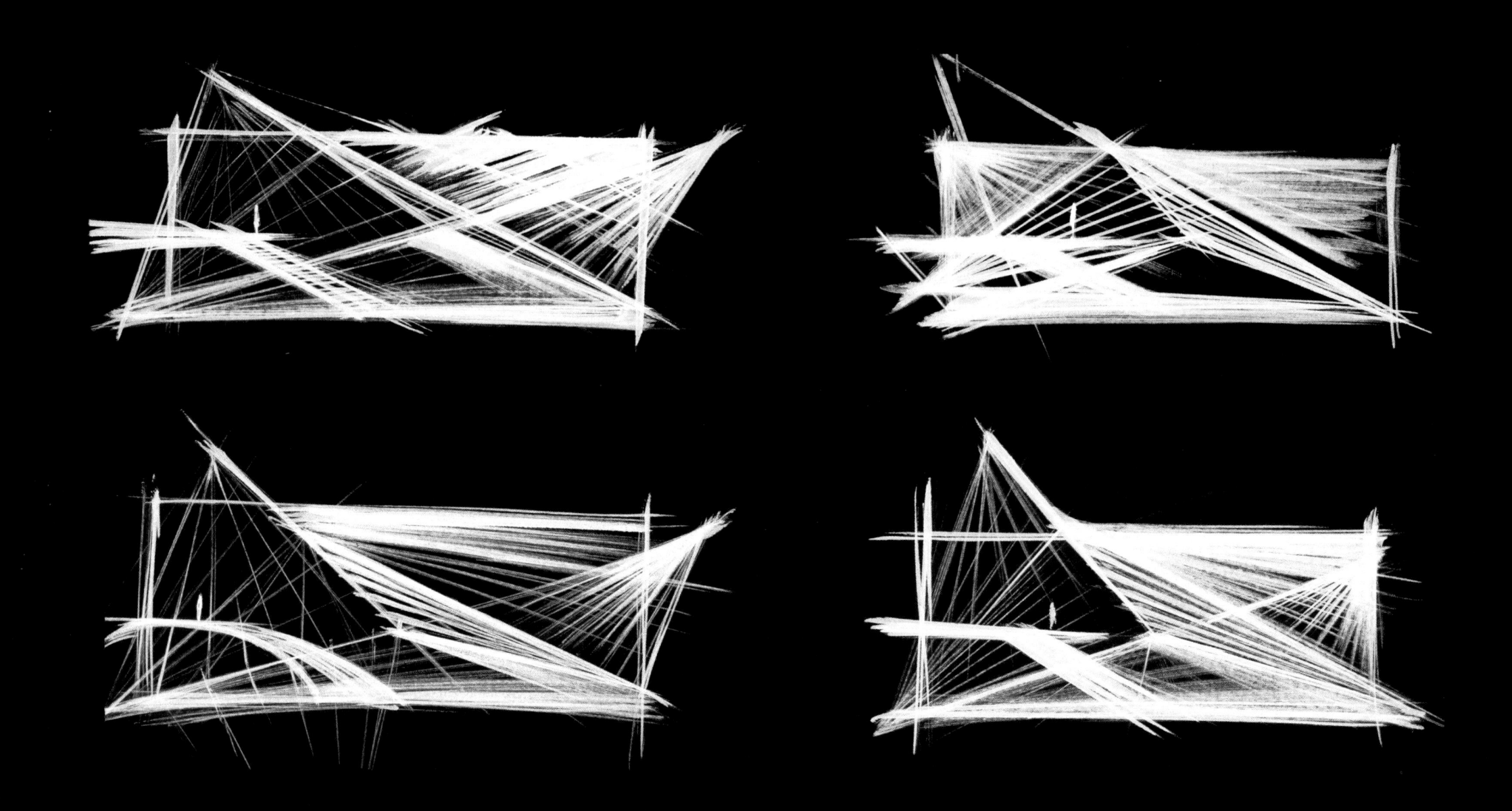

192   **DESIGNING THE FUTURE**

opposite and above **THE MEDITATION CHAMBER** Concept drawings of the Meditation Chamber, with a single human figure inside.

THE CINEMA OF THE FUTURE SPECIAL PROJECT FOR 20TH-CENTURY FOX [1981–82]

Ken Adam worked for a year in Hollywood on a major architectural project. The brief was to create a 'cinema of the future' – an inflatable cinema that would be just one-tenth of the cost of a standard cinema – and to supply twelve or fifteen examples that could be sited in open spaces such as parking lots near major cities in the US. The project aimed to recreate the magic of the golden age of cinema-going, when there would have been a Wurlitzer organ with two films playing, and even vaudeville stage acts. In Adam's version, which was sadly never made, there would have been a pre-movie experience – a lobby, like the interior of a space station – that the cinema-goer walked through before reaching a multimedia IMAX auditorium within a large inflatable structure. Adam's drawings show concepts for the interior of the lobby in the multimedia complex. Though the project never became a reality, 'it became the talking-point of LA'.

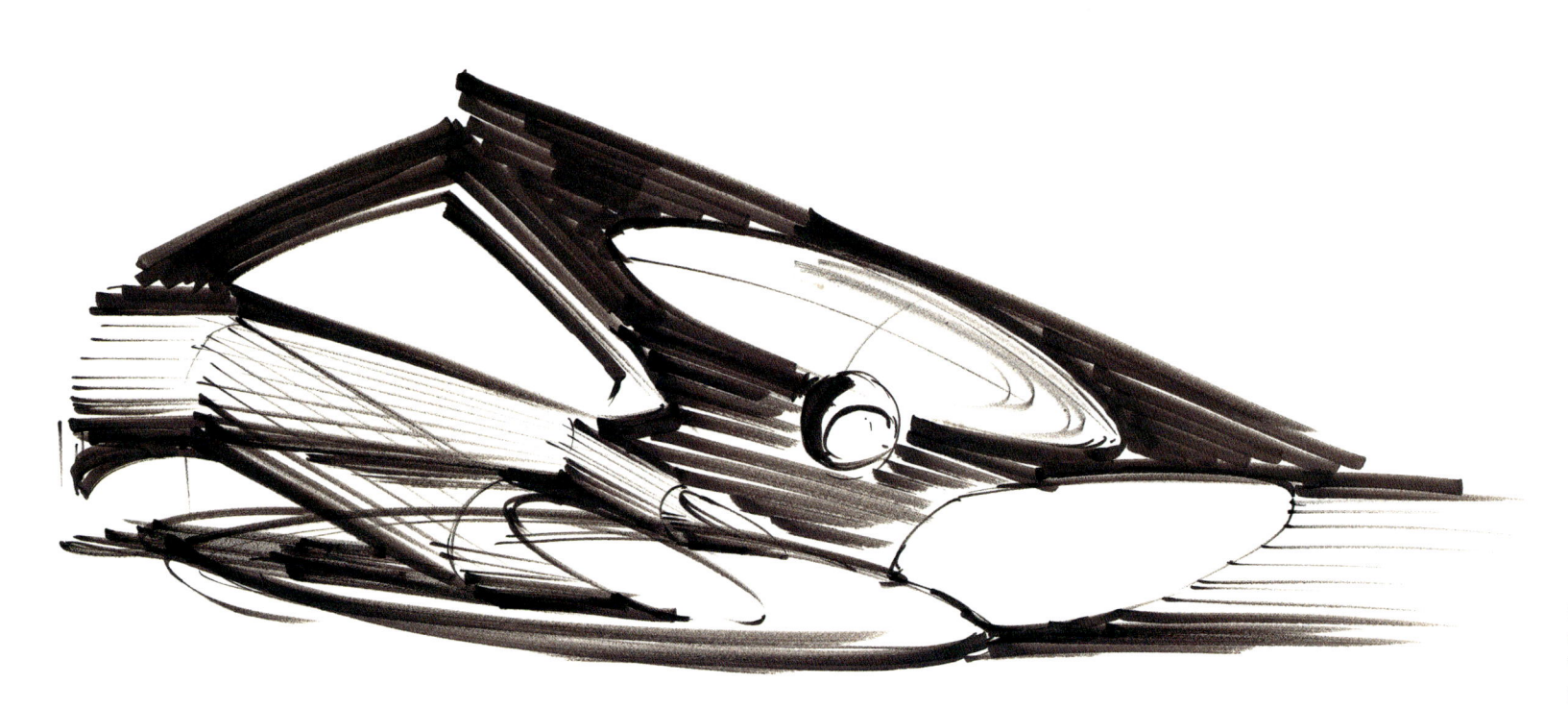

left and right **STUDIES** of the lobby interior (the 'pre-movie experience') in the multimedia complex, 1981.

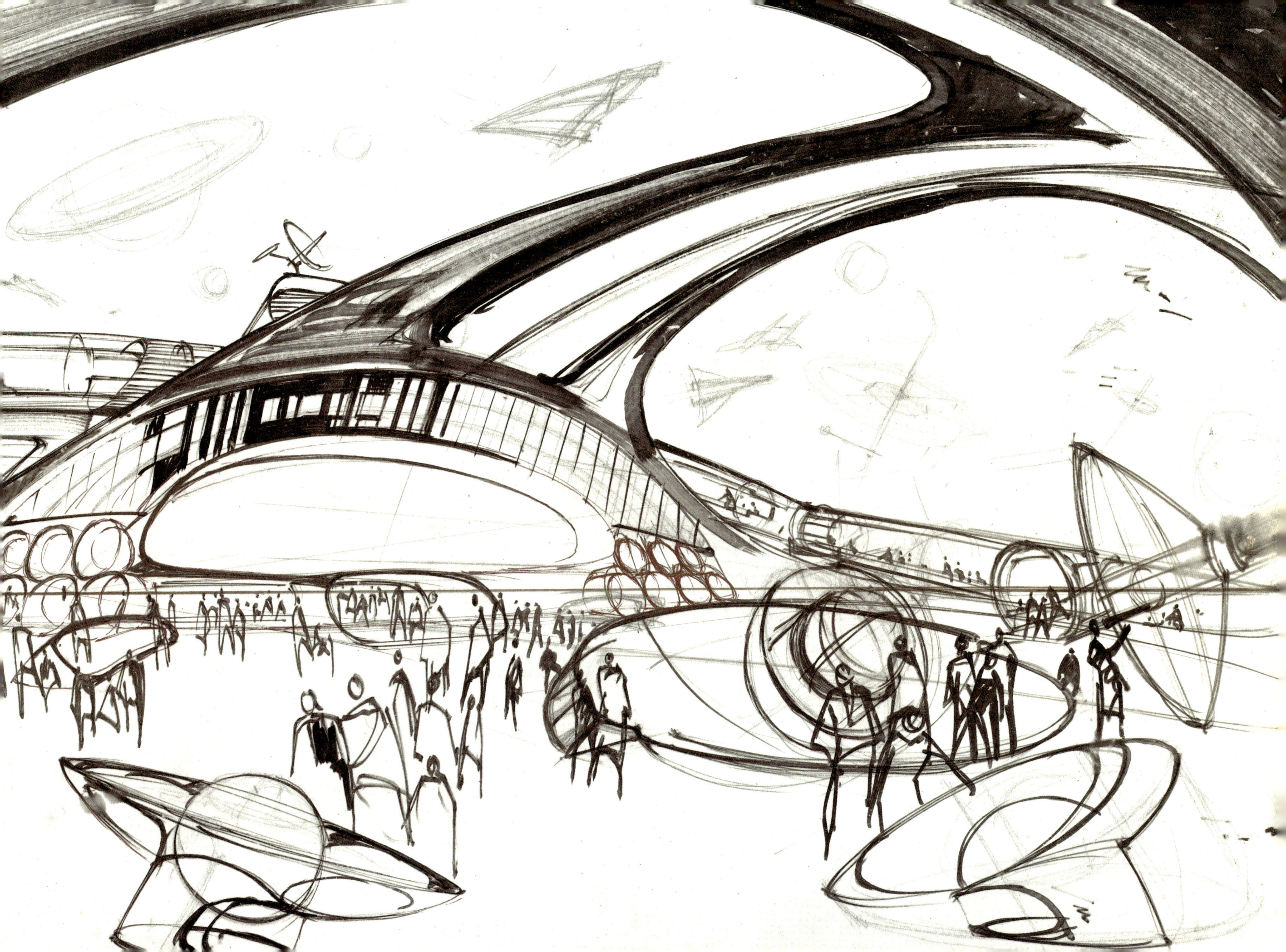

196 **DESIGNING THE FUTURE**

THE CINEMA OF THE FUTURE

'The idea was to design a multimedia theatre that would entertain like the old flamboyant movie palaces of the 1920s, but in a new way. Fox wanted to start with fourteen theatres in the parking lots of large cities. And they asked Dennis Potter to write the screenplay for this new type of cinema experience. And then the whole project collapsed.'

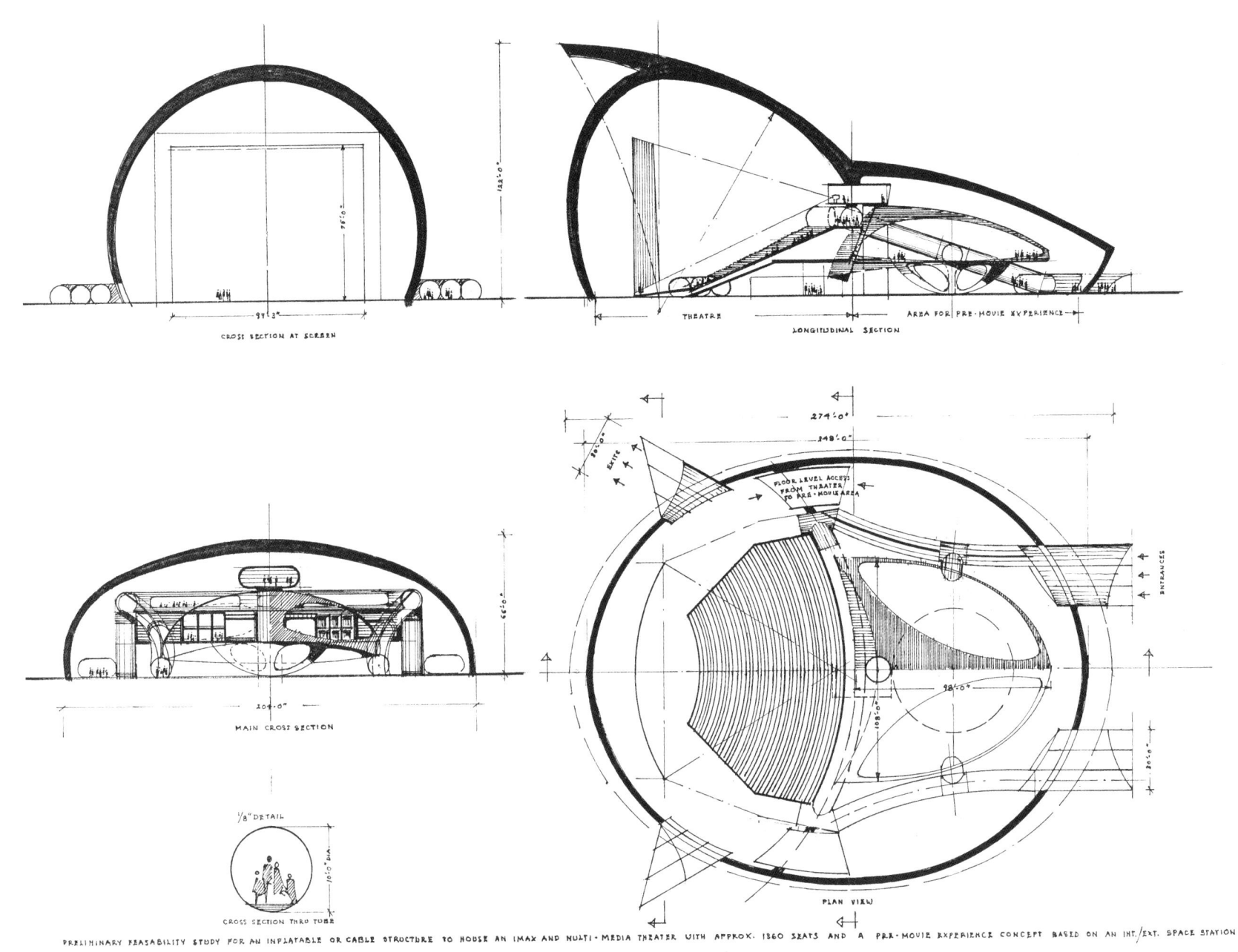

right **TECHNICAL DRAWINGS** of the exterior and auditorium.

opposite **MODELS** made by Ken Adam, of the inflatable cinema in situ, and of the auditorium interior.

DESIGNING THE FUTURE 197

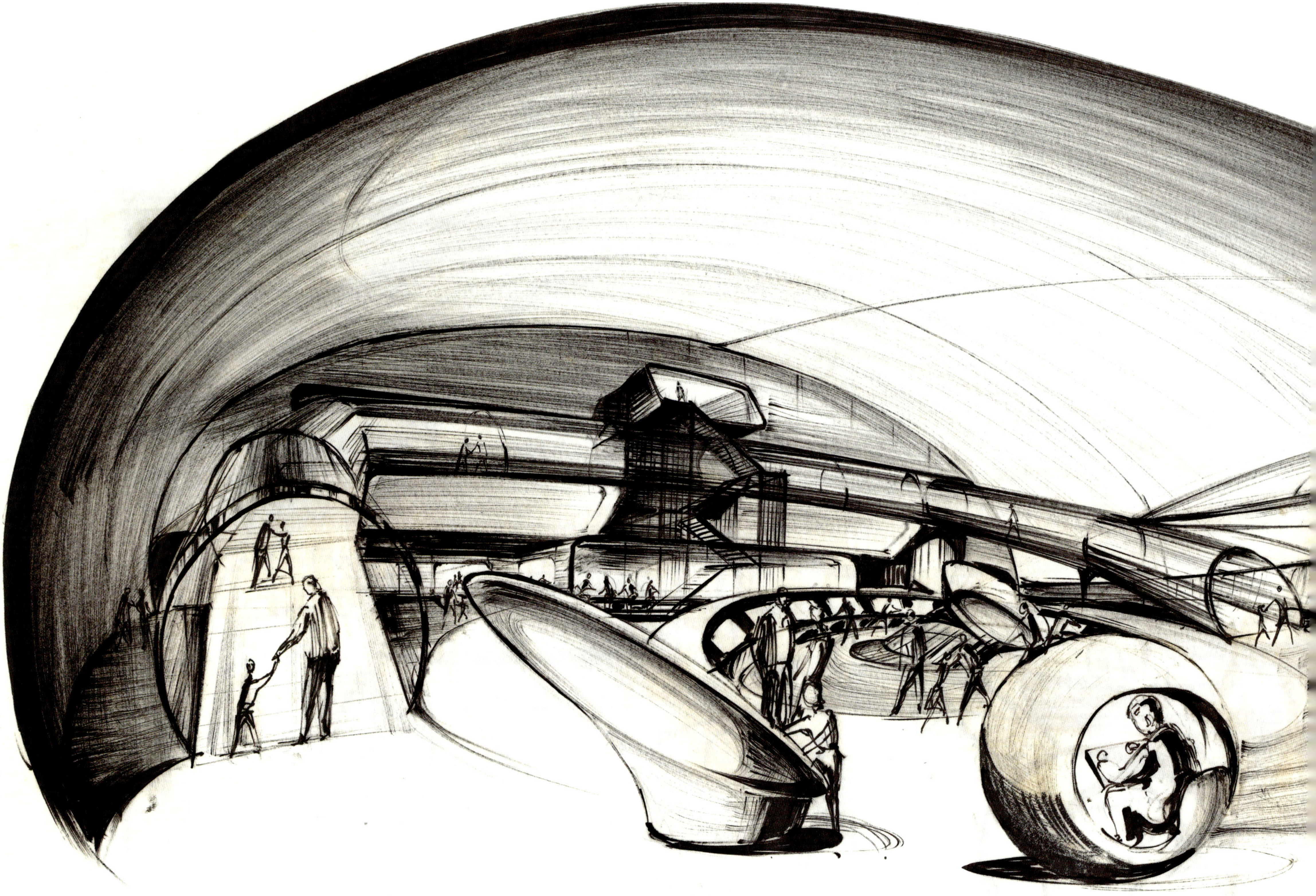

THE CINEMA OF THE FUTURE

left and above **MORE STUDIES** of the 'pre-movie experience', with tubular walkway and viewing pods.

DESIGNING THE FUTURE

THE FANTASTICKS [UNREALIZED, 1982]

This unrealized project was to have been an adaptation of the then-longest-running off-Broadway hit show. Ken Adam worked on it for several months, from Malibu — and incorporated an Errol Flynn-style sword fight on a staircase, a castle, and the basic set, like a Grandma Moses painting, of two identical houses (one well kept, the other neglected) where the two families of the main characters lived. There was never a workable script, the producer disappeared, and a suitable director was never found, so *The Fantasticks* never happened.

'I designed practically the whole film, which was to be all sets in the studio. Fantasy sequences — like the swashbuckling sword duel in the castle — were an important part of it. I did design after design based on the stage musical.'

left **THE CASTLE STAIRCASE** Study of the castle staircase with Errol Flynn-style duel, 1982.

right **THE CASTLE** Proposed castle exterior, for one of the fantasy sequences.

DESIGNING THE FUTURE

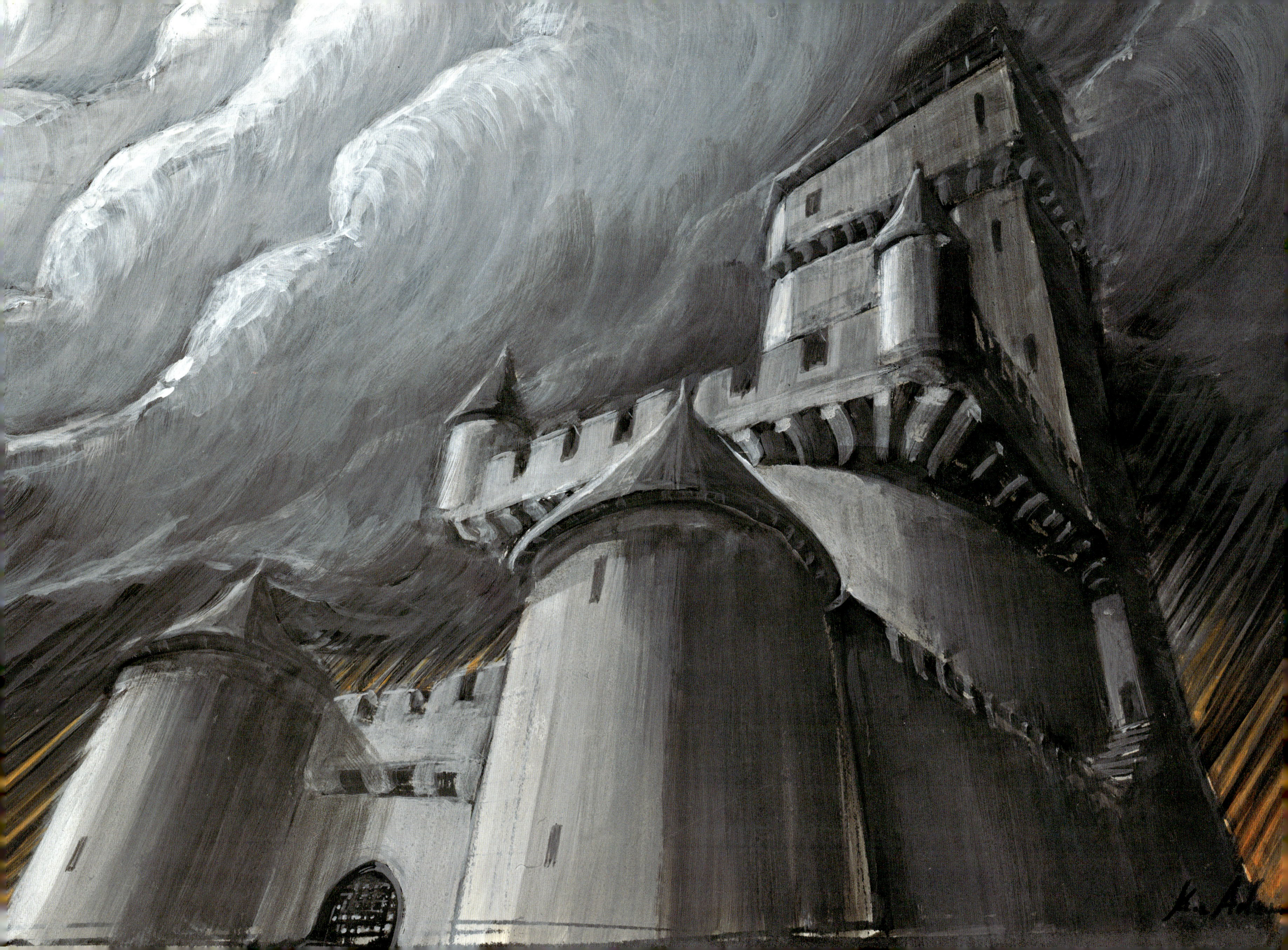

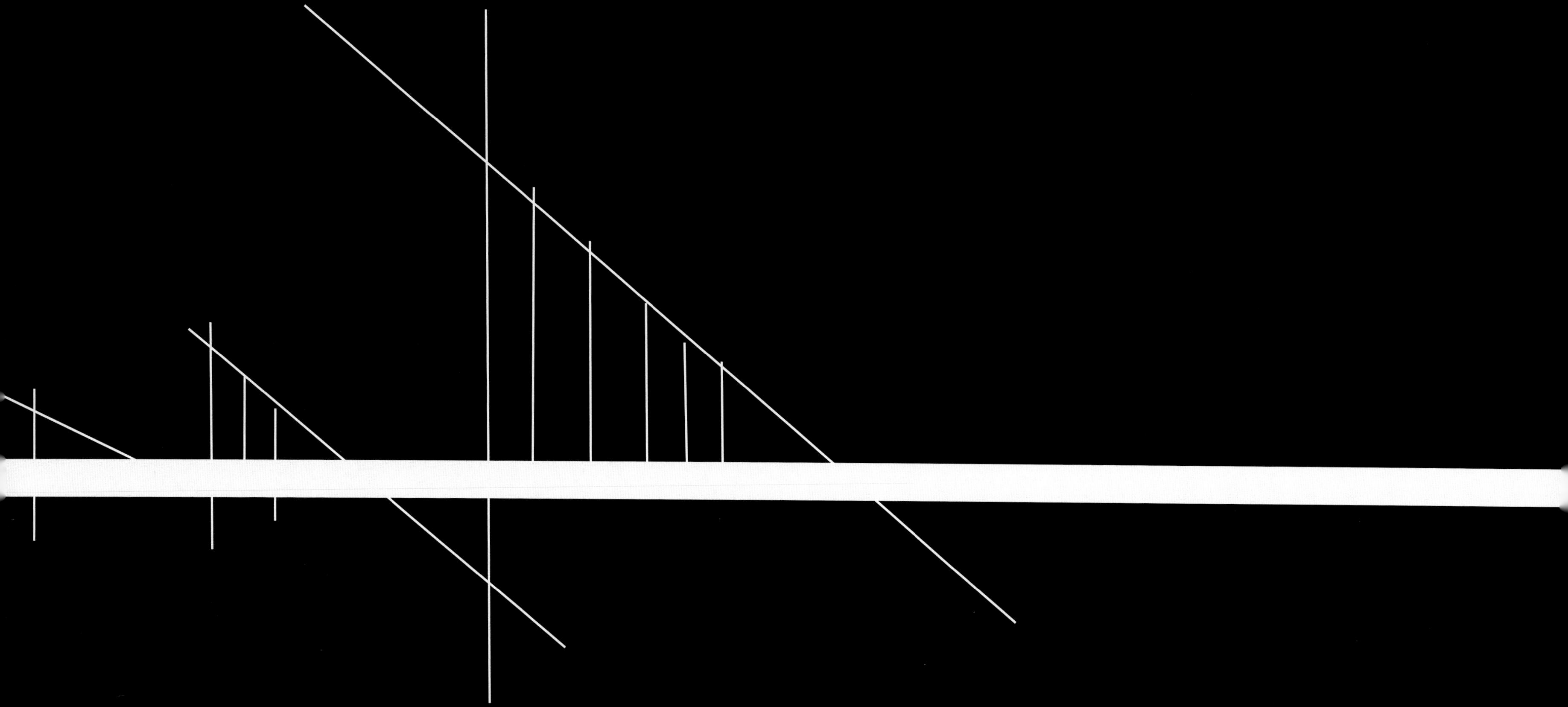

8
BACK TO BERLIN

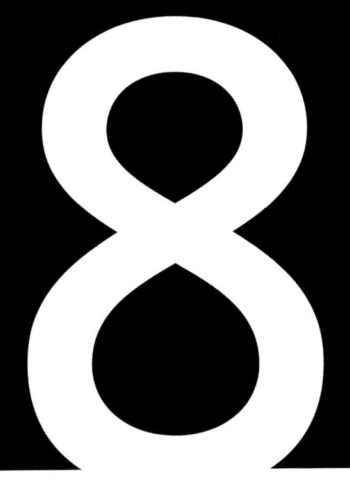

BERLIN MILLENNIUM EXHIBITION [1999–2000]

In 1998, Ken Adam was appointed to design the core of Berlin's Millennium Exhibition at the Martin-Gropius building. The theme was 'Seven Hills – images and signs of the twenty-first century', a celebration of science and technology. The main elements were to include a huge globe showing the outside and inside of the Earth, a stainless steel double-helix sculpture, a simulated brain and a particle accelerator presented like a Gothic rose window. The original plan was for the exhibition hall to resemble a pyramid, but Adam changed this to a cathedral-like steel structure with sloping walls, through which the original Victorian architecture could be seen. 'I was influenced in some ways,' he says, 'by my experiences on the Bonds and on the War Room in *Dr. Strangelove*.' But for the very first time with his fantastical designs, he had to take account of planning permission and building by-laws....

CONCEPT for the interior of the Millennium Expo, 'a pyramid shape inside a nineteenth-century structure', 1999.

'The Berlin Millennium Exhibition was to be about science, technology and the modern world – exaggerated in order to make it understandable by the public. People came in through a large tube, and there were elevators to take them up for the view from above. It proved to be an enormous success.'

overleaf left **THE ENTRANCE** Angled view from the tubular entrance to the Expo.

overleaf right **THE INTERIOR** Photograph of the Expo interior, showing the 'rose window', angled screens and globe illustrating the Earth's core.

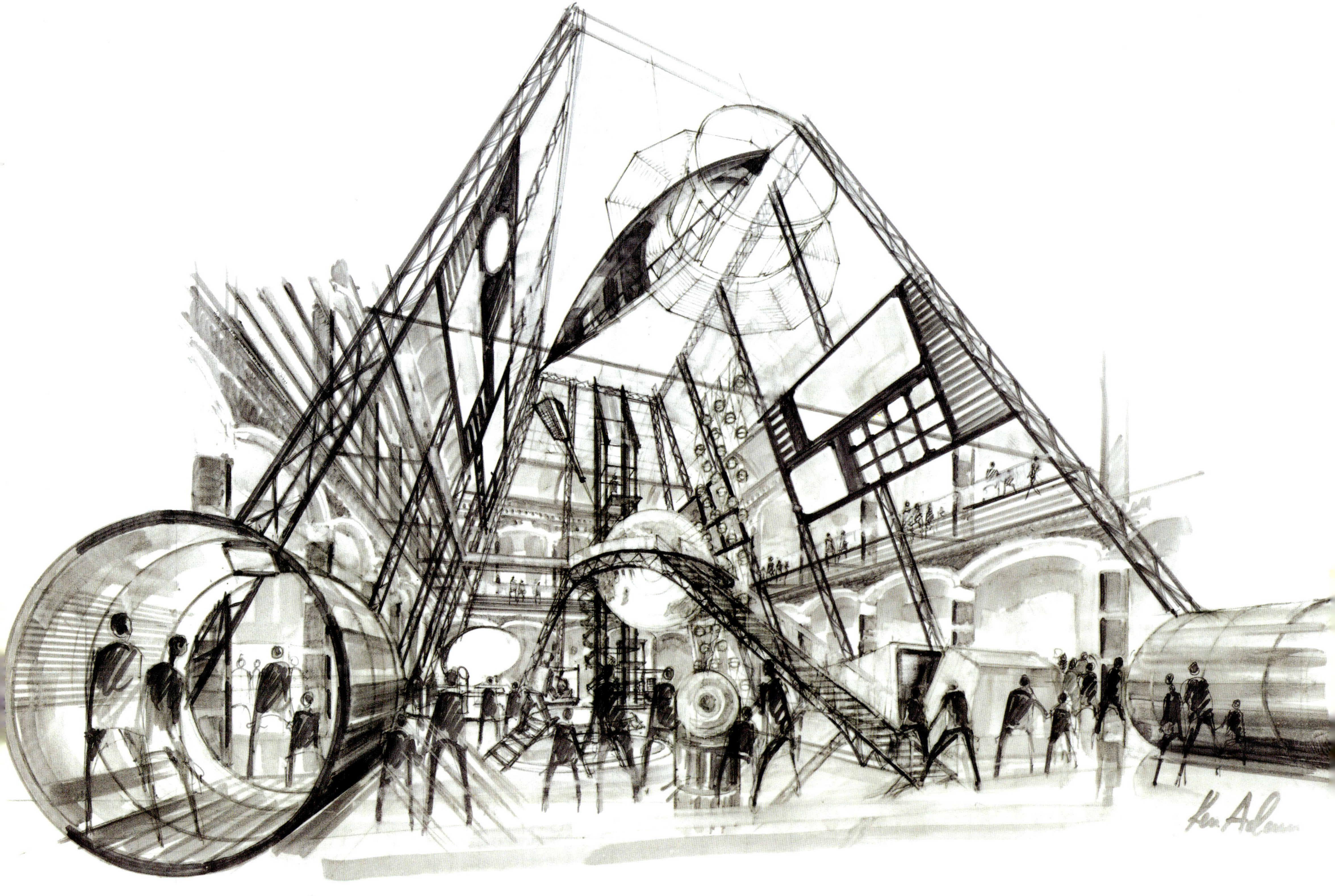
Ken Adam

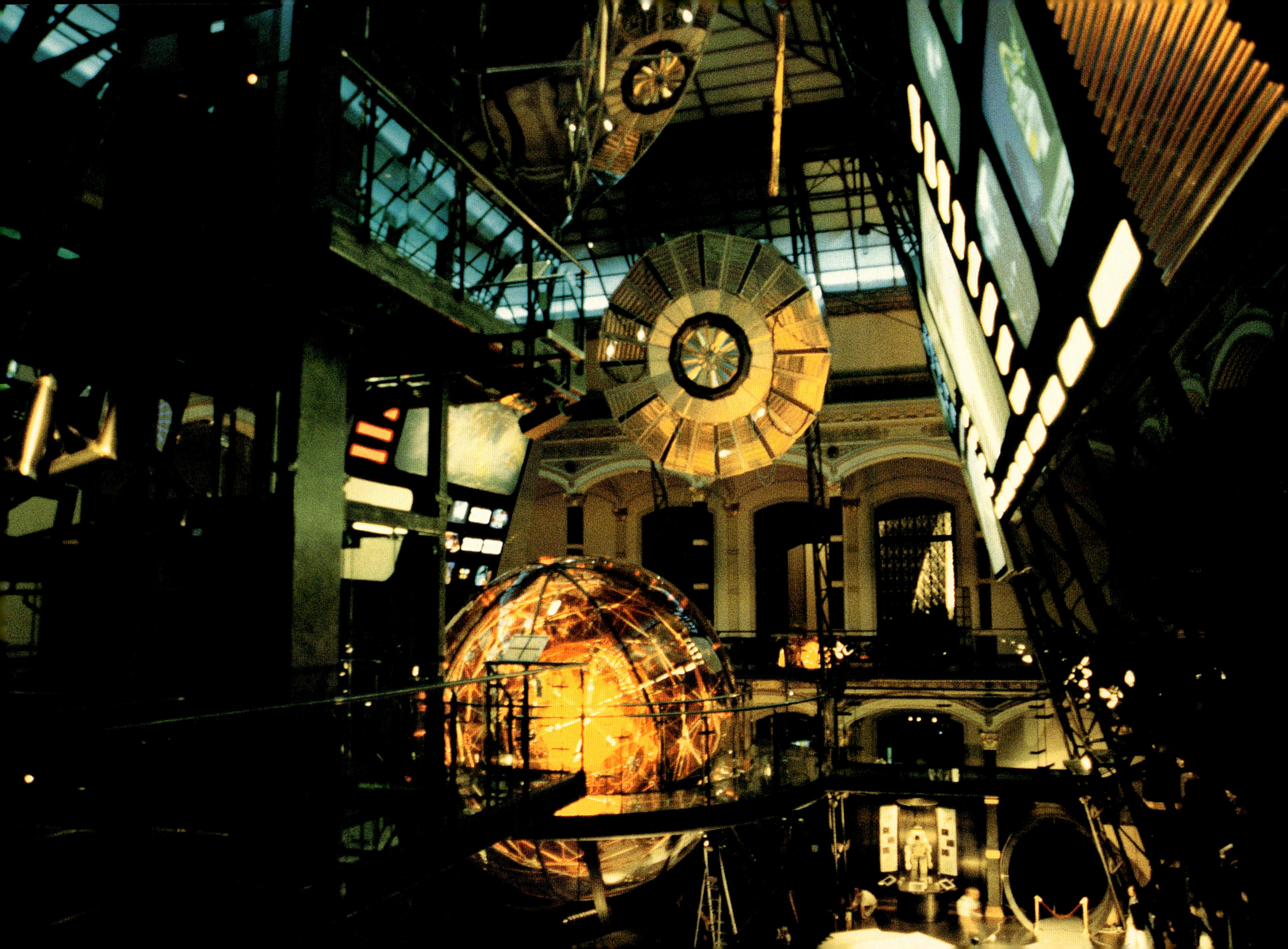

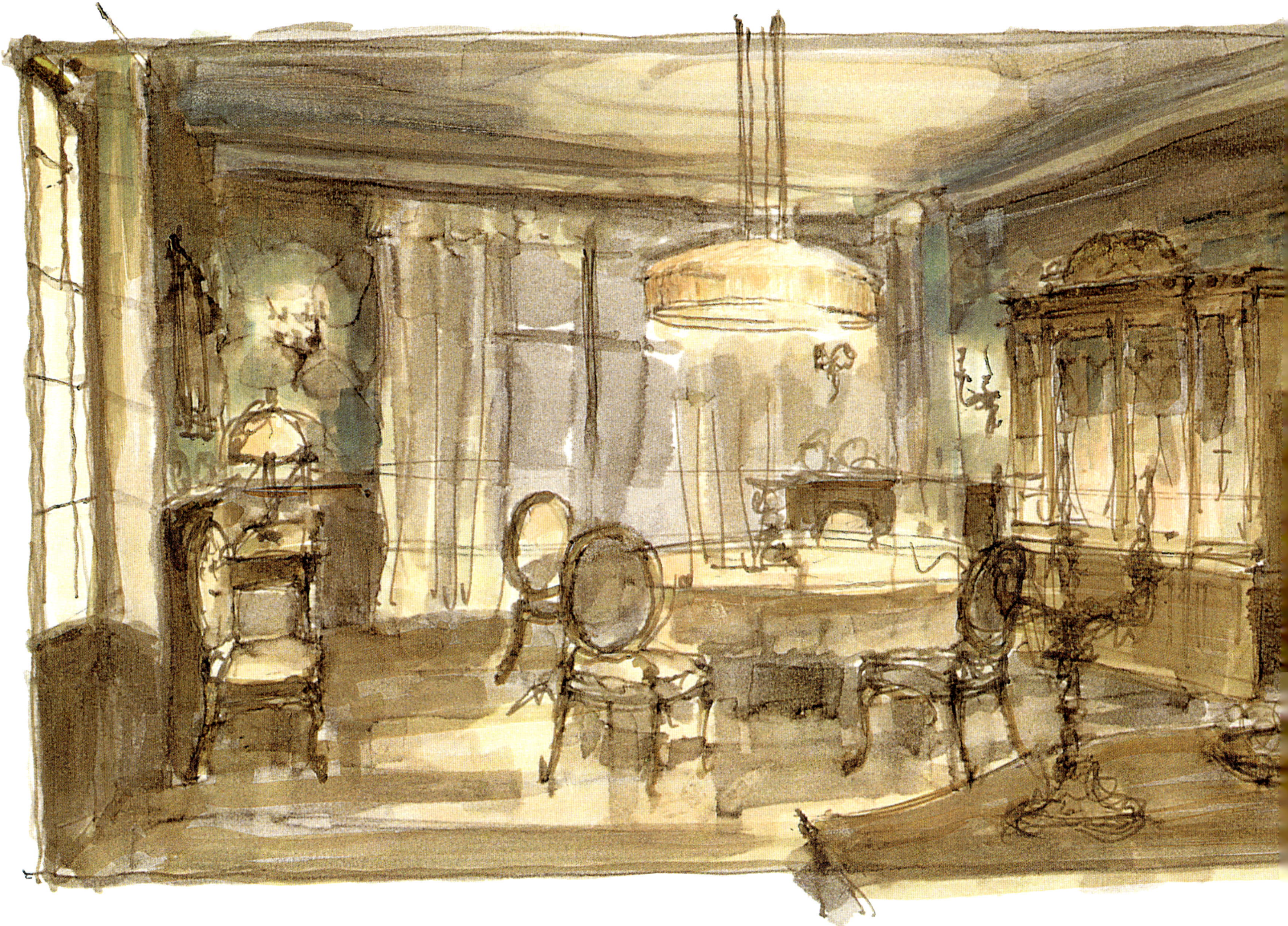

TAKING SIDES [2002]

Taking Sides is based on a play by Ronald Harwood about the orchestral conductor Wilhelm Furtwängler and whether or not he collaborated with the Nazi regime. It is set in Berlin just after the last days of the Third Reich, with a lot of little people in huge baroque rooms. Interiors were filmed at the old Babelsberg studio, with locations in Dresden and Berlin. The ruined streets of Berlin and the 'Interrogation Office' where the American de-Nazification officer (Harvey Keitel) questions Furtwängler (Stellan Skarsgård) presented particular design challenges. Ken Adam also took a great deal of trouble over the look and detail of the old Berlin apartment belonging to Keitel's secretary's aristocratic mother: this was not a particularly important set, but it was based on Adam's memories of growing up in Berlin in the 1920s and early 1930s.

opposite and left **THE STRAUBE APARTMENT** Final concepts of the dining room and the living room of the secretary's mother's apartment in Berlin, based on Ken Adam's childhood memories, 2001.

BACK TO BERLIN

TAKING SIDES

THE INTERROGATOR'S OFFICE
Sketch for the interior of the Interrogator's Office, constructed at the old UFA studio in Babelsberg: 'little people in big rooms'.

THE ARCHIVES ROOM Sketch for the Archives Room, built in a derelict parish church in Berlin: 'I loved the exposed brickwork'.

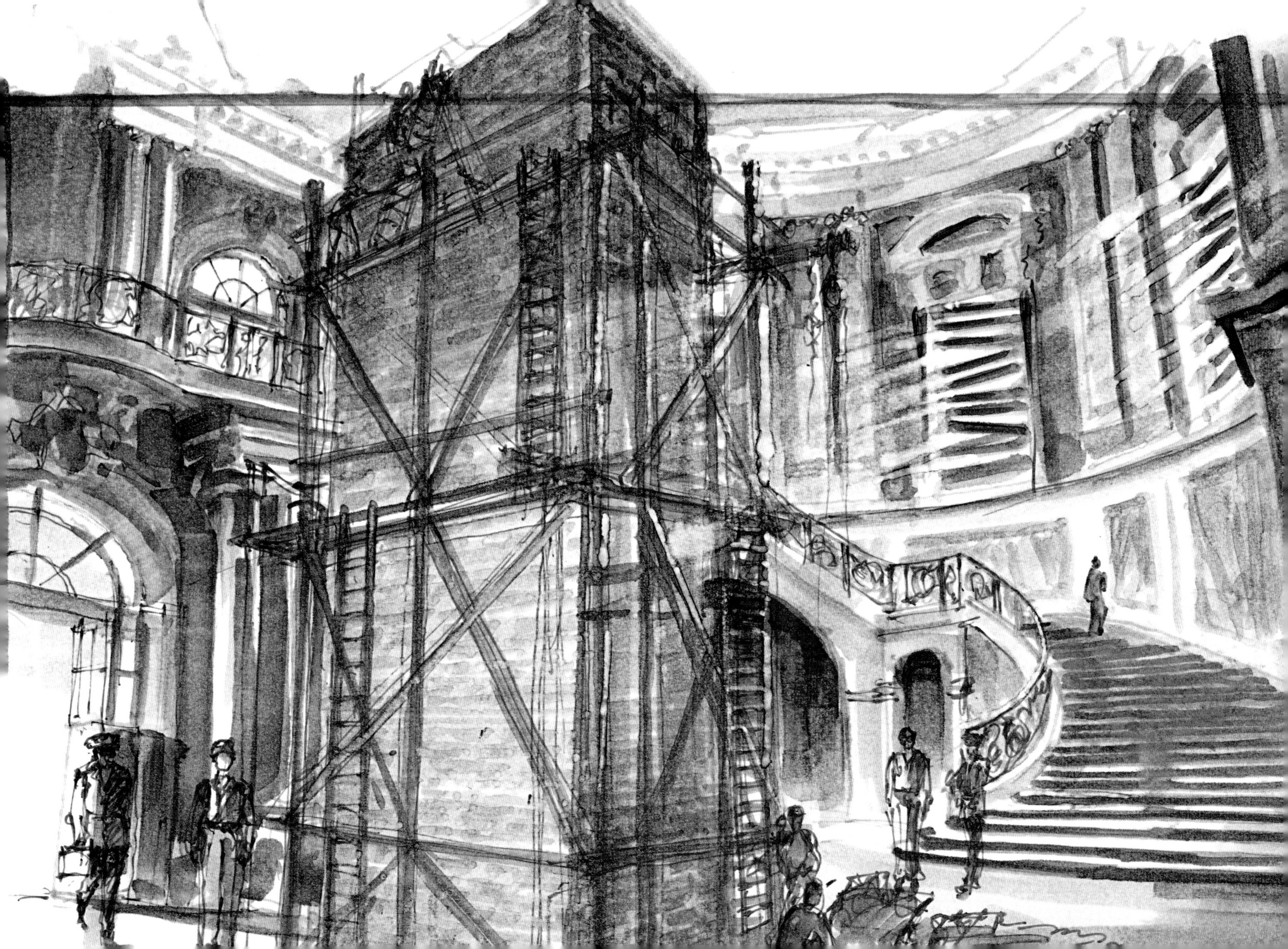

'I got *Taking Sides* as a result of the Millennium Expo, and I was fascinated by the subject matter for many reasons. We used studio interiors and locations. At one of the Dresden locations, I found the lake and I built the destroyed bridge and I put a statue of the Madonna in the water. It was seen floating there, as if blown off a parapet. And when the director, István Szabó, saw it, he honestly thought it was real.'

left and above **THE SCULPTURE** Madonna sculpture 'as if blown off a parapet' in a Dresden lake.

opposite **THE DOUBLE STAIRCASE** Huge neo-baroque staircase in the derelict Bode Museum, Berlin, with scaffolding and blocked windows.

'THE CABINETS OF DR. CALIGARI'

Lecture by Ken Adam at the Renaissance Theatre, Berlin, 4 October 1998

I was a Berliner.

I opened my eyes for the first time on February 5, 1921 in Tiergartenstrasse No. 8. My parents had to leave the six-day bicycle race at the Sport Palast in a hurry so that I could be born at home.

This was the Berlin of the '20s, which I later came to realize formed the foundation of my education. The Berlin of Max Reinhardt and Elisabeth Bergner, of Werner Krauss and Gründgens in the theatre. Of UFA, of Fritz Lang, Lubitsch and Erich Pommer. Of Max Pallenberg and the Soubrette Fritzi Massary, of Grock the Clown playing his miniature violin, of Claire Waldorf of *Cabaret* fame, of the juggler Rastelli and the illusionist Hannusen, and of the architects Gropius, Mendelsohn and Mies van der Rohe who were to influence my future. They became a part of me. The Berlin of the painters Max Liebermann, George Grosz, Otto Dix, Klee and Kandinksy, of Thomas Mann and Feuchtwanger or Erich Kästner and Kurt Tucholsky, of the film stars Hans Albers, Willy Fritsch, Paula Wessely and Lilian Harvey, and of Professor Sauerbruch, the eminent surgeon at the Charité.

My father, Fritz Adam, served during the First World War with the Fürstenwalder Ulans and was one of the rare Jewish cavalry officers decorated with the Iron Cross. He considered himself first and foremost a German.

My mother, Lilli Saalfeld, came from an old Jewish family from Berlin and Stettin, a family that had lived in Germany since the Spanish Inquisition.

My father, with his three brothers, was the owner of the exclusive sports store S. Adam on the corner of Leipziger and Friedrich Streets. Before marrying my mother he had a reputation as something of a 'bon viveur', which may have been why in 1912 he gave a splendid costume ball called 'Fa-Fa' or 'Fritz Adam Fest Abend' decorated by many Berlin artists. My mother was a guest. The ball lasted for two days and two nights and it wasn't surprising that the family of my mother was against her marrying my father; they considered him 'nouveau riche' and a roué. All the same it turned out to be one of the happiest marriages. They had four children, my older brother Peter born in 1914, my sister Loni in 1919, then came me and my younger brother Dieter. My parents were part of the liberal 'Reform Gemeinde' and so we did not have a religious upbringing. To my later regret I had never seen the interior of a synagogue. The old German Jewish families were so assimilated into society that they considered themselves first as Germans—like my father.

Because of his sports store my father participated in a few films such as *The Wonder of Ski*, *Silver Kondor Above Tierra Del Fuego* and *The White Hell of Piz Palu*. He had also equipped the North Pole expedition of the Norwegian explorer Amundsen, and I remember that on camping trips as a boy I was forced to spend nights in a very old-fashioned original North Pole tent. In 1927 he gave a reception at the Hotel Adlon for the American child star Jackie Coogan, who visited Berlin for the première of his film *The Kid*, directed by Charlie Chaplin. For some reason, which escapes me now, I was dressed up and photographed as 'The Kid'. In 1928, my father hosted a reception at the Hotel Kaiserhof for the aviators Kohl, von Hunefeld and Fitzmaurice who, for the first time, had crossed the Atlantic from east to west. For us children these were all exciting adventures, as you can imagine.

I only recently discovered that in 1928 Mies van der Rohe corresponded at length with my father about designing a new building for S. Adam. I had kept for a long time a photo of the model without realizing that this avant-garde design had been created by Mies himself.

My father adored my mother and was devoted to his family. He loved to surprise us children and landed one day in a biplane on a field near our house in the country. At another time he surprised us by arriving in disguise playing a barrel organ. By contrast my mother was frugal and disciplined and tried not to spoil us children unnecessarily. However, we were privileged enough to enjoy the upper-class upbringing of that period, with first a governess, followed by Fräulein Lina, our home tutor—and my first love. At the age of nine, I entered the exclusive Französische Gymnasium where, with the exception of maths, all subjects were taught in French. Much of my early childhood I spent in our country house in Bellin next to Stettiner Haff, an inlet of the Baltic Sea, ideally suited to my kind of imagination, and I discovered there tigers and lions in the surrounding woods. One day I even disappeared with a group of gypsies. Fortunately my parents recovered me after a short time. My hobbies were building rafts from reeds, and ice sleighs in winter to sail across the frozen sea, and I found I could sketch quite well, mainly copying at that stage, which gave me more security. One day I found the courage to paint a stag standing in a field. Proudly I showed the painting to an uncle who was an architect. He said it resembled 'spinach with egg', which did not do much for my self-confidence.

In Berlin we children went riding three times a week with our father in the Tiergarten: he had a beautiful horse called Hadschi. And every Sunday the entire family had breakfast in my parents' enormous bed.

I had the usual piano lessons, but the thick short fingers of Fräulein Müller covered in freckles distracted me so much that I lost all interest in classical music. So I played by ear the *chansons* of the period.

At the start of my schooling my literary knowledge was sadly lacking. I had read all the Winnetou volumes by Karl May, as well as *The Last of the Mohicans* by Fenimore Cooper. I loved *Emil and the*

Detectives by Erich Kästner and directed it as a family play with the help of various cousins. I think I was eleven years old at the time.

I was allowed to see *Wallenstein* and *The Robbers* by Schiller in the grown-up theatre, as well as *White Horse Inn* with Max Hansen and Gitta Alpar. I once visited the Circus Busch with my father. My brother was much more cultured than me, but of course he was older. We weren't allowed to go out to the cinema; my mother insisted we go to the theatre. The first film I saw in a cinema — which I was allowed to go to — was *Chang*, a wildlife movie by the people who made *King Kong*. Before that, at every children's party, there were the films of Charlie Chaplin — with hot dogs and potato salad. *The Cabinet of Dr. Caligari*, *Dr. Mabuse* and Fritz Lang's *Metropolis* I saw shortly after my arrival in England in 1934. They made a great impression, and *Caligari* must have had the most profound influence on my career.

I spent four years at the Französische Gymnasium and had a good education. Gottfried Reinhardt, a son of Max, was with my brother Peter in the top form when I entered the bottom form. For me they were heroes. At night they went to an artists' dive, the Taverne, or played chess in the Romanischen Café. Gottfried, with the help of Max, directed school plays, such as Molière's *Les Fourberies de Scapin* and *Dr. Knock* by Jules Romains. Through Gottfried I got to know his father. It was my first entry into the world of artists and *la bohème*.

But soon my lovely childhood was to come to an abrupt end. I still remember the Christmas Fair at the Potsdamer Platz. I visited a stall with my sister when all of a sudden the owner grabbed the head of my sister, loudly proclaiming to the public, 'Here you see a typical Aryan skull.' My sister had blonde hair and grey eyes, you see, and I didn't have the slightest inclination to change the man's mind.

Many of my classmates were Jewish and emigrated just as I did when the Nazis came to power. Most of them had brilliant careers abroad as academics, doctors, artists and musicians. But even before the Nazi takeover I became aware of anti-Semitism in Germany. Some of the boys I used to play with suddenly wore Hitler Youth uniforms and I was branded a 'Jew boy'. It was a great shock. Then came the boycott of Jewish firms, and S. Adam had to be liquidated. The fear of being denounced at any time made one uncertain and permanently suspicious. My parents suddenly conversed in French at dinner or in the street. '*Pas devant les domestiques*.' On my way to school I witnessed the smoke and ruins of the Reichstag which had burnt down the night before, and foresaw the consequences. One day, at our country place, the local police arrested my father. We did not know why or if we would ever see him again. Ironically, through the intervention of one of his ex-employees who turned out to be high up in the SS, he was released after a short time. That was the last straw.

Christmas was always a great celebration at home, but I will never forget the Christmas of 1933. For the first time I saw my father cry. His world had collapsed and he could not accept what was happening in Germany. The Nazi persecutions had ruined his business and deprived us of our livelihood. The time had come definitely to leave Germany.

In April 1934 my mother accompanied me and my younger brother to a school in Scotland. My brother Peter had been living in London since 1933 and, with the help of a committee for refugees and an English relative, he organized the transfer of the remaining family to London. At the age of barely thirteen, I was a refugee.

My mother opened a boarding house in Hampstead, mainly for refugees. She knew from Berlin how to run a large household. At every dinner 20 to 25 persons were seated around an enormous dining table. Many of the refugees had had interesting life experiences. I learned a lot from them and about what was happening in Germany. They were psychiatrists or lawyers or musicians or visual artists, and I learned much about life in my mother's dining room.

She became the provider of our family. My father tried to earn a living as a glove salesman, but he really felt economically dependent on his wife. He was proud of my mother, and Peter, who by now had grown up, was earning his own living. But my father found it very difficult to adjust to our new way of life. He died from a heart attack on 17 January 1936. He was just 56 years old.

After learning enough English I passed the Common Entrance Examination for St. Paul's School in London. It was, and is, one of the best English public schools and I was reunited there with some of my ex-classmates from the Französiche Gymnasium. I was fitted out with bowler hat, black jacket, striped pants and an umbrella, and suddenly I was 'an English gentleman'.

If I think about my English upbringing of that period, a lot of emphasis was placed on character development — thinking for oneself and the ability to make one's own decisions. Also participating in all types of sport developed a team spirit, which later as a fighter pilot helped to save my life on several occasions.

A good art teacher at my school encouraged my visual and creative abilities, around 1938. At the age of seventeen I became an evening student at the Bartlett School of Architecture. During the day I was articled with a firm of architects for my practical studies and sometimes produced drawings for an architect who was part of a British splinter movement of the Bauhaus, the Modern Architectural Research Group. During this period I was also introduced to Vincent Korda, the famous film art director and one of the three Korda brothers. He confirmed that architectural studies were the best foundation for film art direction and had an influence on my decision to become a film designer. 'Get an architectural background,' he said. 'History, design, composition, draughting. All these will be useful.'

At the outbreak of the Second World War I designed air-raid shelters and illustrated books on air-raid protection and gas masks. But I became restless and wanted to be more actively involved in the war against the Nazis. I had a pretty accurate idea of conditions in Germany and the terror of the Nazis, and had no illusions as to what would happen to me and my family if Hitler would win the war. Furthermore I considered myself British and grateful to the country which had offered me shelter and my family a new life. Later we learned that some of my relatives had perished in concentration camps.

So in October 1940 I volunteered for service in the Auxiliary Military Pioneer Corps — a specialized army unit open to exiles and refugees — after I had several times unsuccessfully applied to join the RAF. Much to my and everyone else's surprise I was granted a transfer to the RAF in the spring of 1941. I was not yet naturalized and I was still under twenty-one.

I underwent pilots' training in Scotland, England, Canada and the USA, and in October 1943 joined a famous RAF fighter squadron flying Hawker-Typhoons, one of the fastest and most powerful fighters of that period. They could fly at 8,000 feet at over 400 miles an hour. As a tactical air force we supported the British and Canadian armies from D-Day, advancing with them through France, Belgium and Holland, and into Germany. At the end of the war I was made officer in charge of German labour units and supervised the reconstruction of the airfield at Wunstorf in northern Germany, near Hanover. During the Berlin blockade, Wunstorf became one of the main supply bases of the Berlin airlift.

In 1947, by chance, I started working in films. My sister Loni, who was working at the US Embassy, helped to obtain some American props for a film production and through her I met the art director at Riverside Studios in Hammersmith, who employed me as a junior draughtsman on a film called *This Was A Woman*.

I have worked for more than fifty years in the film business and collaborated on over seventy films. But to start with, I would like to explain a little about my profession. As production designer I create the visual concept, the style of the film, obviously in collaboration with the director and often also the producer. My work begins with the script and my visual interpretation of it. I look for suitable exterior and interior locations, and design the studio and other settings. I am also responsible for supervising the construction and running my department, the art department.

I also prefer to take part in script discussions which sometimes may result in developing new concepts. A good film is the result of total collaboration between the various creative departments and elements—the only truly collective art form. The director is the captain of the ship, and ideally I try to function as his eyes.

At the beginning of my career I worked as assistant to various art directors. I gained more experience with each film, and my collaboration with Oliver Messel, a famous theatre designer, on *Queen of Spades*—an adaptation of Pushkin's novel with Anton Walbrook and Edith Evans—was important for me, since I did a lot of free-hand sketching and learned a lot about period design. Incidentally Messel's grandfather had designed Wertheim, the famous store in Berlin. I also learned a lot from George Wakhevitch, the Russian opera and theatre designer who had also designed *La Grande Illusion* for Renoir, when I assisted him on the preparation of a film, *World Premier*, for Anatole de Grunwald with Marlene Dietrich. Unfortunately the film was never made. I then worked as assistant and associate art director on a number of films for Warner Bros. in Europe. Amongst them was *Captain Horatio Hornblower R.N.* with Gregory Peck, for which I designed and constructed a frigate of the eighteenth century. Suddenly I became a ship expert and was responsible for designing the pirate galleon on *The Crimson Pirate* with Burt Lancaster. We shot the film on the island of Ischia in the Gulf of Naples. Robert Siodmak of UFA and Hollywood fame directed and Otto Heller, also ex-UFA, was the cameraman. We had many adventures and on two occasions nearly lost the ships in storms, but what I really lost was my heart—to my future wife Letizia, whom I got to know in Ischia. We married in 1952 when again I designed the ships for an Errol Flynn film, *The Master of Ballantrae*, which was filmed in Sicily. In 1954 I worked in Rome on the monumental *Helen of Troy* (it was one of the first films with Brigitte Bardot in a small part) and I had to design the Greek fleet, the thousand ships! After that I had had enough of ships.

On my return to London I was offered Mike Todd's *Around the World in Eighty Days*. To design a film in Todd-AO and to collaborate with William Cameron Menzies was an incredible break for me. Todd-AO was a new wide-screen process in 70mm, requiring a completely new way of thinking about the settings. Menzies was the associate producer on the film. He is considered to be the first-ever production designer, the father of modern production design, based on his work for *Gone With the Wind*, for which he visualized and sketched out every frame, and 99 per cent of it was filmed in the studio. He encouraged me in the stylization of the sets and he taught me not to be afraid to use colour in bold ways. The set for Lloyd's of London was entirely in black and white; only the waiters were dressed in bright scarlet robes for dramatic effect. The Reform Club was treated in green and black. The film offered me the opportunity to stylize reality and to design more theatrically. Mike Todd himself was one of those astonishing larger-than-life showmen. Doubtless he furthered my career, but he could also destroy people. Menzies spent nearly every evening in our London flat of that time. Todd had made him so nervous that he drank all my whisky! Menzies had a big influence on me, as well as Alfred Junge and Hein Heckroth (Michael Powell's designer, the designer of *The Red Shoes*); also John Bryan, one of the top English film designers of the '40s and '50s. But it was Paul Sheriff, the art director of *The Crimson Pirate*, who gave me the following cynical advice: 'Film people are snobs and if they do not understand your sketch they will always praise it, since no one will admit that they cannot understand it.' By contrast, John Bryan was more constructive: 'Roughness of your sketch will bring it to life,' he once said to me. Also my wife Letizia preferred my rough scribbles to lifeless grand perspective renderings. And Lotte Eisner, the director of the Cinémathèque in Paris and ex-Ullstein journalist, selected some of my first roughs for her collection. She much preferred them to my big projections and technical drawings.

I decided to liberate myself from my inhibitions and the rigidity of my architectural studies and to sketch more freely and with less detail in powerful strokes. I altered my technique completely by using a felt pen with a wedge-shaped tip instead of hard pencil, conté or pen and ink. My sketches had more strength and allowed me to experiment with light and shade to guide the cameraman with the lighting of a set. In order to accentuate the 'chiaroscuro' effect, I did my sketches in black and white.

To design a set or scene I always start with a sketch. It is very important for me—however rough the sketch—in visualizing the eventual three-dimensional décor. Then I sketch plans and elevations, and often models are made by the art department.

As a rule, a design which works in black and white will also work in colour, and I believe that it is more difficult to shoot a film in black and white than in colour. Some cameramen have difficulties with black and white, due to lack of experience. But for me certain films are much more dramatic if they have been shot in black and white — films such as *Dr. Strangelove*.

A word on 'stylization'. I find it boring to copy reality, and frequently I attempt to create in the studio a different kind of reality. This is easier to do in a studio than on location, since one can invent anything in designing a studio set. A director like Fellini shot most of his films in a studio. It provided him with the scope fully to realize his ideas and visions.

A theatre or opera designer has to invent a new reality, a self-sufficient universe, since he is limited by the dimensions of the stage and the proscenium arch. He has to use his imagination like any good film designer.

It is much more satisfying for me and also for the audience to try and create a new level of filmic reality. Most films of the '20s and '30s were shot in studios. At that period the technical means to film on location were limited. The sets — such as the elegant art deco nightclubs and the apartments of Cedric Gibbons, the MGM designer — were bigger than life, and offered the audience magic and escape from the reality of the Depression. Nowadays we have seen on film almost everything on earth and in space. But a good film designer still has the opportunity to enchant the public and help them dream.

For the 1960 film *The Trials of Oscar Wilde* (in the USA, *The Man with the Green Carnation*) with Peter Finch, I reverted to using pen and ink and watercolour for my sketches. I felt it to be more suitable for this film. I had £750 left in my budget for the set of the Marquess of Queensberry's reception room in his Scottish castle. The room had to be large so I built it in a forced perspective using elements of other sets. The scene played after the funeral of Queensberry's son and I painted all the walls in a terracotta colour but the floor was painted as a Sienna marble. I treated the rest all in black — columns, doors, fireplace — and the stylization worked, plus I had not exceeded my budget. For the first time the critics mentioned the sets, and the jury of the Moscow Film Festival under the Presidency of Luchino Visconti awarded me the prize for the Best Art Direction.

In 1962 we shot the first James Bond film, *Dr. No*. My total budget was about £14,000 and the cost of the entire film was less than one million dollars, a low-budget film with little preparation time. The script was based on Ian Fleming's novel, and Terence Young was the director. Six weeks were scheduled for shooting exteriors in Jamaica and then back to the studio at Pinewood.

I only spent a short time in Jamaica, since I had to design and construct the studio sets at Pinewood. The film was intended as a thriller, but I had not yet formulated a design concept. I had to fill three or four stages with sets and fortunately the two producers, Cubby Broccoli and Harry Saltzman, remained in Jamaica so nobody could look over my shoulder and I was able to use my imagination freely. I came up with a larger-than-life, tongue-in-the-cheek concept; a reflection of our period where technology was concerned — and also one step ahead of contemporary. I also experimented by using new materials, which up to then had rarely been employed in film design, materials such as copper, brass, steel and plastics.

Naturally I felt a little apprehensive when, on their return from Jamaica, I presented Terence, Cubby and Harry with the finished sets. But it was a 'fait accompli' and Terence was very impressed. I think Cubby and Harry expected something different but basically they also were happy. Suddenly, everyone came up with new ideas like in a democratic debating society. *Dr. No*'s unexpected big success made it become the working model for all future Bond films.

In the '60s and '70s I designed another six Bond films. They became bigger and bigger and more costly. They relied more and more on the sets, gadgets, exotic locations and special effects. They gave an increasing scope to my imagination. Normally the script is the backbone of a film, but in the Bond films I no longer worked according to the strict discipline of the scripts and was able to start dreaming. 'The sky became the limit.' However, in between Bonds I always worked on other films.

Several of my Bond sets are good examples of what I mean by 'stylizing reality': the tarantula scene in *Dr. No*, where Professor Dent gets his orders from the Doctor; in *Goldfinger*, the interior of Fort Knox, the largest gold depository in the world with its gigantic grille and stacks of gold, which are diametrically the opposite of how it is in reality (gold is never stacked so high!); the volcanic crater in *You Only Live Twice*; the interior of the supertanker devouring three nuclear submarines in *The Spy Who Loved Me*, and also Atlantis from the same film, the artificial under- and above-water laboratory of Curd Jürgens.

And then there are the gadgets. Actually I am an overgrown boy scout and I had a lot of fun inventing and designing many crazy vehicles — cars, boats and flying machines (one of the latter as a do-it-yourself kit in crocodile leather suitcases) and a variety of submarine vehicles. I was always most surprised when these contraptions really functioned, since I am not very mechanically minded. But thanks to some brilliant special-effects people in my team and the other specialists we found, someone always made them work.

In *Goldfinger*, Cubby and Harry wanted to replace Bond's vintage Bentley of the early Fleming novels with another car, and we decided on the Aston Martin DB5 — *the* sports car of that period. Since I am a passionate sports car driver myself, I did not find it difficult to design the extra perks for the car such as machine-guns, over-riders like a boxer fist and ejector seat. The super-fast luxury yacht belonging to Largo in *Thunderball* did not exist at that time, except for some very fast hydrofoils which would be easily recognizable. I bought an old hydrofoil in Puerto Rico for $10,000 and designed a kind of catamaran around it to lengthen and camouflage the hydrofoil. Only at the last moment, as the villain escapes, does the catamaran separate from the hydrofoil, which shoots out like a torpedo.

The moon buggy in *Diamonds Are Forever* was supposed to be grotesque-looking with exaggerated, flailing, mechanical arms. To make it look more authentic I used the pattern of the wheels of the original moon vehicle, a decision that almost ended in disaster. On the first day of shooting the wheels collapsed due to the weight of the vehicle and the rough terrain. Fortunately I could replace them with balloon tyres!

The new Lotus Esprit in *The Spy Who Loved Me* was not yet on the market. But I found its streamlined body ideally suited for a sub-aqua vehicle and designed it accordingly. It actually did go under water.

In a way, the gadgets in a Bond film functioned as a sort of pacemaker to the plot. But even for *Chitty Chitty Bang Bang*, several props had to be invented. The film takes place at the beginning of the twentieth century and I had to design a magic car capable of driving, flying and swimming. I loosely based my design of the car body on some old Rolls-Royces looking like boats and added a radiator resembling a Bugatti. It turned out to be more difficult than I thought and I altered the mock-up several times, to the exasperation of my assistants. Ford provided the chassis and engine.

When I designed an airship for Baron Bomburst (Gert Fröbe), I wanted to construct it as a large model but two balloonists convinced me to build it as a real airship. Their cost estimate was only marginally higher than the model. After discussions with Cubby and United Artists we gave them the go-ahead. This was not a good idea. We had nothing but difficulties. The airship was unstable and on one occasion in a gale crashed into some high-tension wires, cutting off all the electricity in Dorset and preventing the local farmers from milking their cows. In desperation I asked some experts from Germany and France for help. They were over eighty years old but full of enthusiasm, and with their assistance the airship finally flew. One day the French expert informed me that the Labaudier airship on which I had based my design never in fact left the ground. I thought, 'So now he tells me.'

Stanley Kubrick liked the look of *Dr. No* and employed me as production designer on *Dr. Strangelove*. It was a black comedy, a satire about the end of the world, triggered by the explosion of an atom bomb. In retrospect I feel sure that it was the most important film of my career. We shot it during the Cuban missile crisis, one of the most dramatic moments during the Cold War. No one knew if at any minute there would be a nuclear war.

Kubrick was incredibly talented. I admired him and we became close friends. We worked in total collaboration, though at times he could be more than difficult.

The War Room set is a good example of stylization. My first design was quite different from the final set. It was a kind of amphitheatre with a surrounding visitors' gallery, on two levels. Stanley liked it at first, but four weeks later changed his mind, when he asked me, 'Ken, what am I going to do with all those extras in the gallery? I don't need them for the scenes. Try and come up with something else.' I nearly lost my composure since the art department had practically completed the working drawings.

So I started scribbling again with Stanley looking over my shoulder. I think he was fascinated with how a creative person functions and was triumphant when he discovered my use of a vanishing point in the sketches. I experimented with various shapes and instinctively arrived at a triangular section with slanting walls. 'A triangle is the strongest geometric form. How are you going to treat the wall surfaces?' asked Stanley. 'As reinforced concrete,' I replied, 'like an underground bomb shelter.' I had convinced him. Later President Reagan was also so convinced of the existence of the War Room that he asked his Chief of Staff if he could visit it in the Pentagon!

I designed a gigantic suspended ring of light-fittings to provide the only light source for the scenes around the huge circular conference table. Stanley wanted to create the impression of a poker game for the destiny of the world.

He came up with another brilliant idea, to recast the captain of the B52 bomber with Slim Pickens, an ex-cowboy star. In the film Pickens rides bronco-fashion the atom bomb into the Russian missile complex. Here, too, Stanley had changed his original concept. The bomb bay was already constructed with non-working bomb doors. Then Stanley wanted them to work. We did not have time to effect the structural changes. Fortunately, Wally Weevers, one of the best special-effects technicians, came to my rescue and made the scene possible.

I worked again for Kubrick in 1973–74 on *Barry Lyndon*. Thackeray's novel *The Luck of Barry Lyndon* was actually the screenplay, since Kubrick believed him to be a better writer than any screenwriter alive. He wanted to treat the film like an accurate documentary of the eighteenth century, and insisted that it must be filmed entirely on location. He felt it was the best way to capture the 'reality' of the eighteenth century for the screen, and also the most economical. It was a new experience for me and I would have preferred to design it in my way, in the studio. A combination of studio and location. In retrospect he was most probably right, since the film had a unique look to it, but in the end, the shooting of actual locations made *Barry Lyndon* so very costly, and so very exhausting for everyone.

To recreate the eighteenth century, we based our research on painters such as Gainsborough, Reynolds, Hogarth, Rowlandson, Stubbs, Chardin and the Polish artist Chodowiecki. We made most of the costumes ourselves, or purchased eighteenth-century garments at auctions. But people tended to be shorter two hundred years ago and most of the period garments served only as cutting-patterns. Stanley wanted the actors to get used to wearing costumes and to treat them as normal clothing, and often he made them wear their costumes even when he was not shooting with them. As production designer I had to supervise the choice of fabrics, colour and wigs, as well as the make up of the actors; to look at how the overall design of the image would work.

Time spent on research was endless and I was not used to working in this way. Normally, in pre-production I sketch a lot. But not on this film. I did not touch a piece of paper, except for some battle-scene sketches for the Seven Years' War sequences: the white coats versus the red coats.

Stanley was personally responsible for inventing a new and very fast camera lens, which he used for shooting scenes by real candlelight. We talked about how much candlepower we had!

Naturally I was delighted with my Oscar for *Barry Lyndon*, though it was ironic that I should have won it for a film entirely shot on location.

Joe Mankiewicz, the famous director of *All About Eve* and winner of four Oscars, and brother of Herman who wrote *Citizen Kane*, greeted me with the following speech after he had employed me to design *Sleuth*: 'Listen, Ken, I employ the best creative talent in the world for my films. We sit down together, so that I can explain my concept for the film. Once that is clear to you, you have a free hand to go ahead with the design, the visual interpretation. I will exploit your ideas and every ounce of talent you have to offer. If the film is a success, I as director will in any case receive all the honours. If the film is a flop, I can always put the blame on you.' Cynical advice, maybe, but at least I knew where I stood! I learned a great deal from him. He was also a brilliant raconteur and as a young man had worked as a journalist in Berlin. His father had been a friend of Einstein.

Sleuth was an interesting challenge. Virtually the entire film was shot in the studio at Pinewood, on one set split into several rooms. There were only two actors, Laurence Olivier and Michael Caine, with the props and set dressing and automata as the third big actor. The complicated plot demanded very precise planning of the sets, which could only be achieved in a studio. Joe Mankiewicz wanted to shoot it all in continuity, and he wanted to go from one room to the other without cutting. Again I attempted to create a theatrical kind of realism. To facilitate set changes, all flats, the staircase and window were constructed of very light fibreglass on castors, so we could move them. After the film came out I was often asked in what country house we had filmed the interior!

In 1981 *Pennies From Heaven* was the last major musical to be filmed at the MGM Studios in Culver City. The action took place in the Middle West during the Depression era. Ninety per cent of the film was shot in the studio to reflect not only the gloom of the Depression, but also the dream world of big money. So I designed the bank as a cathedral built of marble to contrast this monument with the depression in the economy. I also built the Chicago 'El' street intersection and attempted for the first time to bring to life paintings of famous American artists of the period, incorporating the sets as part of the streetscape. I reproduced Edward Hopper's *Nighthawks* café and his usherette in a cinema from *New York Movie*, as well as Reginald Marsh's mannequins in a window for the second-hand fur shop. I also had to reproduce the set of *Follow the Fleet* – the dance scene of Fred Astaire and Ginger Rogers. For the huge backdrop of the 'Diner' I designed a collage incorporating Walker Evans photos of Depression America. It was about sixty feet long and forty feet high.

Herbert Ross directed the film and his wife, the late Nora Kaye – a famous professional ballerina of the 1950s – supervised the choreography. I designed seven films for Herb, a friend of mine, and I believe that *Pennies* was the best.

In the last few years, I've worked a lot in Hollywood, New York and Canada. Hollywood is really the only fully functioning film industry, providing much of California's employment. Most films originate there, even if they are shot elsewhere. The variety offered me the opportunity of a wide choice of films I wanted to be associated with.

Addams Family Values in 1992 attracted me as a designer, since I loved the original Charles Addams cartoons in the *New Yorker* magazine. So I tried to re-interpret them as filmic reality. My designs were also influenced by *Dr. Caligari* and German Expressionism. Almost the entire film was shot in the studio. I had little preparation time and had to construct the sets in three studios at the same time – at Paramount (the main studio), Warner Bros. and Studio City. Even though I enjoyed my work it was only made possible because I had a very good team of assistants, and a fantastic construction crew.

A last word about the art department. I nearly always work with an art director, who, like a personal assistant, is responsible for the practical organization and the budget. Then I have a set decorator, who – based on my designs – has to provide the furnishings and props for the film. His work is difficult; he must be experienced and have good taste. He has to assemble the right furniture, paintings, fabrics, lamps, etc., and generally dress the sets. More than anything he has to understand the parts played by the actors, i.e. the background of the various characters in the script. On top of that he has to satisfy me. Then there are the draughtsmen who have to translate my visual ideas into working drawings and models. The construction department is supervised by the construction coordinator, who also is part of my team.

As production designer one depends a great deal on the efficiency of the art department. Since I have been working all over the world this is always my first and biggest worry. But one normally finds good collaborators everywhere, since the language of film is universal.

In 1994, we filmed *The Madness of King George* in England. It was Nick Hytner's first film as director. He had contacted me in New York to offer me the film, which was originally a play by Alan Bennett that Nick had very successfully directed at London's National Theatre. After reading the Bennett script I did not hesitate for a minute. It was the right film for me.

As so often, we had little preparation time and a relatively small budget of barely eight million dollars. We shot the film partly at Shepperton Studios and in London and surroundings, as well as on locations in the south of England. The actors were superb, since most of them had acted in the play. We all worked well together and this collaboration must have contributed to the international success of the film.

In contrast to *Barry Lyndon*, it was never intended to make this film a 'documentary' of the period. The settings were stylized and theatrical with a little dressing for dramatic effect. A kind of exaggeration in simplicity. We shot the film in eight weeks, and in 1995 I received my second Oscar for it.

Film has become my life. Each film is a new adventure with a new set of people one has to get on with, in order to work together. I have had many experiences and got to know interesting people from all over the world. Fate has been kind to me, and for that I am grateful.

Talent alone is not enough to succeed in my profession. You need a lot of luck, and more than anything the courage and bravado to convince others, to experiment with new concepts, and the right back-up to make the concepts work.

Presently, I am working on the Millennium Exhibition for Berlin, 'Seven Hills – Images and Signs of the 21st Century' in the Martin-Gropius building. I am attempting to design the nucleus of the exhibition in the central hall, as a celebration of science, technology and invention. It is a new challenge for me, but then I have always been attracted by the unknown....

Ken Adam

9
CONCLUSION: THE ART OF KEN ADAM

CONCLUSION

THE ART OF KEN ADAM

A recent survey on contemporary production design and art direction by Peter Ettedgui asked sixteen of the most distinguished practitioners in the business exactly how they would define the role of the production designer.

The consensus was that he or she must have visual flair, plus a lot of technical and historical knowledge, combined with the talents of a quantity surveyor, an accountant and the head of a complex art department.

Dean Tavoularis (of *The Godfather* fame) summarizes: 'Production design requires both sides of the brain.... It doesn't matter how talented you are in creative terms, if you're not well-organized and logical about how you approach the job, or you're unable to manage people or work to budgets and deadlines, it will kill you.... You're making several kinds of decisions apart from the actual design ones. You're listing everything that needs to be researched. You're finding locations. You're hiring your crew. It's essential to surround yourself with a strong team: a good art director and construction manager will take some of the responsibility off your shoulders....'

So it is not only a question of visualizing; it is also a question of designing the way the money is spent, and organizing the effort of building of sets as well as dressing them and filling them with props. Some of Ken Adam's sets (notably the War Room, Fort Knox, the missile volcano, the supertanker) are among the most extraordinary feats of logistics in the history of film, quite apart from their design merits. They required engineers to make them practicable; construction managers, builders, carpenters and plasterers to build them; dressers to decorate them; props masters, buyers and makers; administrators to control the budget – and art directors to help coordinate the visual team.

But it all begins with the drawings, the initial visual responses to the words on the page. Drawings, say all the production designers in one way or another, remain the designer's most important tool. The sketches will in time become to-scale technical drawings and floor-plans for use by the construction manager, or art department models for the testing of lights and camera, or visual maps for the director and cinematographer – but they remain the point of departure.

'You have to come up with the ideas and guide the team,' says Ken Adam. As this book has revealed, his extensive personal archive of drawings (which, incidentally, is very well organized) consists largely of first thoughts and early concepts, stages towards design solutions, and expressive monochrome sketches of entire sets: glimpses of the way in which a great production designer's mind works.

These drawings were often, and distinctively, drawn freely and broad-brush instead of with pencil, conté or pen and ink, which allowed Adam 'to experiment with light and shade', and to develop fluency and confidence as a draughtsman once he had served his apprenticeship. They were intuitive drawings, from the gut.

Adam is most at home designing for studio soundstages, which, he still feels, offer more imaginative possibilities, and which enable him to control the visual information given to the viewer. In the streets, much of this information may be accidental, or full of conflicting signals. In the studio, as critic Raymond Durgnat has written, designers can 'dissolve the conventional distinction between photography (realistic) and painterly (artificial).... In essence they don't photograph a world, they build a painting.'

In Ken Adam's case, this 'painting' is often the result of visual research – in museum collections, archives and architectural monographs, among old photographs, on location, and in the unusual case of *Barry Lyndon*, into histories of eighteenth-century European art. This is visual research, but of a practical kind, to suit the project in hand – where 'the most satisfying design is when it really fits into the dramatic scene or structure'. Giovanni Piranesi's prints of fantastical 'prisons' are favourite sources, and there may also be hints of Etienne-Louis Boullée's vast cenotaphs designed in France in the 1780s. And, from the time when Ken Adam really began to find his voice, there have been the strong twin influences of the Bauhaus and Expressionism, both from the 1920s Berlin where the young Klaus Adam grew up. Fritz Lang, too, mixed Modernism and Expressionism in his gigantic sets for *Metropolis* (1926), the film that bankrupted a studio because the sets and special effects were so elaborate.

But the drawings are also links in a continuous process that begins with the script and script conferences, and ends with the images on the screen – unless, that is, the scripts are rewritten around the big sets and exotic locations, as happened with the later Bonds, from *You Only Live Twice* onwards. But always 'the point of my designs is that they are part of the film'.

This means that the drawings need ideally to be seen in relation to the film sets they are intended to inspire. A 1999 London exhibition of Ken Adam's work was a too-rare example of a major art gallery acknowledging the contribution of the production

BOGUS Storyboard drawings, 1995. The little boy Albert is helped by the fantasy-figure Bogus to come to terms with the death of his mother.

ACADEMY AWARDS
ACADEMY AWARDS

ACADEMY AWARDS
ACADEMY AWARDS

designer to contemporary visual culture. However, it presented Adam's drawings as if they were framed Old Masters, separated from film clips which were screened elsewhere in the gallery. Drawings and film clips really need to be seen together. These drawings are, in the end, tools of the trade.

One of the most remarkable aspects of Ken Adam's career is that it began when the big Hollywood studios were still going strong – with their distinctive 'looks', their art departments, their astonishing craft skills – and it has continued well into the era of independent production, with teams of specialists assembled specially for a particular project; the era of computer-generated images and video games. The intervening half-century has seen the context for the production designer's work change beyond all recognition. Adam joined the industry when it was fifty years old, and he is still working beyond its centenary. His Bond series alone is unique in the history of film, in that it shows the arc of development of a single designer's work – at the peak of his form – over seven films, and eighteen years, from low budget to global event.

Is there a consistent theme? At least, in Adam's most celebrated projects? Is there an 'Adam style'? The architectural curator and historian Donald Albrecht, writing for a Munich exhibition catalogue in 1994, certainly thought so: 'While perfecting his craft as a production designer, Adam conjured a celluloid universe where he exorcised the evil spirits of his youth. Expressionist intimations permeate *Addams Family Values*, the master-of-paranoia's most recent effort, but his work on such movies as *Dr. Strangelove* and the James Bond thrillers best illustrates his well-earned reputation as the Frank Lloyd Wright of *décor noir*. Cool and depersonalized, Adam's looming forms and menacing perspectives conflate the war room and the board room to evoke a post-atomic landscape of limitless power…. To achieve these visions, Ken Adam remembers his childhood and unlocks Caligari's cabinet.'

Dr. No makes his first appearance as a disembodied voice interrogating a professor-henchman in a claustrophobic room where the skylight casts distorted spider-web shadows – just like in *Caligari*. Later, the Doctor will show James Bond and Honeychile Rider around his underground lair – a characteristic mixture of a traditional palazzo, a machine for Machiavelli's Renaissance Prince to live in, and a high-tech laboratory on a vast scale, embodying fantasies of world domination. This wasn't in fact the first of Adam's underground lairs. He had already designed two for visiting Hollywood directors (most of his apprenticeship films of the 1950s were, in fact, made with visiting Americans): *Obsession* (or *The Hidden Room*, 1948), about a sick man who traps his wife's lover in a concrete cellar underneath a bomb site in London; and *Ten Seconds to Hell* (1958), set in and around the sparse bunker headquarters of ex-Wehrmacht soldiers who are disposing of bombs amid the rubble of 1945 Berlin.

Underground, concrete, low ceilings, claustrophobia – surrounded on all sides by the devastation unleashed by the Third Reich…. Later in Adam's career, these bunkers will be joined by intimidating corporate boardrooms, where global organizations with scary Orwellian names decide how to hold democratically elected governments to ransom. And the world outside will come to resemble an upmarket tourist brochure, rather than a bomb site: but not far behind the façade there are those Führerbunkers where mad masterminds play games with weapons of mass destruction, using elaborate gadgets disguised as consumer goodies. The swimming-pool has sharks in it. The aquarium is where minnows pretend to be whales.

The 'Cabinet of Dr. Adam' seems sometimes to provide a visual and thematic link – as did Siegfried Kracauer's controversial book *From Caligari to Hitler* – between the topsy-turvy world of German thrillers in the years following the First World War and the rise of the Third Reich. As critic Philip French has written, the names of Dr. No and Dr. Strangelove 'evoke the megalomaniac world of Dr. Caligari and Dr. Mabuse…. Hitler had his Wagnerian lair at Berchtesgaden and died in a bunker beneath Berlin.'

Is this a case of Ken Adam exorcising the demons of his youth? While acknowledging the visual influence of *Caligari*, with its 'theatricalization of reality', he tends to deny that at a conscious level there's any exorcism going on: 'Well, no, I didn't feel that consciously because I always treated it tongue-in-cheek, with a sense of humour, going bigger and more dramatic. But I don't think it was the result of any persecution. Sure, the world was traumatized by Hitler, and this had an effect. Particularly in the Bond films, where we always had a villain who wanted to conquer the world, or even space. But I think it was an instinctive thing. The only time I took it seriously was on *Dr. Strangelove*….'

Again, pushing the point, I once asked him why he had said, 'I always feel restless, probably because of my past.' He replied, 'Yes, I think that is true. I have suffered all my life from anxieties, and that certainly must go back to something. Obviously I wasn't *that* affected as a child by the Nazis, but when I saw the effect they had…. Yes, without a doubt. I don't like to talk about it, Christopher, but it affected me seriously…. All that took its toll.'

Whatever the deep well-springs of Ken Adam's most famous designs, their purpose – as he has often said – is to make the viewer believe that the artifice, however 'theatricalized', is real; one reason why the work of production designers is not better known.

And when it *is* recognized, this tends to be because the work is set in the historical past or the distant future – as if these involved more talent and more effort than contemporary or 'just ahead of contemporary'. One of the ironies of Ken Adam's career is that his two Academy Awards have been for uncharacteristic work, in the form of two prestigious costume pictures: *Barry Lyndon*, with its carefully observed country houses by candlelight, and *The Madness of King George*, with its combination of sets and 'heightened' historic places. He could and should have won for *Dr. Strangelove*, several of the Bonds, *Sleuth*, *Pennies From Heaven*, *Agnes of God* and *Addams Family Values*….

As Philip French has wittily concluded: 'Fancifully, one might identify Ken Adam with the character of "Q", undervalued, constantly raising the ante, always providing the instruments of survival….' And, like the long-suffering Q, a backroom boy – always a backroom boy, by definition – whose work has often saved the day, not to mention the movie.

Christopher Frayling

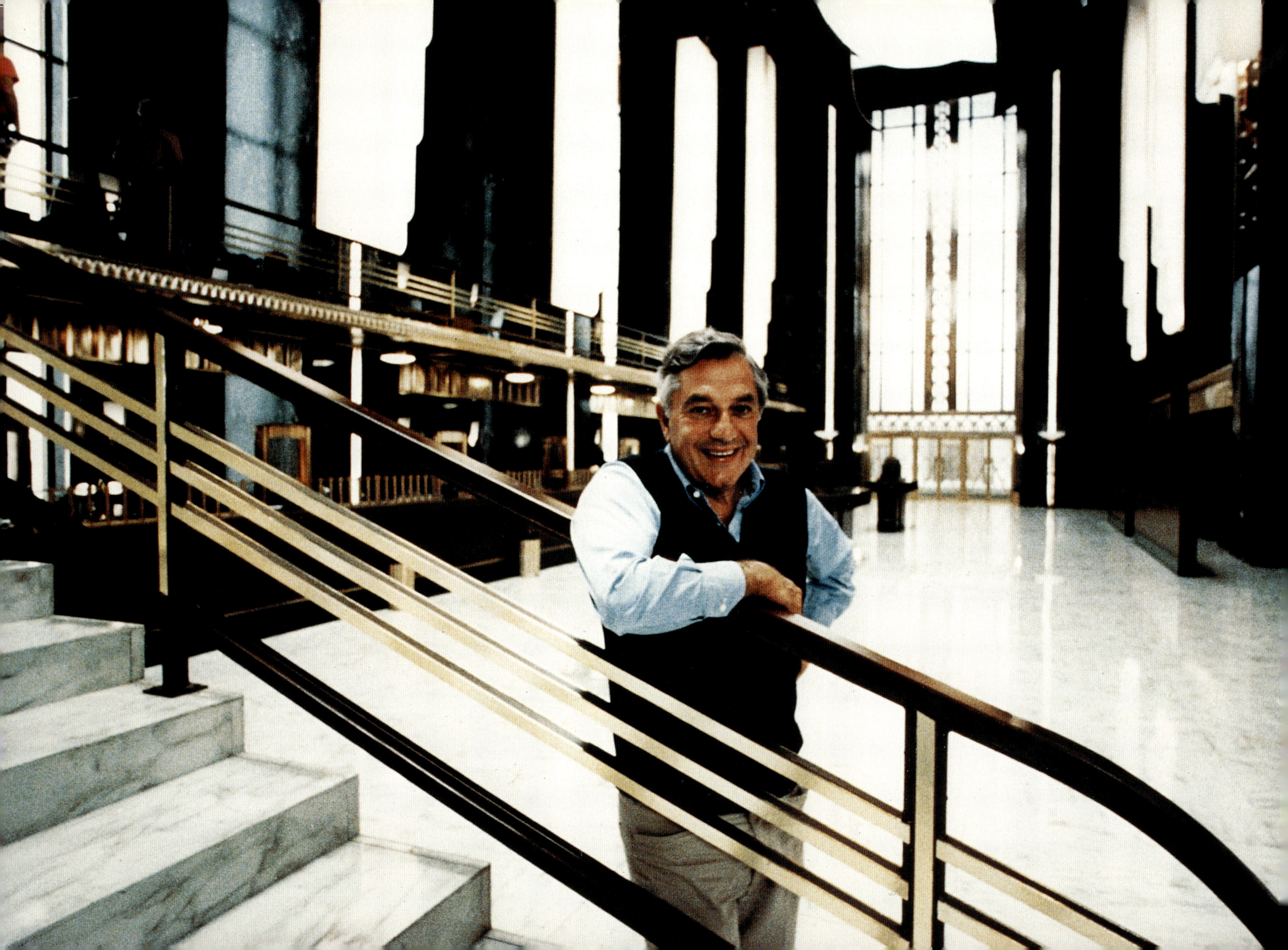

KEN ADAM FILMOGRAPHY

From Draughtsman to Art Director

1948   **THIS WAS A WOMAN** (UK; directed by Tim Whelan), Draughtsman
THE BRASS MONKEY (UK; directed by Thornton Freeland), Draughtsman

1949   **THE QUEEN OF SPADES** (UK; directed by Thorold Dickinson), Draughtsman
THIRD TIME LUCKY (UK; directed by Gordon Parry), Draughtsman
DICK BARTON STRIKES BACK (UK; directed by Godfrey Grayson), Assistant Art Director
OBSESSION (UK; directed by Edward Dmytryk), Assistant Art Director

1950   **YOUR WITNESS** (UK; directed by Robert Montgomery), uncredited Assistant Art Director
CAPTAIN HORATIO HORNBLOWER R.N. (UK/USA; directed by Raoul Walsh), Assistant Art Director

1952   **GOLDEN ARROW** (UK; directed by Gordon Parry), Draughtsman
THE CRIMSON PIRATE (USA; directed by Robert Siodmak), Associate Art Director

1953   **THE MASTER OF BALLANTRAE** (USA; directed by William Keighley), Associate Art Director
THE INTRUDER (UK; directed by Guy Hamilton), Assistant Art Director
STAR OF INDIA/STELLA DELL'INDIA (UK/Italy; directed by Arthur Lubin), Assistant Art Director

1955   **HELEN OF TROY** (USA; directed by Robert Wise), Associate Art Director

Art Director (unless otherwise stated)

1956   **SOHO INCIDENT** (UK; directed by Vernon Sewell)
CHILD IN THE HOUSE (UK; directed by Cy Endfield)
AROUND THE WORLD IN EIGHTY DAYS (USA; directed by Michael Anderson)

1957   **THE DEVIL'S PASS** (UK; directed by D'Arcy Conyers)
NIGHT OF THE DEMON (UK/USA; directed by Jacques Tourneur)

1958   **BATTLE OF THE V-1** (UK; directed by Vernon Sewell), initial designs
GIDEON'S DAY (UK; directed by John Ford)
TEN SECONDS TO HELL (UK/USA; directed by Robert Aldrich)

1959   **THE ANGRY HILLS** (UK; directed by Robert Aldrich)
BEYOND THIS PLACE (UK; directed by Jack Cardiff)

Production Designer (unless otherwise stated)

1959   **IN THE NICK** (UK; directed by Ken Hughes)
BEN-HUR (USA; directed by William Wyler), uncredited design research
THE ROUGH AND THE SMOOTH (UK; directed by Robert Siodmak)
JOHN PAUL JONES (USA; directed by John Farrow), ship designs

1960   **LET'S GET MARRIED** (UK; directed by Peter Graham Scott)
THE TRIALS OF OSCAR WILDE (UK; directed by Ken Hughes)

1961   **THE HELLIONS** (UK/South Africa; directed by Ken Annakin), uncredited initial designs
THE ROMAN SPRING OF MRS. STONE (UK/USA; directed by José Quintero), uncredited initial designs

1962   **DR. NO** (UK; directed by Terence Young)
SODOMA E GOMORRA/SODOME ET GOMORRHE/SODOM AND GOMORRAH (Italy/France; directed by Robert Aldrich)

1963   **IN THE COOL OF THE DAY** (UK; directed by Robert Stevens)
DR. STRANGELOVE OR: HOW I LEARNED TO STOP WORRYING AND LOVE THE BOMB (UK; directed by Stanley Kubrick)
THE LONG SHIPS/DUGI BRODVI (UK/Yugoslavia; directed by Jack Cardiff), initial designs

1964   **WOMAN OF STRAW** (UK; directed by Basil Dearden)
GOLDFINGER (UK; directed by Guy Hamilton)

1965   **THE IPCRESS FILE** (UK; directed by Sidney J. Furie)
THUNDERBALL (UK; directed by Terence Young)

1966   **FUNERAL IN BERLIN** (UK; directed by Guy Hamilton)
1967   **YOU ONLY LIVE TWICE** (UK; directed by Lewis Gilbert)
1968   **CHITTY CHITTY BANG BANG** (UK; directed by Ken Hughes)
1969   **GOODBYE, MR. CHIPS** (UK; directed by Herbert Ross)
ON HER MAJESTY'S SECRET SERVICE (UK; directed by Peter Hunt), uncredited initial design preparation/location research

1970   **THE OWL AND THE PUSSYCAT** (USA; directed by Herbert Ross), Design Supervisor

1971   **DIAMONDS ARE FOREVER** (UK; directed by Guy Hamilton)
1972   **SLEUTH** (USA/UK; directed by Joseph L. Mankiewicz)
1973   **THE LAST OF SHEILA** (USA; directed by Herbert Ross)
1975   **BARRY LYNDON** (UK; directed by Stanley Kubrick)
1976   **THE SEVEN-PER-CENT SOLUTION** (USA; directed by Herbert Ross)
SALON KITTY/DOPPELSPIEL/MADAME KITTY (Italy/West Germany/France; directed by Tinto Brass)
1977   **THE SPY WHO LOVED ME** (UK; directed by Lewis Gilbert)
1979   **MOONRAKER** (UK; directed by Lewis Gilbert)
STAR TREK – THE MOTION PICTURE (USA; directed by Robert Wise), uncredited pre-production design work
1981   **PENNIES FROM HEAVEN** (USA; directed by Herbert Ross), Associate Producer/Visual Consultant
1985   **KING DAVID** (USA; directed by Bruce Beresford)
AGNES OF GOD (USA; directed by Norman Jewison)
1986   **CRIMES OF THE HEART** (USA; directed by Bruce Beresford)
1987   **PU'YI/L'ULTIMO IMPERATORE/THE LAST EMPEROR** (China/Italy; directed by Bernardo Bertolucci), uncredited pre-production design work
1988   **THE DECEIVERS** (UK; directed by Nicholas Meyer)
1989   **DEAD BANG** (USA; directed by John Frankenheimer)
1990   **THE FRESHMAN** (USA; directed by Andrew Bergman)
1991   **THE DOCTOR** (USA; directed by Randa Haines)
COMPANY BUSINESS (USA/Germany; directed by Nicholas Meyer)
1993   **ADDAMS FAMILY VALUES** (USA; directed by Barry Sonnenfeld)
UNDERCOVER BLUES (USA; directed by Herbert Ross)
1994   **THE MADNESS OF KING GEORGE** (UK/USA; directed by Nicholas Hytner)
1995   **BOYS ON THE SIDE/AVEC OU SANS HOMMES** (USA/France; directed by Herbert Ross)
1996   **BOGUS** (USA; directed by Norman Jewison)
1997   **IN & OUT** (USA; directed by Frank Oz)
1999   **THE OUT-OF-TOWNERS** (USA; directed by Sam Weisman)
2002   **TAKING SIDES** (Germany/France/UK/Austria; directed by István Szabó)

opposite   Ken Adam on the art deco Chicago bank set of *Pennies From Heaven*, 1981

BIBLIOGRAPHY

On Ken Adam

Adam, Ken, 'Adam on Colour', *Ideal Home*, December 1968.

Adam, Ken, 'Designing Sets for Action', *Films and Filming*, London, August 1956.

Adam, Ken, significant interviews:
Cinéma, Paris, no. 229, January 1978.
Film Comment, New York, v. 18, no. 1, January–February 1982.
Positif, Paris, no. 191, March 1977.
Screen International, London, no. 74, 12 February 1977.

Berger, Jürgen, ed., *Production Design: Ken Adam. Meisterwerke der Filmarchitecktur*, Munich: Kulturreferat der Landeshauptstadt München, 1994. Catalogue for a Munich, and touring, exhibition.

Frayling, Christopher, *Ken Adam: The Art of Production Design*, Faber and Faber, London, 2005.

Smoltczyk, Alexander, *James Bond – Berlin – Hollywood – Die Welten des Ken Adam*, Nicolai, Berlin, 2002.

Sylvester, David, ed., *Moonraker, Strangelove and Other Celluloid Dreams: The Visionary Art of Ken Adam*, Serpentine Gallery, London, 1999. Catalogue for an exhibition at the Serpentine.

On Production Design

Albrecht, Donald, *Designing Dreams: Modern Architecture in the Movies*, Harper and Row, New York, 1986.

Barnwell, Jane, *Production Design*, Wallflower Press, London, 2004.

Barron, Craig and Mark Cotta Vaz, *The Invisible Art*, Thames & Hudson, London, 2002.

Barsacq, Léon, revised and ed. Elliott Stein, *Caligari's Cabinet and Other Grand Illusions: A History of Film Design*, New York Graphic Society, Boston, 1976. Originally *Le Décor de Film* by Léon Barsacq, Seghers, Paris, 1970.

Berthomé, Jean-Pierre, *Alexandre Trauner*, Jade-Flammarion, Paris, 1988.

Bouzereau, Laurent, *The Art of Bond*, Abrams, New York, 2006.

Broccoli, Cubby, with Donald Zec, *When The Snow Melts: The Autobiography of Cubby Broccoli*, Boxtree, London, 1998.

Carrick, Edward, *Art and Design in the British Film*, Dobson, London, 1948.

Carrick, Edward, *Designing for Films*, The Studio Publications, London, 1949.

Corliss, Mary, and Carlos Clarens, 'Designed for Film: The Hollywood Art Director', *Film Comment*, New York, v. 14, no. 3, May–June 1978. Special 36-page supplement for an exhibition at the Museum of Modern Art, New York.

Eisner, Lotte H., *The Haunted Screen: Expressionism in the German Cinema*, Secker & Warburg, London, 1973.

Ettedgui, Peter, ed., *Screencraft: Production Design and Art Direction*, RotoVision, East Sussex, 1999.

Film Dope, London, no. 1, December 1972: Ken Adam.

Frayling, Christopher, *Things to Come*, British Film Institute, London, 1995.

Hambley, John, and Patrick Downing, *The Art of Hollywood: Fifty Years of Art Direction*, Thames Television, London, 1979. Catalogue for an exhibition at the Victoria & Albert Museum.

Heisner, Beverly, *Hollywood Art: Art Direction in the Days of the Great Studios*, McFarland, North Carolina/London, 1990.

Hudson, Roger, 'Three Designers', *Sight and Sound*, London, v. 34, no. 1, Winter 1964–65.

LoBrutto, Vincent, *By Design: Interviews with Film Production Designers*, Praeger, Westport, Connecticut, 1992.

Mandelbaum, Howard, and Eric Myers, *Screen Deco*, Columbus Books, Kent, 1985.

Marner, Terence St John, with Michael Stringer, eds, *Film Design*, Tantivy Press, London, 1974.

Monthly Film Bulletin, London, v. 32, no. 372, January 1965: 'Checklist 21: Ken Adam'.

Myerscough-Walker, Raymond, *Stage and Film Décor*, Pitman, London, 1939.

Neumann, Dietrich, ed., *Film Architecture: From Metropolis to Blade Runner*, Prestel, Munich, 1996.

Penz, François, and Maureen Thomas, eds, *Cinema and Architecture: Méliès, Mallet-Stevens, Multimedia*, British Film Institute, London, 1997.

Preston, Ward, *What an Art Director Does: An Introduction to Motion Picture Production Design*, Silman-James Press, Los Angeles, 1994.

Sennett, Robert S., *Setting the Scene: The Great Hollywood Art Directors*, Abrams, New York, 1994.

Surowiec, Catherine A., *Accent on Design: Four European Art Directors*, British Film Institute, London, 1992.

Walker, Alexander, *Hollywood England: The British Film Industry in the Sixties*, Michael Joseph, London, 1974.

PICTURE CREDITS

All illustrations come from Ken Adam's personal archive, except the following:

p. 51	Connery and Fleming on the set of *Dr. No*, courtesy of EON.
p. 53	Contact sheet of Dr. No's Reception Room, courtesy of EON.
p. 62	Aston Martin DB5 drawing, courtesy of EON.
p. 66	The Laser Room still, courtesy of EON.
p. 73	*Disco Volante* drawing, courtesy of EON.
p. 77	Bond and Aki, in *You Only Live Twice*, courtesy of EON.
p. 79	Osato's office still, courtesy of EON.
p. 80	Diamond Laboratory still, courtesy of EON.
p. 84	Circular hotel waterbed still, courtesy of EON.
p. 94	Lotus Esprit underwater, courtesy of EON.

Warm thanks to Meg Simmonds of the EON archive, for locating and loaning these film stills; and to Michael G. Wilson for permission to reproduce James Bond material.

p. 128	Caine and Olivier in *Sleuth*. Source: BFI.
back cover	Ken Adam on the Fort Knox set. Source: BFI.

Thanks to Dave McCall, the BFI's Commercial Manager, for making these available.

The fact that you have become a "star" should not cause you to act like one.

Sincerely,
Stanley

Extract of a letter from Stanley Kubrick to Ken Adam.

FOR LETIZIA AND HELEN, OUR LONG-SUFFERING AND ALWAYS-SUPPORTIVE WIVES

Any copy of this book issued by the publisher as a paperback is sold subject to the condition that it shall not by way of trade or otherwise be lent, resold, hired out or otherwise circulated without the publisher's prior consent in any form of binding or cover other than that in which it is published and without a similar condition including these words being imposed on a subsequent purchaser.

First published in the United Kingdom in 2008 by Thames & Hudson Ltd, 181A High Holborn, London WC1V 7QX

www.thamesandhudson.com

© 2008 Ken Adam and Christopher Frayling

All Rights Reserved. No part of this publication may be reproduced or transmitted in any form or by any means, electronic or mechanical, including photocopy, recording or any other information storage and retrieval system, without prior permission in writing from the publisher.

British Library Cataloguing-in-Publication Data
A catalogue record for this book is available from the British Library

ISBN 978-0-500-51414-6

Printed and bound in China by SNP Leefung Printers Ltd